The Sphagnum Moss Bonsai Method

The Sphagnum Moss Bonsai Method

An Illustrated Handbook

GERALD M. LEVITT

McFarland & Company, Inc., Publishers
Jefferson, North Carolina, and London

Also by Gerald M. Levitt

The Turk, Chess Automaton (McFarland, 2000; paperback 2006)

All photos and illustrations are by the author unless otherwise noted.

Library of Congress Cataloguing-in-Publication Data

Levitt, Gerald M.
The sphagnum moss bonsai method :
an illustrated handbook / Gerald M. Levitt.
p. cm.
Includes bibliographical references and index.

ISBN 978-0-7864-6292-6
softcover : 50# alkaline paper ∞

1. Bonsai.
2. Bonsai — Growing media.
3. Peat mosses.
I. Title.
SB433.5.L4725 2011 635.9'772—dc23 2011032541

British Library cataloguing data are available

Manufactured in the United States of America

McFarland & Company, Inc., Publishers
Box 611, Jefferson, North Carolina 28640
www.mcfarlandpub.com

To my wife, Carol … my best friend, lover, and companion on our 34-year journey. Her understanding, tolerance and support encourage me in so many fascinating perspectives of life's delights.

To my sons, David and Aaron, for allowing me to attempt to reveal that varied paths of learning are all worthwhile.

To my dear nurturing mother, Ray Levitt, who with generosity and love set an example of a higher standard for the rest of us.

To my father, Leonard Levitt, struggling with blindness and the outrageous fortunes of growing old, shows me what true courage really is.

And to Brian Batchelder, who showed me the way.

Acknowledgments

The following people were essential in so many ways in the writing and development of this book. Their confidence, support, and good wishes will always be remembered. Isaac Asimov, George Brown, Rosario Coralizza-Peterson, Julietta Darwin, Bette Davidson, Paul Davidson, Joan Dubois, Herman Finklestein, Connie Fotos, Perry Fotos, Fred Goldin, Martin Granoff, Mary Granoff, Donna Harold, Lawrence Harold, Martin Itzkowitz, Paul Kuttler, Ruth Kuttler, Donna Landes, Harold Levitt, Helena Levitt, Jan Levitt, Mary Levitt, Jerry Lidovitch, June Lidovitch, Clayton Dale Peterson, Debbie Peterson, Phyllis Peterson, Steven Peterson, Ayn Rand, Sidney Ravitch, Toby Ravitch, Elaine Sheinmel, Arlene Shore, Bernard Shore, Mark Turetsky, Fred Wasserman, Sandi Wasserman, Linda Weisler, Dori Wexelbaum, Lee Wexelbaum, Andrea Wigert, Eric Wigert, Jeff Zidow, Nancy Zidow.

The following are special people who gave their time, effort, and ideas to the creation of this book: Lawrence Harold, whose knowledge, expertise, sharing, and lessons in life helped make this book possible. Erik and Andrea Wigert, who gave their time, and welcomed me into their wonderful world of bonsai, showed and explained techniques, and help identify specific plants. Carol Levitt, my wife, whose understanding and input, were a major factor in getting this book from my head onto paper. She helped regulate the needed breaks for an author undertaking such a huge and complicated project such as this.

In Memorium. There are two people who would have liked to see this book, but due to their recent deaths, will not be able to.

Eugene Spitzer, who bravely battled multiple sclerosis with humor and determination, was a high school history teacher and a patient of mine. He was always up-spirited, and full of wonderful stories and I always looked forward to making house calls and spending time with him.

Paul Kuttler died suddenly, without warning. His conversation, logical thought, never-ending advice and hands-on attempts to help others, volunteering his knowledge of computers, will greatly be missed by all who had the opportunity to know him.

Table of Contents

Preface

My friend Bernie got a gift of a bonsai from his aunt, somewhere around the late 1980s. I found it most fascinating and began to read about the little trees in shallow pots. I planted lemon and maple seeds, and visited nurseries, looking for damaged and deformed specimens they were ready to throw out, or other specimens that had an intriguing trunk. I soon developed a nice collection of junipers, pines and maples, the usual starting plants for new bonsai enthusiasts.

Then one day a friend told my wife and me about a show on public television, from a New Jersey station (we lived in Philadelphia, Pennsylvania). It was called *New Horizons in Bonsai,* hosted by Brian Batchelder and produced in Miami on WLRN Television. But this was not traditional bonsai with graded soils, extreme wiring techniques, and slow growth. This was for Florida, where the hot weather and long growing seasons made conditions different from the northern climates. Batchelder was a horticulturalist who graduated with honors from Brooklyn's Pratt Institute, with a B.A. degree. He had thirty years' experience working with the traditional method for bonsai. But he noticed that his Florida plants were not doing well. He developed and refined the idea of using unmilled sphagnum moss as a growth medium instead of the graded soil techniques of the traditionalists. He had success and developed an entirely new system for growing bonsai in this amazing medium.

In 1992, Batchelder died suddenly. His fans were shocked that this young talented enthusiast was gone. The series ended, and all I had were the VHS tapes of the series I had purchased from WLRN and his book about the show (*New Horizons in Bonsai*, 1990).

In the meanwhile, I had started using his method, eventually converting all of my approximately 20 to 25 Philadelphia bonsai to the sphagnum moss method. I loved it. It was clean, neat, made logical sense, and the plants were thriving, whether indoors for the winter or out in the shed during the coldest drops in temperatures. Of course as a beginner, you lose some trees, but it is a learning experience.

Back in 1995-1996 we moved to Florida, where I had access to tropical trees and plants, and lost many of my northern maples and pines. But there were so many new and exciting trees here in the humid sub-tropics there was no dearth of material. Using the sphagnum moss method and the tricks I had learned from Batchelder, I was quite successful. Then I started to document my bonsai work on YouTube.com. My screen name is bonsai9723, and in Chapter 18 you will find a listing of my bonsai videos and their URLs. The response to my bonsai videos has become overwhelming in the kind comments and thanks from people who love this new method, the number of views of my videos, and the number of subscribers who get notice of every video I post. I decided to write this guidebook to help those who are interested in learning about a new easy method that is clean and quick, promotes early aging of the tree, and using directional pruning techniques can make their trees into living works of art.

Lots of people seem to like to scare new initiates who want to learn the hobby. People seem to have a fear about the difficulty of raising and caring for bonsai. Nonsense! It is not hard. It is fun and relaxing. It is good for you and the tree. Don't be afraid; just be ready to have fun. With this new and exciting system, things are easy and enjoyable. Taking care of one tree is really an easy task. But beware, like potato chips, you may begin to crave more after you create your first bonsai.

Introduction

My interest in plants started when I was about eight years old. A small patch of our backyard was put in my hands to grow a garden. With guidance from my delightful mother and all-knowing father, I soon had corn stalks, lima beans, peas, carrots, and other vegetables growing. It was a fascinating process to a third grader … to see a seed planted, the young plant break the surface, following the sun on its daily journey across the sky as its stalk twisted in slow harmony embracing the sunshine for photosynthesis. Learning how important water is to get plants to grow, and learning about fertilizer and insect control was a great experience for a curious kid. I had always been and remain to this day an extremely curious person. I use the word "extremely" because in my contacts with other human beings, they have often commented upon my love of doing things of all sorts, and once I was interested in a subject, I went into it full blast. Other interests come along, and we juggle them in the rhythms of our lives, shelving them for a while, often bringing them back when a better time comes along.

My garden lasted a few years, and then puberty was upon me. Junior high school (as it was called in 1962–64), John F. Kennedy's assassination, the struggle for civil rights, the culture-changing Beatles invasion, rock-and-roll, the Vietnam War, were life changing events. I matriculated at Temple University in Philadelphia, receiving a solid education, graduating with a bachelor of arts in Geology. I was going to be a geologist, but I had taken a great interest in biology and physical anthropology. I loved my biology classes, and particularly remember my lab instructor in botany, Mrs. Scheinmel. She inspired me and made me question many of the theories about plants and their lives. That interest in botany stayed with me even though I didn't really use it until 1985.

In 1985, my confidant and friend since being in a high school fraternity at around 15 or 16 years of age, Dr. Bernard Shore, M.D., had moved to upper New York State. He was visiting Philadelphia, where we were both born, and his aunt had given him a gift. It was a bonsai tree. I had familiarity with the miniature trees, as the general public did. But seeing this specimen up close started me on another journey of education and fun. I wanted to raise bonsai. So I did what I normally do in these situations. I went to the library and searched out books (this is pre-internet days and Google did not exist). The books show the rudimentary to the sublime in techniques for growing bonsai, but in the traditional method. This method is thousands of years old, as perfected as a science/art can be, and the results are stunning masterpieces of nature, controlled by humankind. Sometimes it's the other way around, and nature determines the shape and size of trees (hurricanes, earthquakes, infestations, and vegetative pandemics). It is the traditional method I began using for my bonsai creations, as that was the only method of which I was aware. It wasn't that difficult, but the techniques, when I looked at them later, seemed to be almost contra-indicated to the goals of bonsai. In the traditional method there are two goals, at least. One is to grow trees in graded soils and slowly use wires to force branch shape. The other method, the sphagnum moss method, seemed so much simpler, more logical, and actually produced results of a striking character faster than the traditional method. It made bonsai fun and easy. It was not based on some scary set of rules that kept many people away from this amazing hobby and art.

I was using the traditional method when a friend told me about a show on public television on a New Jersey TV station from Trenton that was receivable in Philadelphia. It was called *New Horizons in Bonsai*, and it ran two seasons of 12 or 13 episodes, all of them about using this new method. Brian Batchelder, the host, found his northern traditional plants did not do well in Florida. He experimented with sphagnum moss as a growth substrate, in essence, growing hydroponic bonsai trees. I tried the method and found that it worked. It worked wonderfully for me. My plants thrived. I had fruiting Clementine trees inside during the winter months filled with fruit. I kept other plants in a shed during the cold, freezing winter months. It was at this time that I planted my first seed to become a bonsai, a lemon seed. It sprouted after being planted in soil. I still have that plant today, 25 years later.

So in 1996 we moved to southwest Florida, off the Gulf of Mexico. Our property is 2.8 acres. People have horses, donkeys, emus, ostriches, bulls, cows, and all sorts of interesting flora and fauna on their properties. I had an inviting area under a large and old southern oak, and set up my bonsai area there. I built a stand to hold my trees, and then eventually built two more.

As explained previously, I discovered YouTube, and began airing my videos there. The shows got nice ratings and feedback, so on I went, carrying the method started by Batchelder to a new set of interested people. I found many people who loved this new method and found that they weren't scared of it any longer, thanks to my videos. I was very pleased to hear that and enjoyed making the videos showing people how easy it can be. My following grew, and I even inspired other people who have taken up this method and are spreading it on YouTube via their own videos.

Bonsai is very rewarding to the tree and yourself. Bonsai can be a great equalizer against the ever-present pressures of the world we face each day. Like meditation, working on your bonsai allows your mind to relax and concentrate on something other than the problems that haunt you. That brief respite can be rejuvenating and very helpful with dealing with life's stresses. One of my followers on YouTube is a soldier who had thrown his life into direct danger in Iraq. He wrote to me to tell me how working with the sphagnum moss system and taking up bonsai was a great stress reliever for him and helped him handle the tremendous mental weight that being a soldier in a war can bring to an individual.

I sincerely hope that you the reader, and hopefully established or soon to be bonsai enthusiast, can get something more than just knowledge of how to grow and care for bonsai. Bonsai can help make life better.

This book is far different from all the other bonsai books published. The only book that ever approached this subject was Batchelder's book *New Horizons in Bonsai*, which was a complementary book to his television series produced in Miami by WLRN-TV. My book will be the first detailed compendium about the use of sphagnum moss as a growth medium. It will cover all of the aspects of raising bonsai with this method that I have experienced in my 25 years of using it. We will cover everything from watering, automatic watering systems, building bonsai shelves and stands, fertilization, directional pruning, aging trees prematurely, root care, repotting, increasing growth speed, bonsai styles, diagnosing problems, insects and harmful animals, cold weather care, heating and air conditioning problems, weeds, equipment, tools, pots, drainage, anti-fungicides and insecticides, leaf size, plantings with rocks, on rocks, using surface moss or surface gravel, planting on slabs, planting without containers, wiring, strings and ropes for shaping, and other areas of interest.

The ease of this method versus the difficulties of the traditional methods shall be examined so that the people who wish to do bonsai can leave their fears behind and be successful in growing these miniature beauties. It is fun, easy and rewarding, and requires minimal effort and care compared to the traditional method. This is truly the first major breakthrough in this 2,000-plus-year-old art. Have fun with your bonsai.

1

Bonsai History

What Is Bonsai and Where Did It Start?

"Bonsai is a tree or plant cultured in a container and is therefore small in size, but yet in its entirety expresses the beauty and volume of a tree grown in its natural environment. The literal meaning of bonsai is 'planted in a tray'" (Koide, Kato, and Fuzas, *The Masters' Book of Bonsai* [1989], 9).

Bonsai are often referred to as "those little trees from Japan." They are trees in miniature, designed and sculpted by the bonsai artist to fool the eye and to be appreciated as great works of living art. A common misconception that people harbor is that Japan is the birthplace of the idea and development of bonsai, when in actuality it was China that spawned this horticultural offshoot of today, which has so many aficionados around the globe. (Though in Egypt of 4,000 years ago, there are pictures showing trees in containers and trees growing in rocky crevices.) Like music, it is an international language of sorts, joining people from many cultures through a common interest and appreciation of beauty.

Pun-Ching-miniature forest landscape of Buddha Belly bamboo at Wigert's Bonsai Nursery

"Pun-ching" is a style of landscape miniaturization known from the Han dynasty (ca. 206 B.C. to A.D. 220), and "pun-sai," or bonsai, is referenced during the Ch'in dynasty (221–206 B.C.). In Japan, there are written and artistic references from around A.D. 1195, and it is in this period that bonsai traveled from China to Japan. Previously, in China, dwarfed plants were noticed in desolate areas, such as rocky crags on cliff sides. They caught the eye because of their shapes and size. People use to hunt for such trees and risking death would climb to get them, as they had become valuable. The emperor was rumored to have not allowed anyone else to own the little landscapes, and the penalty for breaking this rule was death.

At some point the realization struck that these trees grew dwarfed in size because of lack of growing space and nutrients, possibly including water. Using seeds and other means of propagation, the Chinese began growing bonsai not secured from the outdoors but cultivated. They developed techniques, later expanded upon by the Japanese, that gave rise to this wonderful living art.

The stories and tales of these "tiny" trees spread throughout the world, and the trees are today recognized and identified on sight by most people. It is an ancient art, and one with a contemporary and enthusiastic following.

The West learned about this fascinating world of miniatures when the Third Universal Exhibit was held in Paris in 1878. The building was located on the Champ de Mars. There were later exhibits that whetted the appetite of the West for these tiny works of art in 1889 and 1900. London, in 1909, hosted a major bonsai exhibit. After World War II a great number of GIs, having spent time in the islands of Japan where they were exposed to this almost surrealistic art form, took the spirit and samples back home. It has been growing ever since with a worldwide following and legions of enthusiasts.

In these early years many Westerners felt that the trees looked tortured, and many openly voiced their displeasure in the way the trees were being treated by bonsai masters. It wasn't until around 1935 that opinions changed, and bonsai was finally classified as an art in the West.

With the end of World War II, bonsai started to gain in popularity in the West. It was the soldiers returning from Japan with bonsai in tow that sparked Western interest in the art, even though most of the trees brought home by these soldiers died a short time after their arrival. They survived long enough to create a desire in westerners to learn more about the proper care of their bonsai. The large Japanese-American population was invaluable to Americans in this respect. Their knowledge of the art of bonsai was of great interest to many Americans learning the art.

Where Is It Now?

Bonsai has now spread worldwide. It can be found on every continent, with perhaps the exception of Antarctica. But it would not surprise me if somewhere at the camps on the frozen wastelands of our southernmost continent, someone has a bonsai tree. We see bonsai trees in the cinema, on television, and in advertising. They are immediately recognizable, and with the new method using sphagnum moss, bonsai should spread even further, just as the roots of our trees spread out looking for new areas to grow into. Bonsai has a wonderful future ahead, and a distinguished past that is honored anytime anyone tries their hand at this exciting pastime.

Traditional Bonsai Techniques

In the past, there was only one method of growing and caring for bonsai ... the traditional method. For more than 2,000 years the art has grown and been developed into near perfection by those practitioners of the traditional method. The traditional method uses techniques such as soil gradation, slow growth, wiring to create specific shapes, and sometimes water deprivation to slow growth and keep the plants miniaturized. When I started in 1985, I used the traditional method because there were no other choices. But time brings change. New things are constantly being developed that in some cases make our lives easier and, in others, more complex but with a greater ability to accomplish goals with lightning speed. So it is a perfectly natural and desirable situation that the art of bonsai has also had some changes. The greatest and most far-reaching change for bonsai is the sphagnum moss method of growth and care. The traditional method will not and should not be supplanted by the sphagnum moss method. It is a beautiful art, and there is plenty of room for the two methods to coexist, one helping the other. The sphagnum moss method, because of its ease and the lack of need for special training, will bring new devotees into the world of bonsai. The number of bonsai enthusiasts will swell, as people see that it is not that difficult to raise and care for bonsai. The sphagnum moss bonsai enthusiasts have much to learn from the techniques cultivated over thousands of years by the traditionalists, and there can be a very happy and rewarding marriage between the two in terms of mutual benefits.

Is Bonsai Cruel?

Many people have expressed the opinion that making bonsai is a cruelty to the plant. I understand people's concern with preventing cruelty or abuse to any living thing. The especially sad increase in animal abuse is appalling. I want people to be concerned, understanding, and tolerant of the many life forms with which we share existence on the planet. The cutting of leaves and branches, the use of bleaches to turn certain exposed areas of wood an interesting white color that contrasts nicely with the rest of the tree, trimming roots, applying insecticides, water starvation, and wiring into shape certainly sound like a torturous path to take with something you purport to care about. Perhaps there is another way of looking at this. Some traditional bonsai artists like to water infrequently to help keep the tree on the small side. They also like to wire branches and bend them into unnatural shapes and positions that Orientalize the tree in their minds, and thus enhances its beauty. The question becomes, in essence, "Can plants feel pain?"

What is pain? Pain is an interpretation made by the brain of a neurologic signal it receives. It is a warning device the organism uses to protect itself. Ignoring a pain signal can have consequences that severely damage, injure, and even cause the death of the individual. So in what I will term "the higher animals," or those with recognized masses of neuronal cells we call brains, the pain signal is one of the most important signaling devices we have to interpret the outside world (apart from our self-known world of body and mind). In these higher animals, there are receptors of stimulation, called nociceptors, that send a pain signal to the brain. They are located on some of the external and internal parts of higher animals. (Hair shafts and the brain have no pain receptors.) Going lower on the scale of complexity in creatures and getting to animals like sponges and protozoa, I have been unable to find any references to nociceptors in these living things. Nor have I been able to find if plants have any similar system to report pain. As these animals and plants lack a centralized sorting center for signals, like our brains, I assume that paramecium or marigolds cannot, and do not, experience pain in the way we humans understand it. (J.C. Bose, noted Indian scientist, invented and used the crescograph. He proved that vegetation has an internal system that responds to sound, touch, damage, anxiety, fear, etc.)

The nociceptors can be triggered in many ways. One way is by temperature changes. Extreme heat or cold can trigger a nociceptor to send a signal to the brain warning it of impending problems if the local affected area is not removed or protected from the source of thermal change, such as pulling your hand away from a flame. Or if pressure is applied to an area that becomes so overwhelming it might cause mechanical breakdown of tissue, this will also set off a nociceptor to signal the brain of impending doom. There are chemical nociceptors that respond with warning signals, and other nociceptors that remain silent until actual damage has occurred, then send their message to the brain. But if plants do not have these pain receptors, what do they have?

Plants have reflexes to stimuli that cause them to act as plants do. They are constantly under attack from wind, cold and heat, insects, falling parts of other plants, rockslides, and humans. Subjected to defoliants, air pollution, and other noxious substances, plants react in an interesting way. They try to repair damaged parts, shut down areas to protect the rest of the plant, grow more branches and foliage, re-grow severed roots, and in essence, fight for their survival. Do they "know" they are doing this? Are they sentient in some manner we cannot fathom, because it is so far below the self-realization of existence that humans have? Perhaps they have a consciousness of existence, a set of reflexes evolutionarily developed to help the species survive. Plants respond well to pruning. They grow fuller, sturdier, and healthier than a leggy, long-limbed plant. Insects are a menace to plants. So spraying an insecticide helps the plant survive so that it can reproduce its kind, which is its main task in life. It is likewise with fungicides. Roots grow thicker and more extensive when pruned, which helps the plant absorb water and nutrients more efficiently, leading to better growth patterns.

So, are bonsai tortured? Are they in pain? Do they suffer? Do they fear the next cutting? Are they anxious about the future? I think not, based on the scientific evidence concerning pain receptors and interpretation of those signals. I think signals are sent within the plant via chemical transmitters that tell the plant to do certain things. For instance, along a stem there are usually many adventitious buds. These are kind of like sleeping areas of the plant that are ready to burst forth in growth if only they receive the signal to do so. So when the leafy end of a branch is pruned, a chemical signal that represses growth is no longer delivered to the branch due to the amputation, and the adventitious buds awake and start to grow. They start to swell and soon some new growth is seen popping out in various places along the previously foliage-free branch.

After I cut off large portions of root balls in making bonsai, when the plant is re-examined a month or two later, it is easy to see the spread of new roots through the plant. A property of sphagnum moss appears to be a medicinal property for roots and a barrier to potential microscopic problems, such as fungus and bacteria.

I think that bonsai should be looked upon as the royalty of the plant world. It is not like a cornstalk, with its ears, loaded with seeds, to be cooked at a barbeque, in essence, "born to die." Bonsai are perhaps the most pampered of plants. They are watered, fed, given light, protected from severe weather and abnormal temperatures. They are grown in beautiful pots, and not stuck in the ground, fighting with the weeds, other plants, and multiple attackers that threaten their existence every day. Grasshoppers, aphids, caterpillars, weevils, and all sorts of nemeses besiege outdoor plants day in and day out. But bonsai are protected by their human friends. We watch over them. We show them off and keep them clean and spruced up. They respond well to out stewardship. They also manage to give back something to us. That is probably no direct intention of the plant, but our own interpretation of the good feelings we get by being with and helping our bonsai.

So, is the art of bonsai cruel? No. It is a heartfelt gift to the lucky few plants that have the honor of being bonsai. If plants could think on our level, I think they would desire a situation like that of a bonsai, rather than being some four- or five-hundred-year-old tree in prime health about to be cut down by the power chainsaw of a Brazilian forester, or being the chemically sprayed dandelion on your front lawn, slowly withering away. Bonsai are the lucky ducks of this world. They have been given a gift, and it is not torture, abuse or cruelty. They are the objects of our affections. It is not such a bad thing to be.

Trees and Other Plants Suitable for Bonsai

People often ask what plants are suitable for bonsai. The basic rule is that plants with woody stems that are perennials are best suited as bonsai subjects. But don't be held back by rules that are often unproven. Palm trees are noted for not being good as bonsai subjects. If you cut their trunks, the palms will die without producing side shoots or growth. But this doesn't mean you can't try to bonsai them. I have found that plants usually not thought of as suitable for bonsai can often be kept in a miniature state by using pots that restrict the growth of roots. In the wild, planted in the ground, they have the ability to grow deeply and find sub-surface water supplies, which helps make them large, full grown plants. As Batchelder did on his short lived series, I, too, started a coconut palm as a bonsai, using the idea of root containment as a way to keep the plant small. I never learned what happened to Brian's coconut palm, as his excellent TV series was cut short by his untimely death. He used to show follow-up episodes on many of his plants, but the coconut palm, unfortunately, was not seen again by the public. The one I attempted to grow was doing well and looked great, but for an unknown reason, died. We have had problems with coconut palm diseases and perhaps that was the cause. It was quite a while ago, and I hope to try again. But I do have a Bismarck Palm that has been successfully kept small by using a smaller pot. It is big in comparison to regular-sized bonsai pots, but the plant has grown a thicker trunk and its fronds are smaller than usual. Pine trees are common bonsai subjects, and I have a rather large specimen, also in a large pot, that does extremely well. I just keep cutting off the top as it reaches the screen on our lanai, and it seems to thrive. All of these larger plants are planted exclusively in sphagnum moss.

I have papaya trees growing out of tiny pots. They are hale and hearty and grow with vigor. I purchased a small Cavendish banana plant because of its small size. It is absolutely thriving in the sphagnum moss in a regular sized bonsai pot. The main plant has died off this year, but it had started growing babies adjoining the main plant before the main plant died, and the babies are doing great. I like to make bamboo bonsai, as they are wonderful subjects for bonsai forests. I grow them from cuttings from my own collection of bamboo that I have spread around my property. There are two kinds of bamboo, running and clumping. The timber bamboo that I have grows about 40 to 60 feet in height, but because they are running bamboo, the cuttings do well. The clumping bamboo, which doesn't spread out like the running bamboo, are sometimes difficult to grow from cuttings.

Bismarck palm, reduced from its natural size because of the small pot

Many succulents, such as the jade plant, make excellent and beautiful bonsai. They are hearty and easily propagated through cuttings. Some succulents are more difficult, such as the Operculicarya decaryi. The Operculicarya decaryi is a wonderfully formed tree with a thick trunk and tiny leaves that makes a striking bonsai. Vines that are perennials and have a woody stem are also excellent bonsai candidates. With directional pruning techniques they can be the stars of your collection.

Operculicarya decaryi interior

Cavandish banana bonsai

Operculicarya decaryi, a variety of jade plant

Fruiting trees make fun bonsai. It is very exciting to see a lemon or Clementine tree with fruit, growing from a small pot. I have had great success with lemons, and some of the other plants develop flowers and small fruit. I have had boxwoods grow fruit, and other species do likewise. Orange, cherry, fig, blueberry, Surinam cherry and several other fruit tree species do remarkably well as bonsai. It is important to select a species well suited to the climate and temperatures in which the normal-sized trees do well. For example, lemon and orange bonsai trees will flourish in dry, sunny California and hot and humid Florida, but not in cold climates. Calamondi orange trees will thrive in nearly every climate, as long as they are brought indoors before freezing. I had a beautiful example of this tree, loaded with fruit, that was placed on my piano during the winter months in Philadelphia. It always amazed visitors to see this miniature orange tree loaded with fruit. The citrus trees, in general, prefer sunny bright areas and can be kept outside or indoors. Cherry trees do well in the South and Midwest, and up into Canada. I have had Surinam cherry trees produce an edible fruit that is often used in South America and other places to make what I am told is a delicious jelly. The Barbados cherry also produces edible fruit and is native to some Caribbean Islands, and does well here in

Lemon tree bonsai

Florida. But the fruit produced is normal size or slightly smaller than usual. But trees such as the miniature pomegranate make small fruit that are proportionate to the tree and its leaves. Using miniature fruiting varieties of trees is an excellent way to make a nicely proportioned bonsai. Some of the trees previously mentioned, such as the Surinam cherry and the Barbados cherry, naturally produce small fruit, so they also are good to use for trees with proportionately sized fruit.

Full-sized lemons on bonsai

Styles and Shapes of Bonsai

There are a fair number of bonsai tree styles that have developed over the years. Many are based on trees that were removed from the wild and were windblown or cascading in shape. Others grew from the imaginative minds of the early bonsai masters who had an eye for style and appeal. Some styles are upright, slanted, cascade, windblown, straight, and twisted, and groupings of two, three, or more are eventually, as the number grows, considered forests. There are trees that grow in water, such as mangroves. I tend to prefer a tree that mimics its larger naturally growing tree in the wild. But this is an art, and you need to determine what you wish to develop. I have many different shapes and styles in my collection.

Upright style at Wigert's Bonsai Nursery

Slanted style at Wigert's Bonsai Nursery

Windblown style forest at Wigert's Bonsai Nursery

Straight style

Grouping of two trees

Twisted style at Wigert's Bonsai Nursery

Cascade style at Wigert's Bonsai Nursery

I urge you to try new shapes and styles, as sometimes the varieties make for an interesting collection, rather than having the same thing repeated over and over. There are trees with exposed roots, which is a very common effect of working with sphagnum moss as the growth medium. As the top layers slowly wash away, the exposed roots harden up and have a wonderful appearance that always seems to delight and amaze visitors. Some people (I among them in my early years of bonsai work) like to Orientalize their trees, copying the beautiful trees they see in pictures. I have grown pines with twisted branches that were very unnatural in shape compared to any living variety of that tree. I used to work with wire to achieve this deformation, and you should consider trying this also, as it will help you decide what you really like. I suggest you do what you like and avoid listening to the comments of others, whether they be friends or bonsai masters. This is YOUR art, and you have artistic license to do what you wish in regard to shape and style.

Group of three or more trees at Wigert's Bonsai Nursery

Forest style at Wigert's Bonsai Nursery

Miniatures in Our Lives

We live in a world where people seem to like the miniaturizing of common or rare items. There are miniature portraits, tediously painted with single hair brushes, that were worn, and are still worn, in lockets, or framed. People have been collecting miniature trains and setting up miniature landscapes and tunnels, along with small-sized people and buildings, to present a view of a world in miniature. There are places where towns and villages are made in small size, and people walk down the streets as if they were Gulliver travelling amongst the Lilliputians. Doll houses are another prime example of size reduction. Many toys for children are smaller versions of their real counterparts, be they cars and trucks, dolls and figurines and their clothes, or small versions of supermarket items they stock on their reduced sized shelves in imitation of a food store. Lincoln Logs and Erector Sets entertained many of us as we grew from childhood to adulthood. It seems to be a human trait that we like to see the world in smaller terms, using maps and globes to give us a view we cannot see unless we are travelling in space, far above the Earth. So miniature trees are just another form of this pastime that entertains and entrances us.

Gift Bonsai

Once one grows bonsai, and especially after appreciating how easy it is to make bonsai using the sphagnum moss method, lots of us like to give our bonsai away as gifts. They are great for special occasions, such as birthdays, weddings, celebrations of accomplishment, or just because you want to do it. But beware, though the intentions are good, often the results are disastrous. Never give away a tree that will sadden you if you see or learn that it has died under the care of the recipient. Of all the many bonsai I have worked hard on and then given away as gifts, perhaps only one or two (and perhaps none) are still alive. People who are not "plant people" will often not take care to water or fertilize their trees, or take steps to correct withering, dying trees, as they are not into that mindset of care. Just as it can be a bad idea to give someone a pet for a gift, especially as a surprise, giving bonsai as gifts seems to have more downsides than successes, from my personal experience. On a macabre note, when a loved one has died and the deceased has been cremated, I always kindly offer the survivor the opportunity to have me mix in a small amount of their loved one's ashes into the sphagnum moss, so that the essence of the lost loved one may be incorporated into the growing, living tree. They may then feel the presence of that person when they see the tree and remember that the person was once a vital, growing part of their own past life. To date, no one has accepted this offer, but I continue to make it, nonetheless. (When our Yorkshire Terrier, Kiwi, died recently, we had her cremated and I incorporated her ashes into the sphagnum moss of a Green Island ficus. The atoms of her ashes will be absorbed into the hardwood of the tree, and she will be with us for many years to come.)

2

The New Easy Sphagnum Moss Method Explained

Brian Batchelder and Sphagnum Moss

Brian Batchelder was the inventor and proponent of this system, which uses sphagnum moss as a growing medium. He had moved to Florida from New York and found that his northern bonsai were not faring well in this sub-tropical environment, with its steady high temperatures and very long growing season, as compared to the northern climates. Many of his trees needed a cold winter, as that was in their genetic background for proper growth. Born (1953) in Biddeford, Maine, he was a descendent of Maine families that had resided in that state since the early 1600s.

Florida was different from his past experiences, and he decided to try new methods to grow his bonsai. He had studied horticulture at Cornell University and was an honor graduate of Pratt Institute in Brooklyn, New York.

Brian Batchelder (courtesy of WLRN Television)

When he was younger he had been exposed to sphagnum moss and the bogs it grew in. At some point after moving to Florida, he decided to try to raise bonsai in sphagnum moss, which he understood was going to be an experiment in hydroponics. He had used the traditional method of bonsai growth for more than 30 years, but that method just didn't work right for him in Florida. He came upon the concept of growing native trees of the subtropics, taking advantage of the long growing season and warm temperatures, with no cold spells like those sub-freezing winters of the northern climates. He found that the sphagnum moss was excellent for growing all sorts of plants, and his bonsai thrived. He reasoned that if he grew trees faster and longer, they would look as if they had matured, but in a much shorter time than with the traditional method. He understood that sphagnum moss was lacking in the nutrients needed for good plant growth, and he determined that frequent fertilization was a necessary part of his system, as it made the plants develop faster and look older than they actually were. His horticultural background enabled him to shape trees using directional pruning techniques, rather than using wire. He had many artistic talents, and this was clearly visible when watching the television series called *New Horizons in Bonsai*, which was filmed and produced by WLRN in Miami and went to national public television because of its popularity. A friend knew that I was raising bonsai and suggested that I watch the show, which I eagerly did. He had two seasons of his show before his untimely death in 1992. The loss of this talented and creative individual was a great misfortune. Those of us who had the privilege of getting to watch him in action will forever feel the wound of his passing, but his legacy will be celebrated for many years to come.

A Different Way of Doing Things

On the tops of bogs grow an interesting organism, sphagnum moss. It has many useful characteristics, one of which is its ability to hold water, kind of like a sponge. As it dies, it sinks into the bogs (covered by the new growth of sphagnum moss), where it undergoes organic changes and becomes peat moss. But the material on top, the maker of peat moss, is long stranded sphagnum moss. It is this material that has helped launch a new way to raise bonsai. In this new way, we use a material other than soil, though soil has been used with utmost success for thousands of years as part of the traditional method of bonsai care. The trees had short growing seasons, and they were often deprived of water and nutrients, growling slowly, but beautifully.

I first heard of sphagnum moss from Batchelder's show, *New Horizons in Bonsai*. He used sphagnum moss as a hydroponic growth medium. I had a few bonsai growing in soil and was very happy to see any show about this fascinating hobby. We also have Batchelder's insight of using sphagnum moss as a growth medium. His vision and devotion deserve the highest accolades. I was lucky enough to see his method, and I started to practice it.

Sphagnum Moss

Peat moss is made from the decaying surface layers of sphagnum moss that sink into the bogs and begin to decompose. It is chopped up into the finely minced material we are used to seeing at garden shops. It makes a great fertilizer, and I always add it to the soil outside in which I plant full grown trees. Sphagnum peat moss is often mislabeled as sphagnum moss, which is an incomplete description. The other sphagnum moss, the long fibered type, is not that frequently seen and is often known only by horticulturalists and gardeners. It is truly marvelous material.

There are about 150 to 350 species of sphagnum moss worldwide. The feature that makes it so good for plant growth is its ability to hold water within its cell structure. Some species can hold up to 20 percent of its dry weight in water. The decaying surface sphagnum moss, called peat moss, is added to soil as a way for soil to maintain moisture and for use as a fertilizing agent. Even when wet, the species have air pockets in the cells that help the organism float to the surface of the wet bog and get the photosynthetic effects from sunlight. It is also an acidic material, which can be quite helpful to many plant species. They depend on surface rains for their water supply. Sphagnum moss does not decay easily because it grows in bogs that do not have much oxygen, which retards decomposition due to phenolic compounds in the moss's cell walls. I have had tremendous success with sphagnum moss as a growth medium, a transplanting medium, seed sprouting material, cutting starting medium, and air-layering medium. I never use rooting hormone (though using it with sphagnum moss certainly does no harm), which is frequently recommended for soil plantings. The results using just sphagnum moss are so worthy and reliable, and have proven themselves to me through empirical experience, that I, too, have become a great proponent of its many horticultural uses. When you have bonsai in sphagnum moss, the work to be done on the plant is so much easier than in a soil-bound plant. When working with traditional bonsai, it is often recommended working with size-based graded soils. In the traditional method the job of replanting or root trimming can easily become a harrowing experience as you try to work the roots into the soils. Many times if you try to take the plants from their soils, the soil growth medium falls apart and separates from the roots. This leaves you to carefully repack the roots, inch by straggly inch, using those graded soil mediums, based on the soil particle size. It is a delicate and can be a therapeutic method, but the costs in time and difficulty frequently discourage potential bonsai artists and cause them to give up their pursuits. Properly packed sphagnum moss using this new method can be easily lifted from its pot for inspection and care, while the soil crumbles from a traditional bonsai should you lift it from its pot. I have found the advantages overwhelming for many reasons. I can, and have, repotted a root bound plant in under one minute. If I used traditional graded soil techniques for bonsai, it might take up to several hours. It certainly can't be done in one minute. Not only can it be quick, it is exceptionally effective and healthy for the plant. They thrive using this simple technique, and the results are nothing less than astonishing when compared to the old-fashioned method of bonsai grown in soil.

Sphagnum moss itself is an item of concern. It has been shown to be involved in a disease known as sporotrichosis, a fungal infection that can enter a break in the skin or be inhaled into the lungs. It can be fatal. Latex type gloves and breathing masks are recommended as a safety procedure. But the talk of diseases from sphagnum moss may be overplayed, though I believe being overly cautious does no harm. It was, and still is, used in surgical dressings because of its great absorption power. After sterilization, it is placed into muslin bags and laid upon open wounds for absorption of exudates and transudates. Because of its excellent distribution of absorbed materials, it does not need to be changed as frequently as cotton or other materials, and ends up being less painful to the patient. So for plants or people, sphagnum moss is a wonderful, multi-use material.

Not all sphagnum moss carries sporotrichosis. In one Wisconsin study, it was found that a batch of sphagnum moss from a specific company was the cause of a small outbreak of workers (four people) with sporotrichosis, while at another nearby plant that used sphagnum moss to make thousands of Christmas wreaths, none of the employees had any signs of sporotrichosis. It is most likely that batches of sphagnum moss carrying sporotrichosis are the exception (and a rather small one at that) rather than the rule. But because you never know what lurks in the microscopic world by visual inspection, better safe than sorry. So it is advised to wear gloves and a mask when working with sphagnum moss. Sporotrichosis is common in many plants, and you can get it from sources other than sphagnum moss. It is an occupational disease of horticulturalists, farmers, and gardeners. Most cases of sporotrichosis are limited to the skin. Central nervous system, lung, and joint involvement are rare. It used to be treated with potassium iodide, but a new medication, Sporanox, has fewer side effects than the potassium iodide. It can take several weeks for the skin lesions to heal.

That being said, I find it still a lot easier to work with sphagnum moss barehanded, though I have taken to wearing a mask when removing sphagnum moss from its bags, as it is dry and many tiny pieces are aerosol in nature and the risk of inhalation is present. I have had no problems in 25 plus years of working with sphagnum moss. I also am careful to keep my mask on while I moisten the sphagnum moss with a hose, as particles are kicked up into the immediate area of work and do present a small but potential hazard. Should you be suffering from autoimmune deficiencies due to disease or medications, you should consult with your doctors about the risks involved.

I order big bales of sphagnum moss on the internet. I do a product search using Google for "long fiber sphagnum moss" (no quotes) or just "sphagnum moss" and look for those labeled "long fibered" or "un-milled." Available are large bales and smaller hobby bags. I find the hobby bags usually sized as 100 or 432 cubic inches (which is really not that much). I have also seen the small bags described as .33 pounds, another small amount. The bales that I used to get were 8 cubic feet, but unwieldy and overly large for storage or transport. Now I buy compressed 3.5 cubic feet rectilinear bales that are very densely packed with the best quality sphagnum moss available for a reasonable price. I am often surprised at the fine and fresh quality of the moss in these easily stored and stackable bags. The hobby sized bags are usually available in garden centers in the orchid section and buying them there may save the costs of shipping, but they are very expensive when compared to what you get by purchasing in bulk. I used to order the large bales from a local garden shop, but they had to special order it, and it often didn't come in. In addition, the prices were spiraling upwards every time I went to purchase a bale. I found the internet more competitive, and even when you added the shipping costs, it was still less expensive than the garden shops.

When I have too much sphagnum moss mixed for a particular project, I save the excess in a large plastic specimen pot (5–10 gallon size) for the next time. It just dries out in the dry season and is ready for added water the next time you use it. During the rainy season, it stays moist and ready to go at a moment's notice, as I leave the excess sphagnum moss in the containers outside in the rain. My dry bales are stored in a shed.

Learn to get used to the appearance of fresh sphagnum moss compared to aging, decomposing sphagnum moss. At some point it will be time to repot. It is so much easier when compared to the traditional method. You just take a hose and wash out the decomposing sphagnum moss, which breaks apart and washes off almost instantly. And any pieces left can remain, though it is best to try to remove all the old material, which as stated, really is quite easy to extract from the roots by the force of the water coming from the hose sprayer. I use an adjustable hose controller to regulate the size and force of the spray. You just add new sphagnum moss and repot. We will discuss this in more detail in future chapters.

Sphagnum moss is a wonderful material for bonsai. It has opened up new worlds for me, and I think it will for you also.

Afraid or Not Afraid? That Is the Question

I have spoken with many people about bonsai. There always seems to be a great interest in these miniature trees, but most people have a fear of this art and are only familiar with the older, traditional method. They don't want to invest the time or money in dealing with a hobby that on its surface appears difficult and for which training by professional bonsai artists is recommended. And therein lays the beauty and simplicity of the sphagnum moss method presented to you in this book. You don't need professional training. You don't need special pots and instruments, nor do you need to learn wiring techniques. The idea of grading your soils and dealing with sensitive roots becomes a non-issue with this method.

The fear is not necessary, and people recognize this. The cost to start is fairly low. I used to go the garden shops in Philadelphia and look for plants the stores were going to throw out because they just didn't appeal to their customers for landscaping. But they were great for anyone who wanted to try their hand at bonsai using this new and easy method. Many of my first bonsai cost about one dollar, as the stores were glad to get anything for these plants to avoid a total financial loss. The more bent and deformed (to their eyes) the better they looked to me. As you work with these plants, you develop an eye for what you want and what you will attempt to make your tree look like. The point of this hobby/art is to have fun and enjoy what you are doing. It is greatly frustrating to go to a traditional bonsai nursery, pay a lot of money for a good-looking specimen, and then have it die. No wonder people are scared of the traditional bonsai method. Soon after I switched to the sphagnum moss method, I realized just how easy and fun this new method is. I began switching all of my bonsai to sphagnum moss and have been enamored by it ever since. It is easy. It is fun. The scare factor is gone. As my dentist frequently tells my wife and me, "Don't be afraid, little boy (or girl)." Likewise I tell you, that there is no need for fear using this method. You will find yourself doing rewarding work with bonsai, and it will not only be evident in propping up your self-esteem, but it will become a method of relaxation that you can take advantage of far into your old age. I have a YouTube viewer who suffered great mental anguish from his role in the military while fighting in Iraq. Bonsai is his way out of the difficult mental memories and feelings. So throw your hesitations and fright away and join the legions of followers of the Sphagnum Moss Method of bonsai growth and care.

Roots

Roots can be scary to deal with on any plant, from orchids to common house plants. If handled roughly, or if you damage them by cutting or accidental breakage, they can cause problems. Overwatering, underwatering, or fertilization burns can kill your plants, especially if you use soil. It is not easy to transplant a specimen from one pot to another using soil. The soil falls out, leaving hanging and vulnerable roots, and replacing it, even if using orchid growth medium, can be a daunting task. Those problems disappear when using sphagnum moss as a growth medium. There appears to be a medicinal quality to the sphagnum moss, and its natural low acidity seems to make plants of all sorts just love to grow in it. Plus, it doesn't fall out when you remove the plant from its pot. When properly planted using the simple techniques in this book, the plant and its root structure come out as a

Sphagnum moss root ball after easy removal from the pot

unit, with the roots holding the moss in place. Repotting or transferring a plant or tree to another sized pot becomes an exercise in simplicity. All one needs to do is to cut off the bottom of the root ball with a sharp knife, place fresh sphagnum moss on the bottom of the new or old pot, and place the bonsai in the pot on top of the new sphagnum moss. If going to a different shaped pot, add additional sphagnum moss to fill in the voids.

It is virtually impossible to overwater a plant in sphagnum moss. The moss will swell as it sucks in the water and, when it reaches its maximum absorbency, will allow all of the excess water to flow out. But one needs to make sure that the drainage holes in the pot are large, and sometimes multiple, compared to the usual small holes found in terra cotta or ceramic pots sold in garden shops. The techniques for enlarging drainage holes will be explained in this book. It is not difficult and will help your plants avoid any overwatering. If you persist in constantly watering your plants, even in sphagnum moss, you run the risk of root rot, caused by roots sitting in water for too long a time. Most plants like to go through a cycle of watering and drying out. That is the natural state of things. It doesn't rain every day or at the same time. Droughts come about, as do heavy periods of rain. Plants in soil with small drainage holes can easily suffer from overwatering, though they will hold on longer in under-watering situations because soil holds water longer. You do not have to water soil plants as often as plants grown in sphagnum moss. Yes, the sphagnum moss will hold about ten times its weight in water, but it gives it up easier and faster, so watering in extended hot periods needs to be more frequent than with soil plants. Is this a detriment to this system? It is in one way, as you will have to be more aware of how your plants are doing water-wise. But this also allows you the great pleasure of seeing your plants more frequently and being aware of the many changes plants go through. I have some plants that act like the canary in the coal mine. I have a silver variegated hibiscus that will have droopy leaves before the other plants show any sign of water deficiency. It is my canary, and when I see the leaves drooping, I know it is time to water the bonsai. You will learn the tricks of determining if your sphagnum moss is too dry by sight and by touch. Look at your sphagnum moss when it is dry and in the bag. It is light colored and light in weight, and when you touch it, it feels dry and warm or room temperature. When wet it looks darker, is heavier, and has a recognizable coolness to the touch. Pick your plants up before and after watering and feel the difference in weight. It takes longer for water to saturate sphagnum moss than soil, so you may be watering the surface and the water may not be getting to the deeper roots, which can cause a deficiency that can ultimately harm your plants. I like to give the surface a fair watering, switch to another plant as the water settles into the first plant, then come back and water it again. This helps ensure a more thorough watering. By picking up your plants, you will learn what is normal and good in terms of water content of the sphagnum moss root ball inside your pot. I always overwater my bonsai, because I know the excess will run out of the large drainage holes, and the plant will be properly saturated, without the usual fears of overwatering. Just remember they need periods of dryness also. Get them into a cycle and your plants will be contented and delighted with their care. They are pampered pets in a way, and with the sphagnum moss method, it is easy to keep them that way, relatively free of problems.

Acidity and Alkalinity

Plants have differing requirements for the medium in which they are grown. For instance, many orchids need to grow on an orchid mixture consisting mainly of bark and wood chips. Trees can grow in many environments, from deserts to tropical rain forests. The desert environment is usually an alkaline environment, meaning its pH is high. PH measures the amount of acidity or alkalinity in a substance. The lower the pH, the more acidic it is. Likewise, the higher the pH number, the more alkaline it is. The neutral point between these two conditions is pH 7.0. Most trees and plants like a slightly acid growth medium, and sphagnum moss has a natural acidity that works well with most of the trees you might use in creating bonsai. I have plants called Foxtail Palms near my driveway. The original driveway was stone chips made from limestone, an alkaline material. I planted three of them at the same time that had all been grown from the same batch of seeds. They are about seven years old, and the growth rate has differed for all of them. The one farthest away from the driveway has grown the most, while the other two are stunted due to being

Two stunted foxtail palms near the limestone bedded driveway

too close to the underlying use of limestone. If you have a desert tree, or one that needs an alkaline environment, you can add a small amount of Epsom salt to the top of your growth medium. Watering the plant will carry the alkaline material into the growth medium over time and make for a more hospitable environment. The other trees should do well in the sphagnum moss without the addition of any additional substances. If you have a tree that needs a more acidic environment, you can add pine needles, sawdust, peat moss, or dried leaves on the surface as an acid source. Watering will percolate the acidity into the sphagnum moss. Do not add these to the sphagnum moss and mix it in, as this may create areas of bacteria or fungus growth. Just layer a little on top of the sphagnum moss and let the

A foxtail palm planted at the same time as those on the previous page, but away from the limestone driveway

percolating water carry it down to the roots. Fertilizing with chemicals also makes the medium more acidic.

Foliage Care

The leaves, collectively known as foliage, are a very important aspect of bonsai. There are many different kinds of plants and trees, and they are often put into categories depending on the type of foliage they have. For instance, there are evergreen trees (gymnosperms), which keep a major portion of their leaves all year around, versus deciduous trees (angiosperms), which lose their leaves during the fall and cold winter months, and then start out with a new set each spring. Those two major classifications have many subclassifications.

Evergreen tree leaves are designed to maintain and conserve moisture. The leaves are usually needle-like, being long and narrow, as in the pines, but sometimes may be rounded, fan-like, flattened, or scaly. Deciduous leaves have many shapes and sizes. They are classified by leaf type and their arrangements. There are simple and compound leaves, and each of these may be arranged opposite or alternately along the stem. In the fall, as the temperatures fall and the days become shorter, the chlorophyll, which gives the leaves their green color, begins to break down and leaves the other components of the leaves, such as the carotenes (orange and yellow) and the phycoerythrins (red), unmasked and visible. The chlorophyll is broken down to obtain nitrogen compounds that are stored in the tree for the next season of growth in the spring. Bonsai, either in soil or sphagnum moss, will also have these color changes. My gingkoes turn a beautiful yellow, and the maples I used to have when I lived in the northern climates would turn to red or orange, depending on the temperatures.

Foliage care is mainly that of pruning or cutting certain leaves and/or branches off of the tree. One may do this to improve the artistic shape of the tree or to have a better appearance as the yellowing or bigger leaves are removed. Proportion of the tree parts is an important part of bonsai principles. Keeping the leaves small by pruning methods helps keep the tree in proportion.

The foliage is almost continuously attacked by insects or disease. They are controlled by the use of insecticides, fungicides, or bactericides. Sometimes these leave a residue that can usually be wiped off with a dampened rag to give a better appearance.

Transplanting

The sphagnum moss method has a great advantage over the traditional method when it comes to transplanting a nursery specimen from its original pot to its new home. The traditional method has the bonsai enthusiast using different combinations of grit and humus for evergreen versus deciduous trees, and depending on the species, sometimes adding clays, sand, peat moss, pine bark, compost and/or coconut components. With the sphagnum moss method, we use only unmilled sphagnum moss, and nothing else. That makes transplanting easier and eliminates the complications with various needs of different species and the soils they prefer. It is also quicker and neater. You should never add anything to the sphagnum moss, as the introduction of other materials, no matter how well intended, may cause problems. The techniques we are generally discussing here will be explained in greater detail in the chapters ahead.

Repotting

Repotting trees is similar to transplanting but even easier using the sphagnum moss method. If your tree is root bound or has decomposing sphagnum moss, repotting is necessary. In the traditional method you need to carefully remove the soil it either came in from the nursery, or that to which you have transplanted it, to protect the roots from damage. With the sphagnum moss method, you intentionally cut down the roots and don't worry about breakage or damage as the medicinal characteristic of the sphagnum moss not only encourages root growth and spread, but protects and defends against the problems encountered in the traditional method. It is as simple as sawing off the bottom of the root ball with a knife and placing the tree back in its pot on a new bed of fresh sphagnum moss. I can repot most trees in under one minute, while the traditional method may take hours or days.

Root-bound tree in sphagnum moss that needs repotting

Increasing Tree Growth Speed

Another difference in the two methods is that the traditional method encourages slow growth and wiring to shape the trees, and sometimes uses water deprivation to keep growth slow. In the sphagnum moss method, we do just the opposite. We want fast growth so that the trunk develops more quickly, making an older looking tree. Wiring is okay if you want to use it for shaping trees, but I find that by directional pruning, which is the cutting off of branches so that the new growth goes in the desired path, you can obtain trees of great beauty. Tying and roping the trees can also have this effect. Because of the fast growth with the sphagnum moss method, wiring needs to be examined frequently and closely so that the tree does not scar if it grows into the wire. As I have many trees, I sometime would forget where I wired and would have damage to my trees. If you wire one tree at a time and keep a careful eye on it, it can be an exciting way to shape your tree. Personally, I prefer to have my trees look like they do in their natural environment, rather than have the unnatural but beautiful appearance of trees from the Orient. But it is your choice, as it is your tree, and that is one of the enjoyments and artistic rewards of creating your own bonsai rather than buying one that has been already trained.

We help our trees grow faster by frequent fertilization. I usually fertilize every week to ten days during the growth season and once a month during the winter. The sphagnum moss has few nutrients, and the frequent fertilization is necessary for good plant growth and health. I will describe in detail the methods used in later portions of this book.

Making Trees Look Older More Quickly

The goals in bonsai include making small, proportionally sized trees that have the appearance of age. The traditional method has different techniques for doing this compared to the sphagnum moss method. In the sphagnum moss method, we encourage growth by frequent fertilization, making the tree look older, faster. We achieve proportion control by directional pruning, to shape the tree as we wish it to appear, and by using leaf size reduction techniques. In both methods the addition of surface moss gives an appearance of grass and a natural setting for the small tree. Rocks and gravel paths can also give a pleasing appearance. All of this helps the tree appear older than it really is. The sphagnum moss method does this more quickly than the traditional method.

Inspections

Bonsai need frequent inspections in both systems of bonsai development. But the inspection process in the sphagnum moss method is easier and quicker in regard to roots. The foliage inspections are the same. Checking the roots of a traditionally planted bonsai means removing it from the pot, which has inherent problems when working with soils. When you remove the traditional tree, a good deal of the soil may fall away and have to be replaced in replanting. With the sphagnum moss method, the root ball is easily extracted from the pot with no loss of sphagnum moss and inspection is quick. If there has been too much root growth, as briefly explained above, one merely cuts off the bottom edge of the root ball and places it on a new bed of sphagnum moss. Root rot is something I rarely run into but is easily spotted during an inspection of the root system. Sometimes pests are seen in the root inspection, such as ants, and these issues will be addressed in later chapters of this book.

When inspecting the foliage, look for insect problems, such as leaves that have been eaten or the insects themselves. You need to look for fungal infections or bacterial infections, which present themselves in many guises. Old leaves need to be removed when spotted. The appearance of the leaves can tell you how your plant is doing. If you are watering too much or too little, it can show up in the leaf appearance. I have a hibiscus that shows wilted leaves if the water is insufficient, and it acts as a warning sign. The advantage of the sphagnum moss in terms of watering is that by using big drainage holes, it is virtually impossible to overwater a sphagnum moss bonsai. Keep your eyes open and learn the signs your plants will give you, and you will have robust and healthy bonsai.

3

General Plant Care with the Sphagnum Moss Method

The Sex Life of Plants

Angiosperms and Gymnosperms—Seed Bearing Plants

There are two types of trees used in bonsai. One is the angiosperms, or flowering trees, and the other is the gymnosperms, or naked seed trees. Their difference arises in leaf structure and sexual reproduction methods. Both produce seeds for reproduction.

Angiosperms—Flowering Trees

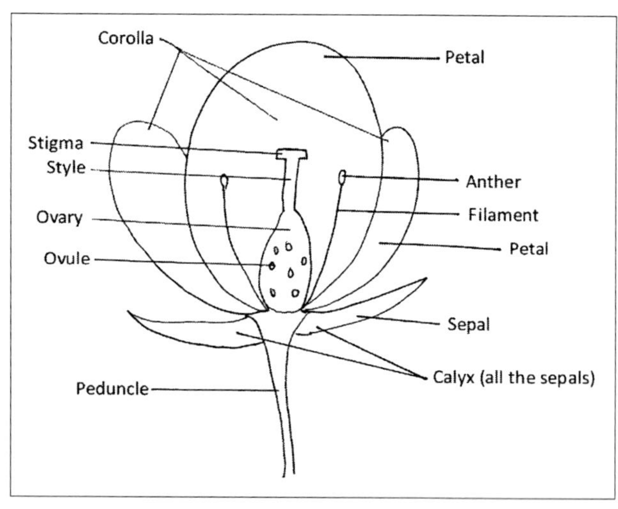

The parts of a flower

The sex life of plants is the same whether planted in soil or sphagnum moss. Plants have different ways to reproduce. In the angiosperms there are male and female reproductive parts, called the stamen (male) and the carpel (female). In the flower there are numerous parts. The stamen consists of the anther, which makes pollen, the male reproductive cells; and the filament, which holds up the anther. The carpels consist of the stigma, which receives the pollen; the style, which supports the stigma and attaches at the ovary (the female reproductive organ); and the ovule, which is the reproductive part that will become the seed after the pollen fertilizes it.

The process in which seeds are started is called pollination. The pollen of different plants is spread to ensure genetic diversity by wind, rain, insects, and animals, such as bees, wasps, and bats. The wind spreads the pollen by simple air movement, rain carries pollen, and the insects and animals spread the pollen by moving from plant to plant in search of nectar. Once the pollen lands on the stigma, pollen tubes grow down toward the ovary where they fertilize one of the ovules. This fertilized ovule will develop into the seed. The seeds are then spread about by wind, birds and other animals that eat the fruit, or by gravity, dropping the seed to the ground.

There are different types of flowers. The perfect type of flower has both the male and female reproductive organs. The imperfect flower has either the male or the female reproductive organ, but not both. Complete flowers have stamens, a pistil, petals (the thin plates, surrounding the male and female reproductive parts, which form the corolla of a flower) and sepals (small leaves under the flower). An incomplete flower is lacking one these components. Many plants have male or female parts. If we want a tree with fruit, it is best to have a female plant developing fruit that contain seeds. In some plants the females have messy flowers that drop, dirtying lawns or cars and are therefore not desirable. The gingkoes, which often line streets because of their hardiness to auto pollution, are usually males, thus avoiding the odiferous female seeds. Some male plants can have some complete flowers, meaning they are able to produce some fruit but not as many as the female can produce. The flowering plants (angiosperms) are a recent development in the evolution of plants, though still millions of years old.

Palm trees are angiosperms. Most of us recognize the exotic appearance of palms, with their long, unadorned trunk, ending in a spreading crown of long leaves known as fronds. They often resemble the cycads (which will be discussed below). Frequently they have thick, stout trunks, but these two types of trees are very different in their reproductive styles, which places them in different areas of plant classification. They have evergreen, compound leaves, usually large in nature. There are many exceptions, as there are over 2,600 species recognized. Their branchless trunks (though some have multiple trunks growing from one area) and top-hat appearance has been used throughout history in the warmer temperate climates, the tropics, and sub-tropics. Used as symbols for victory, peace, and fertility, they have appeared on coins and in art through the ages, just as today they often represent vacations and the tropics. As angiosperms, they use flowers for reproduction. They are usually greenish, on the small side, and many times difficult to notice. Each female flower contains only one egg, and though the trees are usually unisexual per individual tree, they often switch gears and produce male flowers one season and female flowers the next. This helps ensure cross pollination and a diversity of genetic material combinations, assisting them in their evolutionary development. They are not well suited for bonsai growth because cutting them shorter, to keep a thick trunk

Palm tree on ancient coin

while restricting height, will usually result in the plant's death. Brian Batchelder had a coconut palm that he was trying to keep restricted in size by keeping the roots contained in a small pot. Those who saw his television series saw this plant perhaps once or twice, but his death prevented us from seeing how it worked out. I started growing royal palms, a spectacular species from seed, the first year I moved to Florida. They sprouted easily in the sphagnum moss, and I eventually planted them outside to let them develop fully, instead of trying to have them remain as bonsai because their growth was too massive for the pots. I envisioned that they would not be miniatures of the beautiful royal palms I have now because their stem development takes many years to show the usual ring structure, and they were just outgrowing their containers. This is an area well worth experimenting with, and I will continue to try.

Gymnosperms — Naked Seed Trees

The gymnosperms are an older classification of trees that do not produce flowers. Their male and female reproductive organs mainly form cones, such as the pine cones with which we are familiar. Gymnosperm means "naked seeds," as their seeds have no ovary wall to protect them, as in the angiosperms. There are four main classifications within the gymnosperm group: conifers, cycads, ginkgoes and gnetales. This grouping is known to have existed since about 380 million years ago from the fossil record, during the carboniferous period. They are a part of the carbon and oil forming processes that have given us the fossil fuels of today. The conifers are also known as evergreens, mainly producing cones, with some using brightly colored and sweet fleshy fruit, often eaten and spread by birds. The cycads have a crown of leaves and a thick trunk, and are often mistaken for palms or ferns. The ginkgoes were thought to have been extinct, but Englebert Kaempfer discovered living specimens in Japan in 1691. They are the only living species left in this group, though there is fossil evidence of their relatives. Found in China, where they had probably been planted by monks, they spread to Japan and eventually the rest of the world. The gnetales comprise three genera, and their classification is still evolving. They are woody but have vessel structures similar to the flowering plants.

Female pine cone

Male pine cone

The gymnosperms produce seeds

but not flowers. Their male and female reproductive organs mainly consist of cones. They release pollen into the air, which is spread by wind to reach the ovules. Some of the gymnosperms, such as gingkoes, produce a nut-like fruit, while others produce a fleshy colorful fruit that is sweet and attracts birds and other animals to help spread the seeds. All gymnosperms have a similar reproductive method. The adult trees form male pollen cones and female egg cones. Some species of trees have male or female cones, and some have both types. The female cones are bigger and more noticeable, and may hang on their parent trees for many years, while the male cones drop off soon after they release their pollen. Release of the pollen is followed by spreading of the pollen through the winds in the springtime. The free pollen lands on the open scales of the female cones on a sticky fluid that leads to the egg chamber. Once pollination occurs, the cone closes, and the pollen fertilizes by growing a tube that travels to the eggs. Once contact is made, fertilization occurs. When mature, the scales of the female cones open, dropping seeds. This procedure usually takes two years in most species. The seeds are dispersed by gravity and animals. The gingkoes make a nut in a similar manner, in that pollen, or sperm, reaches the eggs where fertilization occurs. The ginkgo sperm are motile, having a flagellum that helps propel them to the eggs. The cycads reproduce in two manners, asexual or sexual. The asexual method produces offshoots or suckers, while the sexual method produces male and female cones, with pollen and eggs. In the gnetales, there is a process called double fertilization, in which one event forms an embryo and the following event produces an endosperm, which is the outer layer of the seed, surrounding the embryo, providing nutrition for the seed.

The conifers are represented by the pines, the cycads by the sago palm, the gingkoes by the gingko, and the gnetales by the Ephedras.

Getting Proper Species for Your Area

Where you live makes a great difference in how certain trees will grow. It seems obvious that if you live in Alaska or Siberia the trees of Florida or the rain forests of Brazil will not be good candidates for bonsai. Likewise, if you live in the tropics trees from the frozen tundra of the north will likely not flourish. But this is not completely true. Because we live with heat and air conditioning, the possibilities are much more varied than you might think. But it will take a great deal of care and effort to have a well grown and successful tree from an area that is so far away from where you live. It is easier to keep trees warm using indoor heating in cold climates than it is to keep trees from the more frigid parts of the world cold enough for a sufficient period of time to simulate the winter conditions that they need. I had tried to bring my northern Maples, Oaks, and others down to Florida, but the heat was too much for them to bear. When I had the great fortune to visit the sequoias in California, I purchased some seedlings at the gift shop. They all died because the conditions were so different from what they needed.

In the long run, it is best to keep to the trees that are native to your area, but remember that you can have trees adapt from other areas, and it is worth the try to raise species that appeal to you. Some trees seem to do well no matter where they are. But tropical trees are accustomed to warm temperatures and long summers, with virtually no real winters, other than weather spells blowing cold air from the north. My advice is to shop in local nurseries and garden shops, and ask what trees are native to the area. Usually if they are selling trees, they are trees that will flourish in their area; otherwise, they could get a bad reputation from selling plants that die easily, no matter what care the owner gives them. If you live in the North, then the pines, maples, and poplars will usually do quite well. They may have to be protected during the cold winter months, as they have root systems in pots, which make them more susceptible to damage from the freezing temperatures. Plants in the ground have a natural insulation that the pots do not provide. If you live in the South, look for trees of a southern nature. Avocados, fruit trees, eucalyptus, and calamondin, for example, will generally do well in southern climates. Likewise plants of the southwestern United States, such as the Texas ebony, Joshua tree, pistachio, apple or peach trees, can also fare well there. There are trees that do well in the desert, or other places of extremes. Your bonsai will do best when it is acclimatized to the area it comes from. But by all means experiment. I was told you can't grow a northern mimosa in Florida. I obtained some seeds, and I have a magnificent mimosa that I have had for 15 years. But I usually find when people trade seeds with me from other climates, the seeds I receive do not grow well here. Likewise, the seeds that I send them do not fare well there. A greenhouse helps, but one is not always available. So stick to the locals in most cases and experiment with the exotics and see what you can accomplish. Even though the oaks, hollies and maples did well up north in sphagnum moss, that alone was not enough to bring them success In Florida.

Watering

Trees need water, and there are different ways to accomplish this. I always liked the idea of showering my trees with a spray from a hose or sprinkler, as it simulates the natural rain they are accustomed to. It also has benefits in that it helps wash away pests and superficial diseases. It also keeps the plants clean longer and, by washing away dirt that might clog the stomata (pores) on the bottom of the leaves, helps keep the trees in good condition. Junipers are susceptible to mites, and I find that a good washing keeps mine relatively clear of these pests. Sphagnum moss grown trees usually need more frequent watering than soil based trees. Soil based trees, if overwatered will often develop root rot. The extra water that inundates sphagnum moss plants and trees runs harmlessly out the big drain holes, but the needed frequency of watering is increased. In the hot weather I water my trees every day, as long as we are not in the rainy season, when I let nature do the watering.

Some people like to use an automatic water system to take care of watering and/or fertilizing their trees. I find the trees still need water delivered to the foliage for cleansing purposes, as discussed above. In many of the automatic systems, the water is directly deposited into the soil or sphagnum moss on a regular basis, and the foliage is ignored. If you have soil plants and travel for an extended period, your automatic system may unintentionally provide an excess of water that may cause problems, as natural rain may oversaturate your trees. With the sphagnum moss method, overwatering is not a problem as long as it is not a constant thing. As stated before, the excess runs out, and the large drainage holes help keep the roots from living in a watery environment. I have constructed a PVC pipe system that goes to my bonsai tables and stands. I will turn it on and let the spray do its job for five to fifteen minutes. I then go around with a hose and spray any plants that the spray could not reach because of their position. My system is hooked up to hose lines and easily controlled. Later in this book we will go into greater detail if you wish to set up your own automatic system that can deliver water and/or fertilizer in the amounts you want, or the semi-automatic system that I use. Sometimes I like to just go out and use a hose to water my plants individually. It gives me a chance to see how they are doing, and I find it relaxing and enjoyable. There are watering bulbs that can be filled and inserted into the growth medium, supposedly giving the plants just the right amount of water each day until the bulb is empty and needs refilling. I have not used those particular watering devices, as I wonder about the delivery of water to all parts of the root system and not just to the area where they are implanted.

You need to get a feel for the sphagnum moss planting because it can take time for the water to saturate all parts of the medium. I usually start with a brief surface watering, allowing the surface to be saturated. This enables the second watering to be transported into the deeper medium and not just run off the top surface, which can happen if you are not careful. The tops can look good, but the bottoms may be drying out without your knowledge, and that can be as dangerous to your plants as root rot. After you water, it is a good idea to pull your plants out of their pots, one by one, and see how the water is working its way downward. That way you will establish a proper time span for watering and keep your plants healthy.

Fertilization

Some of the most common questions my YouTube watchers ask me are how often to fertilize and what to use. I keep it simple, and it works well for me. I always use the fertilizer in half strength as opposed to what the manufacturer suggests. This avoids root burn, which can be very harmful, if not deadly, to your tree. In the summer I fertilize my bonsai once every seven to ten days. The rains and the frequent watering will wash out the fertilizer, and using this method of frequent fertilization, the plants grow faster and healthier, having the nutrients they need. In the wintertime, I fertilize only once a month; because of the shortened periods of available light, the trees' growth rate slows down naturally, and they do not need the more frequent fertilization schedule.

I use a combination of a dry fertilizer, such as Miracle Grow, mixed with SuperThrive, a vitamin preparation you can get at garden centers, nurseries or on the internet. Lately I have been adding a locally produced fertilizer called Grow, which seems to really help plants do their best. Grow is new and in a testing stage now. Perhaps one day it may be available to you.

The fertilizers I use can all be used as media fertilizers, being deposited on top of the medium to soak in, or sprayed onto the foliage, where it is absorbed by the plant. I often go back and forth between these methods, ensuring a thorough delivery of the nutrients to the bonsai. I used to sometimes make a soup of water and fertilizer in a big plastic container that could accommodate my larger plants. I would then gently lower the plant into the water with the fertilizer combo until the water just hit the bottom of the trunk. You will be covering up your surface moss when you do this, and if it is not well attached to the sphagnum moss below, it may float away. Just stick it back where it came from after you remove the plant, and it will look fine again very soon. You will see bubbles escaping as the water/fertilizer mix seeps into the medium, replacing the air with water. Just wait it out until all the bubbles stop and slowly pull out the plant. You should easily notice the increased weight of the bonsai due to the great absorptive properties of the sphagnum moss. This is probably the best method for fertilization, but it is not always practical due to time constraints in your life. It takes more time but is more thorough. If you only have one or a few plants, this method is recommended. The other methods will also do well.

When I am out fertilizing my fruit trees, with citrus fertilizer, I will often sprinkle a little bit onto the surface of my bonsai citrus trees. Likewise, if fertilizing my ornamentals, I will sometimes add a bit of that fertilizer to those species that I have made into bonsai.

The plants are quite attuned to cyclical events. They seem to respond best when events like watering or fertilizing are carried out on a regular basis, as to day and time. Haphazard watering or fertilization may slightly inhibit plant growth, but as long as you are watering or fertilizing on a fairly regular basis, you should see no problems. If you are on vacation, you can skip a week or two of fertilization without worry. Better to skip the week than have a friend, who means well, damage your plant by thinking that extra fertilizer is better than less.

Fertilizing is important, so try to get on a regular schedule and don't overfeed.

Leaf Shapes and Classifications

Leaves are some of the components of the foliage of a plant or tree. The leaf is a specialized organ, and its main job is to carry out photosynthesis. Photosynthesis is a process by which the leaf takes in carbon dioxide and water, and produces compounds, such as sugar, by using the energy it receives from sunlight. A byproduct of this chemical reaction is oxygen, which allowed the young earth to develop life as we know it, based on carbon, hydrogen and oxygen. The loss of water is known as transpiration.

Leaves are usually flat, though many of the conifers have rounded leaves that resemble toothpicks in a general way, while others look like small scales. Ferns, palms, and cycads have structures that appear leafy but are referred to as fronds.

There are many different leaf shapes. There is no need to learn all of them, as they get quite detailed, and sometimes the differences are small. For our purposes, we will discuss the various leaf shapes and show you what they look like.

There are two main classifications of leaves, simple and compound. Simple leaves consist of a single leaf (such as oak, maple, gingko, and the like), which is attached to a branch of the tree. Compound leaves have two or more simple leaves attached to a leaf stalk.

Simple Leaves

In alphabetical order, some of the simple leaf shapes are:

Acular look like needles, thin and pointed
Acuminate far end tapers to a point
Aristate far end tapers to a spine or thorn-like end
Cochleate shell shaped
Cordate heart shaped with the stem attaching to the cleft of the heart
Cuneate wedge shaped
Deltoid triangular with the stem attached to a side

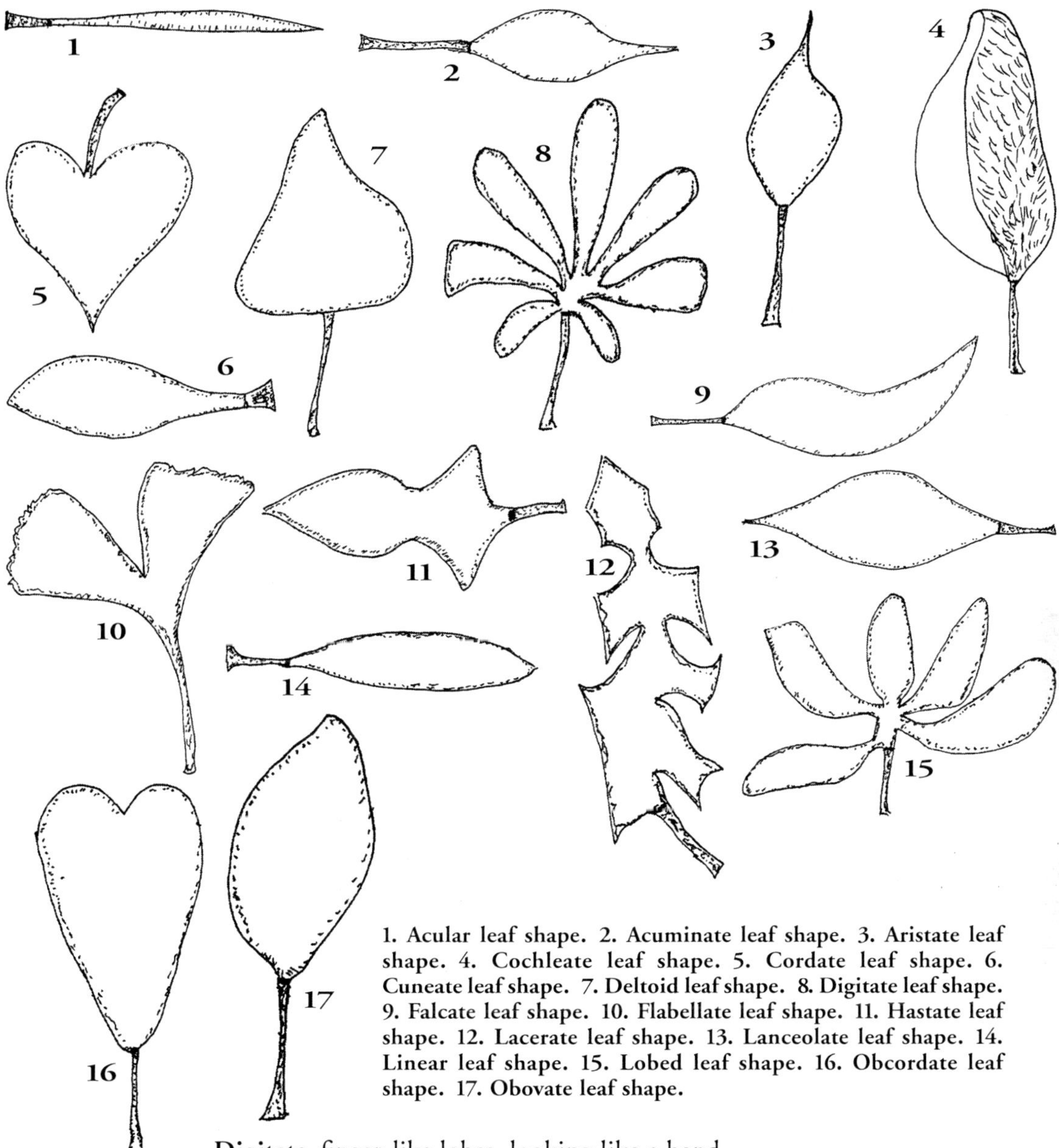

1. Acular leaf shape. **2.** Acuminate leaf shape. **3.** Aristate leaf shape. **4.** Cochleate leaf shape. **5.** Cordate leaf shape. **6.** Cuneate leaf shape. **7.** Deltoid leaf shape. **8.** Digitate leaf shape. **9.** Falcate leaf shape. **10.** Flabellate leaf shape. **11.** Hastate leaf shape. **12.** Lacerate leaf shape. **13.** Lanceolate leaf shape. **14.** Linear leaf shape. **15.** Lobed leaf shape. **16.** Obcordate leaf shape. **17.** Obovate leaf shape.

Digitate finger-like lobes, looking like a hand
Elliptic oval shaped, with a little, or absent point
Falcate shaped like a sickle
Flabellate fan-like in shape
Hastate triangular with lobes at the base
Lacerate leaf appears to have been torn
Lanceolate pointed at both ends, shaped like the tip of a lance
Linear long and narrow
Lobed has deep indented margins
Obcordate heart shaped, with stem attached at the point
Obovate shaped like a teardrop with stem attached at the point

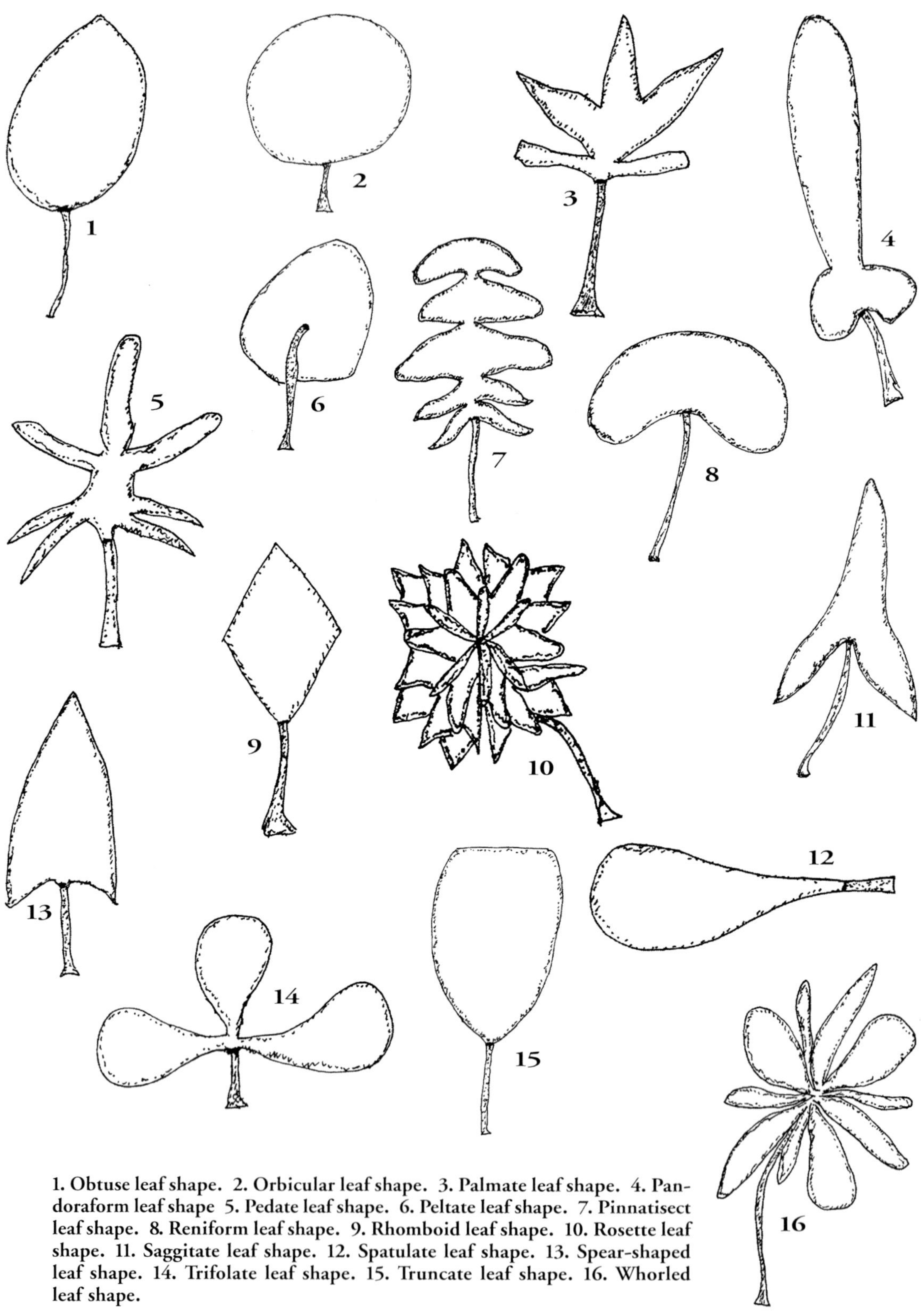

1. Obtuse leaf shape. 2. Orbicular leaf shape. 3. Palmate leaf shape. 4. Pandoraform leaf shape 5. Pedate leaf shape. 6. Peltate leaf shape. 7. Pinnatisect leaf shape. 8. Reniform leaf shape. 9. Rhomboid leaf shape. 10. Rosette leaf shape. 11. Saggitate leaf shape. 12. Spatulate leaf shape. 13. Spear-shaped leaf shape. 14. Trifolate leaf shape. 15. Truncate leaf shape. 16. Whorled leaf shape.

Obtuse having a blunt tip
Orbicular round, paddle shaped
Palmate lobes or leaflets radiating from the base of the leaf stem
Pandoraform violin shaped
Pedate palmate shaped but with divided lateral lobes
Peltate rounded with stem attaching on underside of leaf
Pinnatisect having deep, opposite lobes
Reniform kidney shaped
Rhomboid shaped like a diamond
Rosette leaflets in tight circular rings
Saggitate shaped like an arrowhead
Spatulate spoon shaped
Spear shaped shaped like a spear point
Trifolate divided into three leaflets
Truncate having a squared-off end
Whorled rings of three or more leaflets

Compound Leaves

Compound leaves consist of multiple simple leaves arranged on a leaf stalk or multiple leaf stalks in various ways. There are many fewer trees that have compound leaves than have simple leaves. This is used in identification of some trees because of the limited number of compound-leaf trees. The type of leaf that is repeated on a compound leaf (e.g., palmate, trifoliate) can be very helpful in determining what type of tree you are looking at. For instance, if your tree has palmate leaves on a compound leaf, it is either a buckeye or a horse-chestnut.

This book is not a study in botany, so I will present a few of the types of compound leaves so you have a general idea of leaf shapes. If you seek further and more detailed knowledge about the various compound leaf types (such as tripinnate) or the descriptive classifications based on leaf edges (e.g., serrated, dentate) or the surface of leaves (e.g., hairy, tuberculate, verrucose) seek it out on the internet or in books, as it is an interesting field of study.

Even pinnate single leaflets in rows, with two at the tip
Odd pinnate single leaflets in rows, with a single leaf at the tip

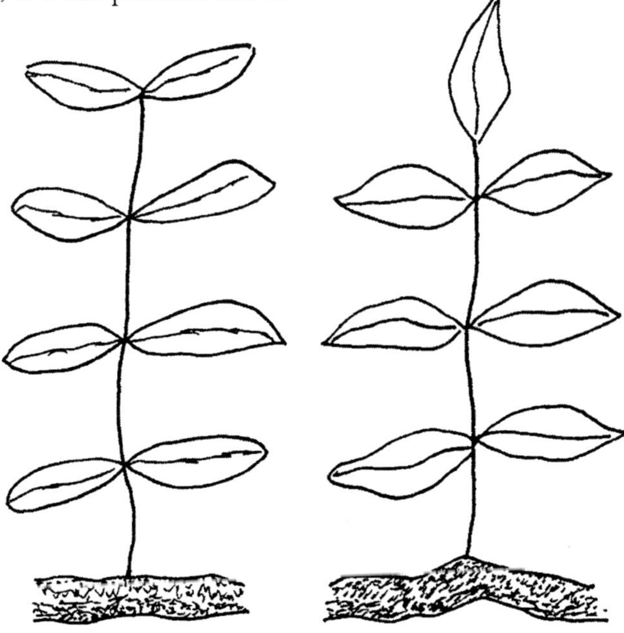

Left: **Even pinnate leaf shape.** ***Right:*** **Odd pinnate leaf shape.**

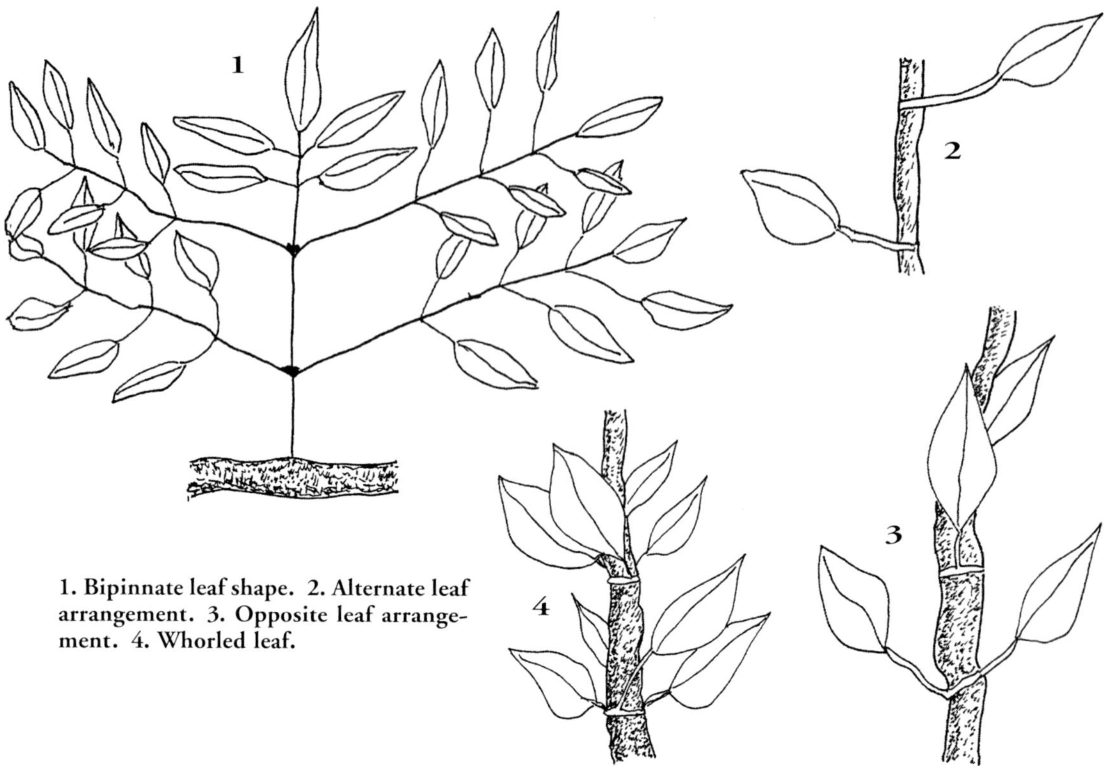

1. Bipinnate leaf shape. 2. Alternate leaf arrangement. 3. Opposite leaf arrangement. 4. Whorled leaf.

Bipinnate the leaflets are also pinnate
Alternate leaf arrangement leaflets arranged alternately
Opposite leaf arrangement leaflets opposite one another
Whorled leaf arrangement three or more leaves at a node

Lighting — Sun Requirements

Plants have various needs, such as water amounts (cypress want a lot of water), salt (sea grapes have a high tolerance of salt, while others have none), fertilizer (the Venus flytrap, pitcher plants, and other carnivorous plants require a nitrogen poor soil because these plants capture animals for their nitrogen), and sunlight. Some trees like full sun or about six hours a day of direct sunlight. Others like part sun, which is four to six hours a day of direct sun, mixed with some shade, usually in the morning or afternoon. Some trees want dark shade, such as on the forest floor, being protected from the sun by the canopies of trees that like full sun above them. Most deciduous trees like a medium shade. There are also those that like light shade, as on the north side of a building (in the Northern Hemisphere and opposite in the Southern Hemisphere), where they receive indirect lighting as the day progresses.

In Chapter 20, you will find a listing of trees and their usual light requirements. Some trees can do well in differing light amounts, which allows us to keep some plants indoors, while others do best outdoors.

Deciduous Versus Evergreen Trees

Deciduous trees are those that lose their leaves on a seasonal basis, usually in the winter months. They are able to determine that the length of the light received during the day is lessening, and that sends a signal for the leaves to shut down in preparation for the cold months ahead. Evergreens usually have green growth the year round, though some are considered semi-deciduous, meaning they lose old foliage as new foliage develops. Any of these tree types seemingly do well using the sphagnum moss method.

Examining for Problems

With the sphagnum moss method, it is easier to examine your trees for the problems that might occur. Because they are easily removed from their pots without fear of soil dropping from the roots, and easily replaced into those pots, the sphagnum moss method has many advantages over the traditional method.

One problem that might occur is root rot. This is usually due to a condition where the roots are in water for extended periods of time, causing the roots to die. The roots are unable to get the air they need, and thus they decay. This is often fatal in plants located in soil medium. It is a common problem in houseplants and bonsai because of poor drainage. Because we use large drainage holes, and the sphagnum moss only absorbs a limited amount of water before allowing the excess to drain off, if examinations are frequent, it is a problem that rarely occurs with this method. If you catch it early, it is easily repairable by merely cutting off the lowest root portions where the rot starts and replacing it with fresh sphagnum moss for the roots to grow into. When you see your sphagnum moss turning a dark color and decomposing, it is always good to examine your plant closely and then replace the old decomposing sphagnum moss with new sphagnum moss. We will discuss the techniques for this in later chapters.

Physical damage can occur to your trees. Breaks caused by wind or animals, such as squirrels or birds, can be noticed by visual inspection of the plant growing above the growth medium. There is not much to do for these breaks. It is best to remove the broken piece, preferably with a clipper so the exposed surface area is small, rather than pulling off the piece and perhaps making a strip of exposed branch that can become infected by bacteria, fungus, or viruses. You can use a pruning sealer to cover the freshly cut end for protection. I rarely do this on smaller branches, but on larger ones I will protect the exposed area in this manner. In some trees you may develop a hole in the trunk. Sometimes they are aesthetically pleasing and can become part of the tree's configuration, adding an aged look. But if it weakens the tree so that it faces the possibility of breakage, it is best to fill up the hole with a waterproof material so that water does not collect in the hole and cause water rot. In my bigger trees outside, I use cement to fill in holes of this type. In bonsai, careful watching and drying of the hole may allow it to form a scar tissue that will keep the tree looking natural. But the trunk may be compromised in strength, and there is always the possibility of severe breakage when a bird or squirrel lands upon the tree. You can keep partially broken limbs as they are, and often they will form an interesting shape. Sometimes you might like the looks of the broken branch or deformed trunk and wish to use other techniques, such as jin or shari, which will be discussed in greater detail in future chapters. I have found that trees in sphagnum moss recover from these incidents quicker than soil raised trees, brought about by the quick growth due to the frequent fertilization used in this method.

Insects also can be quite destructive to bonsai, as can other invertebrates. Worms of various types can infect the growth medium but can usually be cured with proper chemical treatments. Grasshoppers, caterpillars, and other leaf-eating insects can be very destructive. But use of insecticides on a periodic basis can eliminate this problem. Ants can also be destructive when they live within the sphagnum moss. That is why frequent inspection is a deterrent to ants. You merely pull out the plant to examine its roots as discussed above, and if there are any ants you will usually see them scurrying around in great numbers, carrying their eggs to hide. I find that a sprinkling of fire-ant killer and then watering is sufficient to drive the ants out. But keep an eye on neighboring plants, as the ants make take up residence there. Ants sometimes use aphids to suck out the juices of plants, and you need to be able to identify them so that a spray insecticide can be used to kill them or drive them away. Bees, wasps and hornets can be a danger to the bonsai enthusiast, who may accidently stumble upon them, and the stinging insect responds by protecting itself. I have rarely found stinging insects to attack without reason, other than yellow jackets, which are mean and can sting repeatedly and not lose their stinger, as a bee does. Bees only sting once because the barbs on their stingers stay in your skin, and when the bee pulls back, it rips out its internal organs causing death. Wasps and ants can sting or bite repeatedly, so look out for these creatures.

Insect eaten leaf

Lizards, if big enough, can damage limbs because of their weight or leg propulsion, as they push off to escape the threat of a human or predator. We have many anoles that are very territorial here in Florida, and the same ones inhabit their own tree without damage. In fact, as insect eaters, they help protect the trees. I often find the white, pea-sized eggs of anoles buried in the sphagnum moss root ball. You can leave them or remove them. They will do no harm.

Snakes are occasional visitors here in Florida, and you may have them where you live. I never saw any in Philadelphia when I lived there, but here in Florida they are a fairly frequent sight. I have never seen them in my bonsai, though it is always a possibility. I usually see them on the ground, or occasionally winding around a shrub or bush. They are probably more scared of you and will usually try to escape from your presence. If accidentally cornered, however, they may often respond with hostile behavior. But because my outside bonsai are out in the open, I find they almost always run away. If crawling around bonsai they may cause breakage. If left alone, they will move on, and later you can assess any damage that might have occurred.

Spiders can and will bite, and I believe all have some degree of poison in their bites, and some can be extremely dangerous. Keep your eyes open for webs and look to see if the builder of the web is home. Some spiders do not build webs, so just looking before you touch is a good practice with anything growing outdoors.

Fungus, bacteria, and viruses can also be a problem. You may see signs on the bark, or the leaves may develop spots, discoloration, crinkling, or similar manifestations that you notice are not normal. When examining the root ball look for discolorations, such as white areas that may indicate fungus. Cleaning out the sphagnum moss with a strong hose spray and repacking the area is usually sufficient, as is cutting out the infected area and replacing it with fresh sphagnum moss. There are usually easily treated by spraying, but at other times, nothing you do will prevent the loss of the tree.

If you overfertilize, or use too strong a concentration of fertilizer, you can get root burn. Often fertilizers contain urea as a source of nitrogen. It is a synthetic compound that can be dangerous to root systems. You may see signs, such as leaf yellowing, slow tree growth, or lack of flowering, but it is relatively easily cured if caught early. That is why it is important to examine your plants frequently and be on the lookout for changes, such as leaf yellowing. Especially with the sphagnum moss method, the treatment is easy. Merely overwater your plant a few times. The water will dissolve the extra fertilizer and wash it away through the large drainage hole or holes. The sphagnum moss will only absorb its usual amount of water, and the rest will pass by harmlessly, washing away the excess fertilizer. Do this for a couple of days, and you should be fine. With soil grown trees, the excess watering may cause a washing away of soil if the drainage is sufficient, or root rot if the water is retained in the bottom of the pot. This is another advantage of the sphagnum moss method over the traditional method.

Heating and Air Conditioning Problems with Indoor Bonsai

Raising bonsai indoors presents its own special problems. There are certain plants that can do well indoors, such as schefflera or ficus. But other trees may be adversely affected by either the heating systems in northern climates or the air conditioning systems in southern climates. Northern climates that have warm summers may also present air conditioning problems.

Heating systems may cause problems due to low humidity. A humidity of 50 to 80 percent appears best for house trees. Plants suffering from heat problems indoors may not be getting enough fresh air, as recirculated air can be a problem. The plants may not show the usual growth or just look like something is not right. Sometimes yellowing of the leaves will occur or an inability to flower. You can attempt to raise the humidity by frequent misting or placing containers filled with water around the room. A mechanical humidifier may also help. Opening windows to allow fresh air to circulate may also be of benefit. If your tree is in the direct path of the heat as it comes out of the ductwork, it may be getting overheated or overdried. Move it to another location and keep a close watch on it. Some trees need to be outdoors but protected in a shed or by some other cold weather protective system, such as burying the plant in hay or other material that will help keep the winds from lowering the temperatures too much. The trick is to protect the roots as they are not in the ground, which provides a natural protection, but are in pots that allow for a complete freezing of the roots. The water in the roots will expand as sharp ice crystals form, damaging the cell structures of the roots beyond repair by puncturing the cell walls.

Air conditioning can cause plants to be overcooled, especially if the cold air blows directly onto the plant. Air conditioning also tends to lower humidity, which as noted above needs to be in the 50 to 80 percent range. These plants need to be moved out of the line of the blowing cooled air. It is best to keep the plants outdoors, where the humidity is usually very good for them. You may see symptoms similar to those found on trees that suffer from overheating, such as yellowed leaves, loss or nonproduction of flowers, or lack of growth and a generally unhealthy appearance. If you cannot replicate the natural conditions for your specific tree, it is usually best left outdoors. That is another reason to try to raise bonsai that are local trees rather than exotic trees from areas with special climate conditions, such as the foggy Northwest or the hot, arid deserts.

Overwatering and/or Underwatering

These two topics were mentioned above, but let's go over them again, as they can easily damage your trees. With the sphagnum moss method, if you have sufficient drainage holes it is virtually impossible to overwater your trees. The excess will drain out, and the sphagnum moss will absorb a proper amount of water to keep your plant healthy. Underwatering with sphagnum moss can be a more serious problem if not detected early. It is very easy to see if your sphagnum moss has enough water by merely touching and looking at it. The fresh dried sphagnum moss will be light colored and dry, or warm to the touch. Watered sphagnum moss will be darker in color and cooler to the touch. It is a matter of examination and learning what your sphagnum moss looks and feels like. There are some plants that can act as a canary in a mine by showing wilting or leaf drop earlier than other trees. If you see this particular tree with wilted leaves, it is a warning that you need to water your trees. I have a silver queen hibiscus that tends to transpire heavily and get rid of water faster than other plants. I look at this tree frequently, and when I see its leaves drooping, I know it is time to water. The other trees may not yet feel the effects of the lack of water, so they may be deceiving. So it is best to learn to look at the sphagnum moss for color, feel it for coolness, and watch leaves of plants susceptible to water lack. Once you get a feel for it, it becomes second nature.

Weeds

Weeds can be a problem. They can take away needed nutrients, such as fertilizers, from your tree, and they can also take away needed water. Sometimes weeds seem to give an interesting appearance to the surface of your bonsai, such as artillery fern or clover. But their roots often travel a good distance below the surface and need to be removed. Artillery fern is a common and pervasive weed in the South that needs to be constantly removed or it will soon overtake the entire surface of your bonsai growth medium. They produce tiny flowers and seeds and spread easily. To remove weeds from sphagnum moss, it is best to water the plant and then gently pull out the weeds with forceps or your fingertips. I generally walk around examining my plants after a watering, and when I see weeds I pull them out by hand. If you have a surface moss covering your sphagnum moss, be careful, as quick pulls can take a section of the surface moss with it. If I have a special plant that I want to give a crisp and manicured appearance to, I use forceps and pick out all the weeds, no matter how small. If you do this every day, you will soon be weed free for that tree. But you must keep an open eye for weed growth, as they are constantly attacking your plant. Don't use chemical weed controllers on your tree growth medium because they may well do more harm than good and kill your tree. A few occasional weeds will do little harm, so just try to control them as best you can on a steady basis.

Clover, a common weed

When Your Bonsai Dies

It can be difficult to be sure if your bonsai is dead or just playing possum. If the leaves have all dropped off, you need to examine the branches. If the branches are dry and snap off when you bend them, those portions are usually dead. Work your way towards the trunk to see if it is just the peripheral branches that are dead. If the branches closer to the trunk have some play in them or when you break them you see signs of green, there is a decent chance your tree is still alive. Sometimes they are just going through a difficult time due to underwatering, and with time and patience they may return to full growth. I have had a number of trees that appeared to be dead but were in reality alive, but not well. I always take my dead-looking trees and put them aside, out of their pots on the ground, often for months, and up to a year, at a time. And I have been rewarded many times by suddenly seeing a leaf or two growing from the presumed dead tree, which was not really dead at all. I will often give them up to a year like this to see if they are really dead. Sometimes they have died, and that is an unfortunate reality we have to learn to accept. If your tree had a really nice structure to the trunk and branches, I have occasionally actually spray painted them, often gold or silver, which can make for a nice display piece that needs no water or fertilization. These spray painted trees do better indoors than out. The elements will wear away the paint. But, of course, they can always be repainted. Using a clear overcoating, such as polyurethane and no paint, in an attempt to preserve a natural look may leave the tree below to change color as it decomposes, looking bedraggled. Paint, on the other hand, will usually keep them fresh looking, even as they slowly decompose.

4

Pots and Containers

Materials

Bonsai can be pronounced bon-sigh or bone-sigh, depending on who is speaking. This one word in English is two words in Japanese. According to Paul Lesniewicz, "The word 'bonsai' is formed of two words, 'bon' meaning tray or dish and 'sai' meaning tree or plant, so its literal translation is 'tree planted in a dish.' A bonsai is, then, a tree — a miniaturised tree — grown in a dish and resembling in all respects its large counterpart in nature." Susan Resnick says, "Bonsai [pronounced, according to *Webster's* and contrary to popular belief, 'bone-sigh'], literally means 'planted in a tray' or 'potted dwarf tree,' depending on the translator." In *The Master's Book of Bonsai* the directors of the Japanese Bonsai Association, "The literal meaning of bonsai is "planted in a tray."

Choices, choices ... what does a person put their tree into ... or onto? The tree and its holder are a pair. They go together in our minds like bread and butter, Fred and Ginger, or Yin and Yang. Most often, it seems, the holder is a pot. Here and there you see bonsai planted on slabs of stone, metal, or wood. Occasionally a natural material, such as driftwood or bamboo, is used as a substitute for the usual materials we associate with pots: plastic, composite, ceramic, terra cotta, metal, and others. I have grown bonsai in driftwood that had natural cavities in their trunk centers, held upright by the driftwood roots. They are quite appealing visually, but the constant watering cause decomposition of the driftwood, and they eventually collapse under their own weight.

An assortment of plastic pots

Plastic pots are the cheapest. But when I was a kid, there was a commercial for Yuban Coffee that said, "You get what you pay for, 'John Arbuckle.'" In general, plastic pots that are used for garden shop specimens are useful for seeds or for planting cuttings to propagate plants.

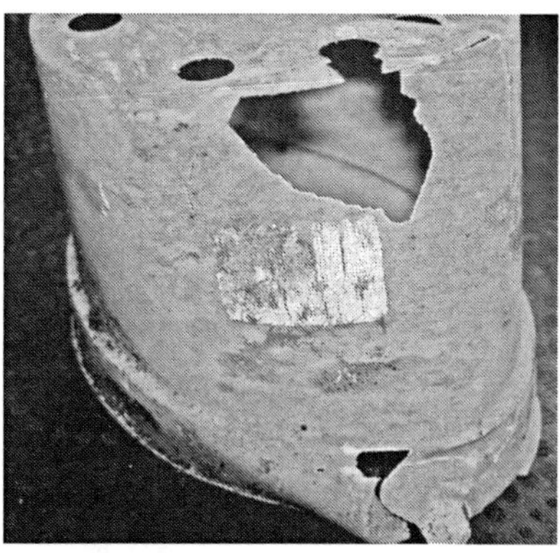

Plastic pot deterioration attributable to the climate

I have at times, I must admit, used a thinner plastic pot as a bonsai container. But they weather poorly, look cheap and bio-unfriendly, and break down in a relatively short time. They crack and often chips fall out.

But there are bonsai pots made of plastic that are well constructed and can last many years. I have a number that are 14 years old and have outlasted ceramic pots, surviving falls from shelves caused by the wind and animal acrobatics. The ceramics would break, but the plastic would not. Most have an acceptable design and an attractive appearance that people comment about in a positive fashion. They are sturdy and in most cases are safe for your plants. (Some orchid hobbyists will not use plastic or internally glazed pottery [because it acts like plastic] and they like terra cotta.) Plastic pots are good if you want to keep the growth medium damp for seedlings or plant cuttings. So if you spend a little more and get a decent plastic pot, you do get what you pay for.

A better quality plastic pot

There are pots made of composite materials. They are very tough and have a great durability. They are molded into classical and modern styles, and there are many types available. From small to large, ornate to plain, expensive and reasonable, they are more and more common. Sometimes, however, they are available only in dark brown or black.

A strong composite pot

Ceramic pots are the classic standard of good taste. They have a life of perhaps thousands of years. Even when thrown away as trash, with sometimes only shards surviving, after 2,500 years they still drive our imaginations. They certainly look great and, to me, present the best looking partners for the best looking plants. They are made from clay, which is exposed to great heat in a kiln. This is the first firing, or the "bisque" firing. Once cooled, a liquid glaze can be painted, sprayed, or dripped on, or the vessel can be dipped into a glaze bath. The glazed pot is allowed to dry and then fired again. The glaze consists of exceptionally tiny glass particles suspended in water. This is the silica, like the sand that makes glass. There is the flux, an alkaline material that lowers the melting point of the silica, making it easier to control the process. There is also the refractory, which helps stiffen the silica so it can stick to the clay aspects that are vertical during melting and not run or drip. This is usually aluminum oxide. Then there is the color. Silica is clear, so color needs to be added. There are a wide range of colors and combinations available, including multi-color glazes that dazzle the eye. The glazes make the surface of the pot they cover waterproof.

Terra cotta saucer made into a tray pot

Typical shape of a terra cotta pot

Some people prefer terra cotta as a bonsai tray or pot. Terra cotta is Italian for "baked earth." It is clay that has been exposed to heat, or "fired," and thus hardened in the process. It is porous, and it is that quality that some growers like. It is usually in the brown-orange family, and it too can be glazed.

Metal pots are seen, mostly as a decoration, but some people use them for plantings. Galvanized pots, iron pots, aluminum pots, all are used. But I prefer not to use metal. The sphagnum moss is of a slightly acidic nature, and acids and metals often do not mix well.

Then there are the natural materials. I have used driftwood and bamboo as pots. As mentioned before, the driftwood I found at a nursery stood up on its roots and was about 12 inches high. The bonsai was planted in the trunk, which had a natural hollow in it. I planted a tree in sphagnum moss in the hollow, and it did quite well. But the driftwood, in a humid, rainy environment like Florida, decomposes, and eventually the moisture broke down the roots of the driftwood, and it would stand no more. I raise bamboo. Called "timber bamboo," it towers nearly 60 feet tall, its beautiful glossy green slowly aging to the tan and browns we recognize. I have tried to preserve the green color after cutting, as it is magnificent, but have been unable to do so. The chlorophyll just decomposes. The bamboo can be cut into sections of various shapes and used as pots.

You can use stone slabs, such as granite or marble. Acid rain will dissolve the marble, but it may take many, many years, as evidenced in cemeteries. You can also use relatively flat trays of metal as a support for your plant. These plantings have no pot sides to help constrain them, and special care must be taken (such as ropes or string) in these situations. Other materials that can be used are wood or even cork bark. But these do not hold up well to the elements.

Perhaps the most important thing when considering pots is drainage. The more and bigger the hole or holes, the better it is. Using the sphagnum moss growth medium, a very well drained pot is the best thing. As the water contacts the sphagnum moss, it gets absorbed by the moss causing it to swell. When it reaches its maximum capacity, it stops taking in water, and the water washes over the top surface, through the bottom of the sphagnum moss, and out of the pot. The sphagnum moss has the water it needs stored inside its cell structure. There is rarely a problem with root rot because of this.

Large drainage holes in a pot made by the author

Tips About Pots

The pots I like the best are the pots I have made myself. There is a certain satisfaction in making such a utilitarian item that will most likely last beyond your lifetime. But best of all, I make them the way I want them. I like them thick walled, heavy, beautiful, designed to be able to lift a plant out easily, and especially having excellent drainage. The heavier the pot, the less likely it is to fall over in a stiff wind gust or by a squirrel or bird landing on it. Making it with a lower and wider base of support will make it less likely that the wind will affect it. But these factors are quickly offset by the tree in the pot. If it is large, with heavy foliage, and lots of air resistance, the wind will blow it over anyway. A wintertime denuded deciduous tree in a less stable pot may have the wind whistle through its empty branches, not stirring it a bit. My pots are thick and clunky, and they last a long time. Sometimes the thinner ones I made in the beginning of my pottery courses broke down, so I quickly learned that thick and heavy meant long lasting. I cut out big drainage holes in the bottoms. If you are using a pot with a small drainage hole, as you often see in terra cotta pots, there is a danger of clogging and problems with excess water.

I also use plastic pots, the ones you get seedlings in. They are thin and don't hold up well, but they are great for taking cuttings from plants for propagation or seed plantings. I

A ceramic pot made by the author

also use the better plastic bonsai pots for my less developed bonsai. Sometimes the plants mature as the years roll by, but the pots are acceptable to me, until I make or buy a replacement pot.

I got my first composite pot recently at a local bonsai nursery. I got a large size for a large plant. I like the look and feel of the pot. It is very sturdy and strong and should have an extended life span. Try them, as I think you may like them.

I get slabs of marble and granite from a local company. They give me the cutout ovals left over after cutting counter tops for kitchens and bathrooms as well as irregular slabs and pieces. If you take it away, they don't have to pay for having it removed as trash, so visit local countertop companies for free slabs.

I have some pots simply standing on a shelf. My bigger bonsai, the ones more prone to wind, bird, or squirrel problems, are tied down with stretchable bungee cords. I get these at dollar stores or flea markets. Depending on your local weather conditions, the rate of decomposition of bungee cords differs. Because they have the power to blind and/or greatly injure you, ALWAYS take proper safety precautions before using bungee cords. They can and do snap back, and are extremely dangerous. Wear protective goggles and work cautiously and slowly. You can of course tie down your plants with string or rope. Be careful and check on restraints that will not expand as the plant grows to avoid damaging your trees. In tropic or sub-tropical climates, the fast growth can cause unwanted scarring along surface roots or trunk bottoms by restraints that are not flexible.

5

Tools

Tools play an important part in the art of bonsai. They are mainly cutting tools, but there are a few other tools that can come in handy when working on your trees.

I have found that only a few tools are really necessary for me. But you may find that a variety of tools do a better job for you. One of the points I like to make is that this is a hobby that is yours, to do with as you please. Some people may try to lead you down a different path than that which you find comfortable. I find it is a good idea to evaluate what they say and show you, as they may lead you to a better way to do things. But remember, no one holds a patent on the manner and methods you choose to use. Some ideas may be time saving and more precise, so be ready to be flexible and open minded, as there is always room for improvement. I do things my way, and you, I hope, will get the confidence to do things your way. I would urge you to be open to new ideas and learn from the advice of others. But above all, I hope you gain the confidence to work on your bonsai without fear or anxiety.

Traditional bonsai scissors

Scissors

I use a minimum of tools. I use scissors, clippers, and a knife for most of my cutting tasks. I have some other tools that I use as the occasion demands. Being a podiatrist has helped me gain a feel for the scissors that I like, as we in that profession are very frequently cutting materials. You may be somewhat familiar with the scissors used by bonsai masters. They have those large curved handles, with an elegance of the Art Nouveau style. Sometimes the cheaper versions are not so good at cutting, because of poor manufacture. The better-made ones will have a fine shearing ability, enabling you to feel the difference as you use them. If you only have a few bonsai and are not cutting too frequently, these scissors may appeal to you, and they will be fine for cutting leaves and thinner branches. But I have found that I prefer scissors that are more ergonomically designed, as I have many bonsai and sometimes am working for extended periods. I find these scissors help me avoid strain on my hands and do the same job that the "bonsai" scissors do. I like to use scissors that are well made and have a good feel about them. As a professional who used cutting tools many hours a day, I always got the best quality that was available. But the bonsai artist (you) may find a less expensive pair that does the job without the expense. I liked to use German scissors, as I found them well designed and easy to use, and they have a long shelf life. I also used the finest clippers I could find when working professionally, but as a bonsai artist, I find I don't really need the precision of the superbly machined tools. I have purchased the tools I use at flea markets or hardware stores. I use the thumb and third finger to control the force of the cut, and I like to use the forth finger, on the flange to help direct my cutting. It is a choice that you will need to make, and there is no right or wrong way. Find what is comfortable for you, but try other ways, as you may find them better than what you have been using.

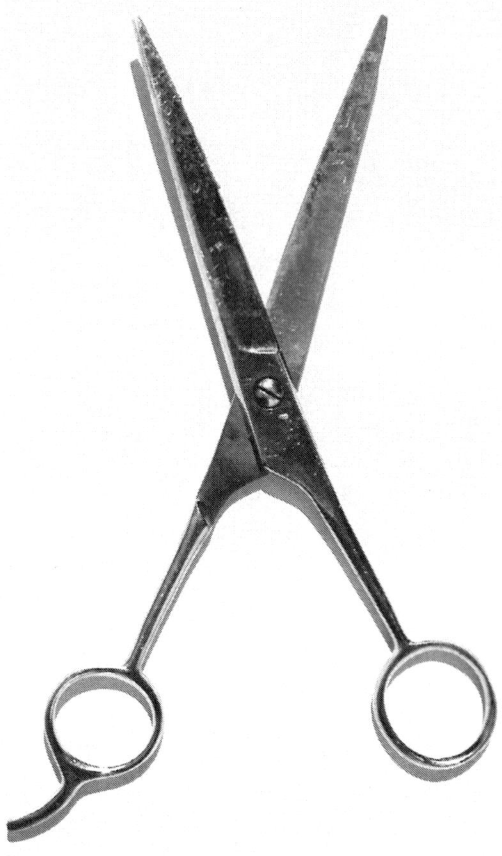

The author's favorite scissors

It is best to make clean cuts, either fast or slow. As you practice you will get to know what is best for you. Of course you need to be careful using any sharp object, and scissors can do major damage to your body if they accidently cut or stab you.

Clippers

I had many different kinds of clippers as a podiatrist, each with special tasks to perform. There are many different kinds of clippers that a bonsai master may use for different cuts and different effects. I find that a simple, inexpensive pair of clippers is fine for most circumstances, though I like to have different sizes available for differing branch diameters. I will use small clippers for small branches and work my way up using larger and larger clippers

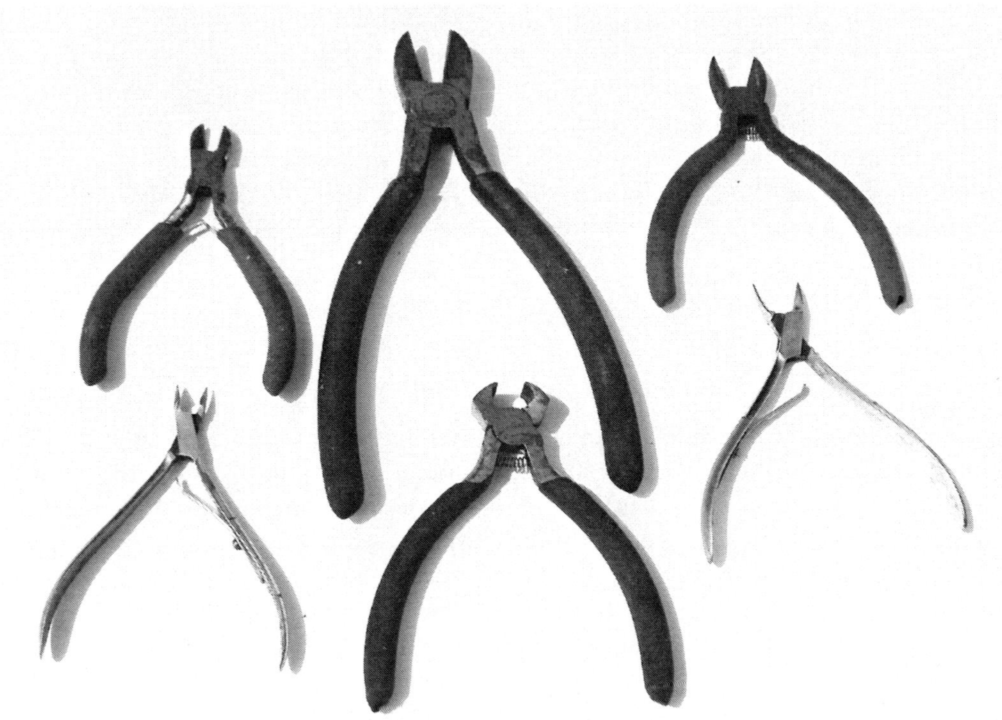

Various sized clippers

as the situation calls for. Eventually I will get to using pruning shears, and even loppers for the really thick boughs. I would urge you to find clippers that feel good in your hand and do not exert undue pressure on your fingers, as pressure points can lead to repetitive stress injuries, such as tendonitis, nerve damage, or unsightly callous formation. You may find that padding your clippers with a spongy material lessens these stress points. Clippers with a spring that opens the clippers between cuts is a handy design.

Knives

A good, serrated knife is very useful in the sphagnum moss method of transplanting or repotting your trees. In the traditional method, the use of a knife is not recommended, and clippers are used more frequently to reduce root size. That is because of the nature of the growth medium. I find frequent tasks, such as repotting or transplanting, are far easier

A Ginsu knife

with the sphagnum moss growth medium than with the traditional method of graded soils as a growth medium. Any good serrated knife should be sufficient. Find one that is about 12 inches in length with a comfortable handle. I like and use exclusively a Ginsu Knife for this purpose. They were commonly sold from 1978 to 1984, and you can find them at garage sales or flea markets. They never seem to get dull and, with a very durable plastic handle, are one of my favorite tools. They cut straight and clean, and work exceptionally well with the sphagnum moss method. A penknife is also handy if stripping bark for jin or shari (to be discussed later).

Saws

Sometimes you will need a saw to cut branches that are too thick, or have a situation in which a clipper is too unwieldy or large because of dense growth and a desire not to damage adjacent structures. A coping saw can be very useful in circumstances such as these, and the ability to undo one of the ends of the saw blade, placing it through the tight space, and then reattaching it to the saw, allows for precision cuts without damaging adjacent

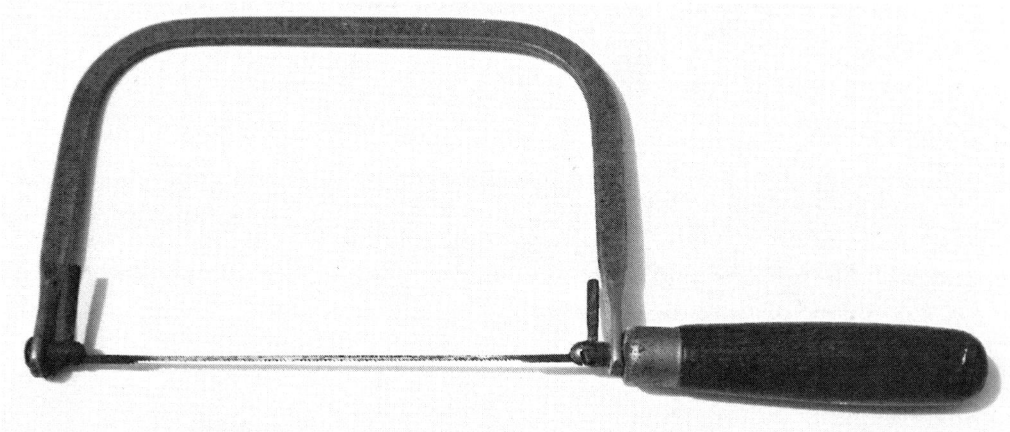

A coping saw

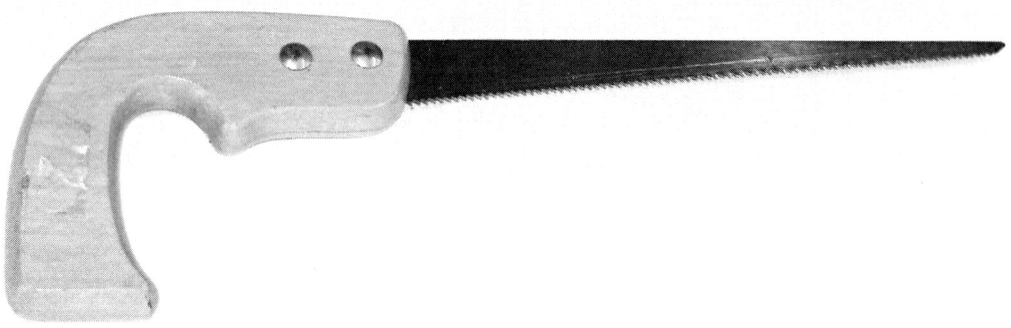

A fixed-blade saw

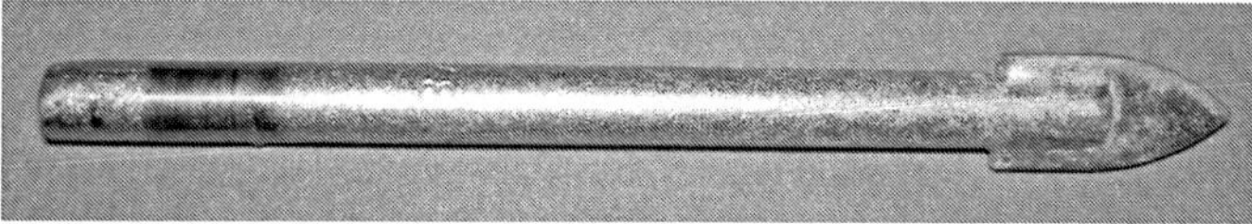

A drill bit for ceramic pots. These can generate a lot of heat, which can cause burns, or crack the pot being drilled.

areas. Be aware if your blade is becoming worn and replace it when necessary. The same advice goes for any saw blade that you use. With a fixed saw blade you can often sharpen the blade or have it sharpened for you by a professional. Many times these fixed saw blades are inexpensive enough that you can replace one with another more cheaply than it would cost to have it sharpened.

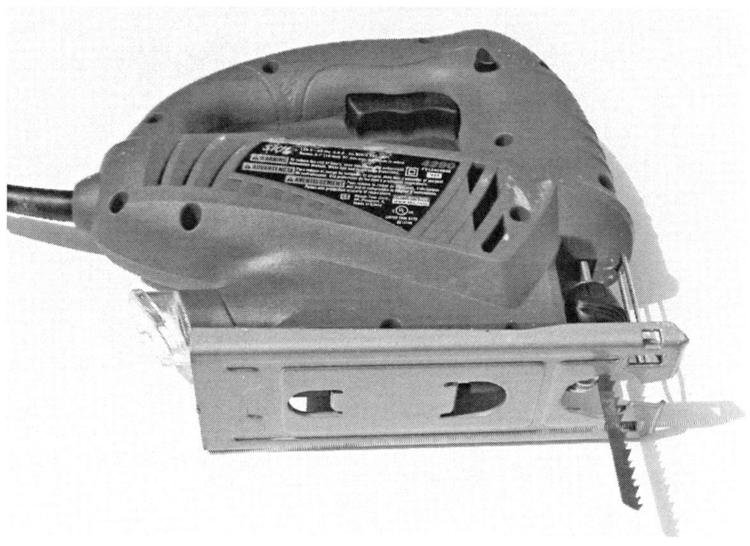

A power jigsaw

In some instances, you may want to use a power saw for your cuts to save time and effort. But beware, for power saws can move too fast, creating a great deal of friction that can produce enough heat to damage the surrounding tissue of the tree. If it shakes the tree too much, the sphagnum moss can fall out from the vibrations. It is best to keep the root ball in its pot while cutting with a power saw, and even cover over the surface of the planting with a plastic film wrapped around the pot. I use a jigsaw occasionally that has a built in speed control so that the blade is not moving at high speeds and creating an overdose of friction. When doctors have to drill or cut bone with power instruments, they are careful to avoid too much friction as it can easily cause cell death and subsequent risk to the patient. They will have the power tool work slowly or give it time breaks attempting to avoid friction. Dentists use water to keep the tooth cool. The blade or drill bits can easily become too hot, so be careful. You also need to be very careful that you do not injure yourself, as power tools can jump or lurch in unexpected ways. And make sure your tools are properly grounded and avoid water so you don't receive a lethal or debilitating shock. Be especially careful if you have heart problems, or have a pacemaker, defibrillator, or other device that is sensitive to electrical fields. It is always safer to use a hand powered saw rather than a power saw.

Woodcarving Tools

When carving out topographical features for jin or shari to assist in "aging" or giving the appearance of damage (such as lightning or breaking of branches or trunks), I find that a set of woodcarving tools to be very helpful. I urge you to practice on spare pieces of wood to get a feel for how these tools work. NEVER have your less dominant hand in a position so that if the tool slips it can cause injury to that hand. ALWAYS wear a protective glove on that less dominant hand for protection. A slip can be very costly to your well-being. If it cuts a tendon or nerve, you can end up needing surgery to repair it, if possible, and may have a lifelong disability. If you hit a bone, osteomyelitis (bone infection by bacteria) may occur, and even a septicemia (blood poisoning) can be initiated, which can cause loss of life. If you are careful, and work unimpeded by drugs or alcohol, with diligent care and concentration, you should not have any problems. Take the time to be safe. The consequences of hasty or careless actions can forever change your life.

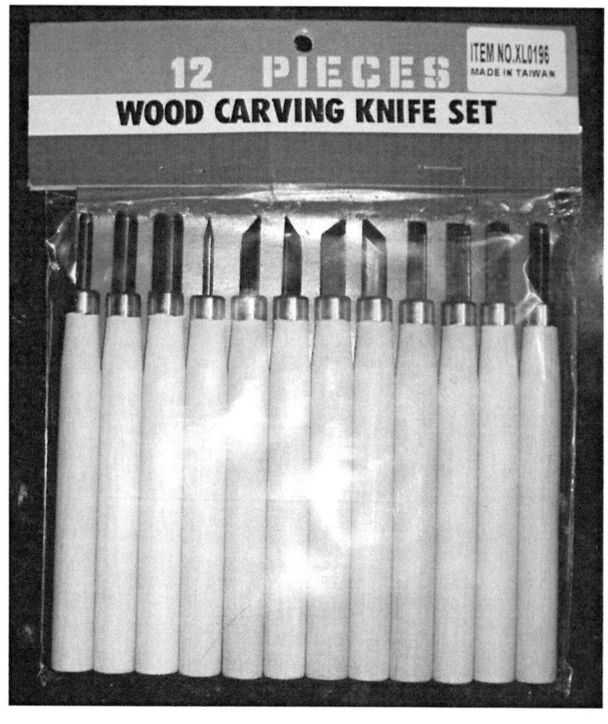

A set of woodworking tools

Chopsticks and Edgers

Once in the pot with the sphagnum moss, the tree may need additional sphagnum moss in some areas for a firm setting, but your fingers are restricted by the pot's shape or the tree's location in the pot. I find that chopsticks, either wood or plastic, are a great tool for getting into these areas your fingers can't reach. Plastic chopsticks hold up better from the ravages of water than the wooden ones, but either material will usually give you years of service (wood) or even decades (plastic). Either the wide or narrow end can be used, depending on the spot you need to push down. You can use a good amount of force in packing the sphagnum moss, as any roots you cause incidental damage to will recover nicely due to the medicinal qualities of the sphagnum moss.

Once you have placed the plant in sphagnum

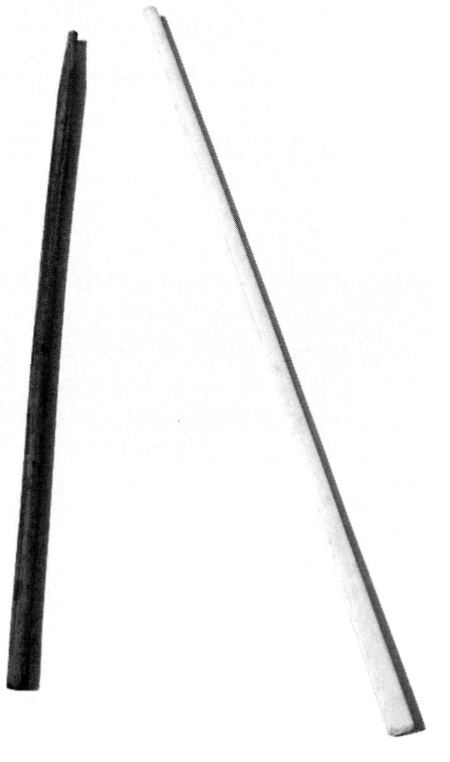

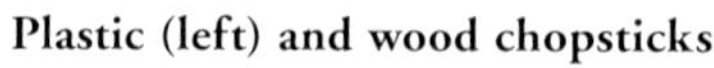

Plastic (left) and wood chopsticks

Three wooden spoon edgers (left) and one wedge edger

moss and set it in its pot, often sphagnum moss will protrude over the rim of the pot. I use an edging tool, which is nothing more than a small slab of wood (or plastic if you want) measuring about two inches by three to four inches, with one end sanded to a slight bevel. I also find that wooden spoons, which can often be purchased inexpensively, make great edges if you cut the tips off to form a straight edge. I then sand the edge to a slight bevel. If you use either of these tools to press downwards along the edging of the plant, pushing down the sphagnum moss that is hanging over the side, it gives a clean finished look to the sphagnum moss. I often do this after I place surface moss on top of the sphagnum moss to give the appearance of grass. Once the edging is complete, a fine spray of water from a hose or misting bottle will clean up the pots exterior surface, and you can then sit back and admire the finished product.

Lazy Susans

Working on your bonsai will be made much easier if you use a lazy susan. These are usually round plates, positioned on top of ball bearings, so that the top can turn easily. They allow you to see and work on your tree from all angles without having to pick up the plant and turn it, or walk around your work table. They run from fairly inexpensive ones made of plastic, to more elaborate and precision designed wood models. If you will be leaving your lazy susan outdoors, then plastic is recommended so that weather does not cause problems, such as warping or wood rot. The wooden ones are more expensive but usually have a better feel about them, and they should be cleaned after each use and stored indoors.

Fertilizers

Bonsai planted in sphagnum moss need fertilizing more often than plants in soil. Soil will hold water longer, and it has nutrients as part of its makeup of inorganic and organic materials, which the plant can access when needed. Soil based bonsai are usually fertilized four or five times a year at the bonsai nurseries and by the traditional bonsai artists. Sphagnum moss in its fresh state has very little nutrient value. Once it starts turning to peat moss as it decomposes, the nutrient value increases, but the structure for growth is weakened. Plus the decomposition leads to bacterial and fungal growth, and an overly wet growth medium as it begins to act more like soil than sphagnum moss. I have found that keeping your sphagnum moss on the fresh side will keep your tree growing hearty and full. You need to be aware of the condition of the sphagnum moss by frequent examination of the growth medium, which is made very easy by the nature of the sphagnum moss and the ability to pull the root ball out of its pot without it loosing shape. You can then return the root ball to the pot if it looks healthy. But sphagnum moss needs nutrients added more frequently than soil. It is an essential part of this method in that it also helps promote faster growth and the apparent aging of the tree in less time than the traditional method. Fertilization is recommended every seven to ten days in the summer months, and monthly in the winter months. Once winter sets in, a monthly fertilization will be sufficient in areas with extended growth periods.

I use a water based fertilizer such as Miracle-Gro, Peters, Scotts, or others, mixed to half strength. I prefer Miracle-Gro as it has a good balance of nitrogen, phosphorous, and potassium. These are usually indicated on the label in numbers, such as 15-30-15 (nitrogen-phosphorous-potassium) as in the case of Miracle-Gro. These numbers indicate the percentage by weight of the ingredients necessary for plant growth. Too much nitrogen will inhibit flowering. Some fertilizers are labeled 30-5-5, which will be good for grasses or other ornamental plants, but not for bonsai. Use fertilizers that are designed for water addition, and not dry, time-released fertilizers that could cause problems because the dosage may be too strong for your trees planted in sphagnum moss. Most trees or vines are flowering and do well with Miracle-Gro. The others also appear to do well with this combination of nitrogen, phosphorous, and potassium. The main thing for the sphagnum moss method is not to overfertilize by using strong concentrations of fertilizer. Less is better, as it stops the burning of roots that can occur with fertilizer that is too strong. If you accidently use a strong fertilizer, all you need do is overwater your plant for a while, as that will wash out the extra fertilizer. I also add a drop or two of a vitamin supplement called Super-Thrive to the fertilizer and water mixture, which is available in most garden shops or bonsai nurseries. It is a simple combination that I find works well and gives good results.

Watering

Watering of your bonsai is and should be a fun and relaxing experience. Some people like to submerse the pot of the plant into a container of water, watching for the air bubbles to stop. Then they know the roots have been thoroughly soaked. The plant is gently picked up and placed back on its resting area. If your surface moss has good adhesion to the sphagnum moss below, it will usually stick tight during this method of watering, but if an occasional piece floats off, simply replace it into the bald spot. Make sure you press down firmly to get good contact between the surface moss and the sphagnum. This is a good method of watering if you only have one or a few bonsai in your collection. I have lots of bonsai and cuttings, and have made a watering system using PVC plastic pipe construction and watering

Water supply

sprayers designed for sprinkling systems, available at hardware stores. I hook these up to hoses or other water outlets and turn them on to spray all my plants at once. But while this is going on, I am also walking about looking for plants that are either not reached by the sprinklers or just not getting enough water. I have a hose with a spray end that I can control, and I hand water these trees. You can also just use a hose with a sprayer and water each plant individually. Use a spray that is not too forceful, as you may accidentally wash off the surface moss with a spray that is too strong.

Sprinkler attachments

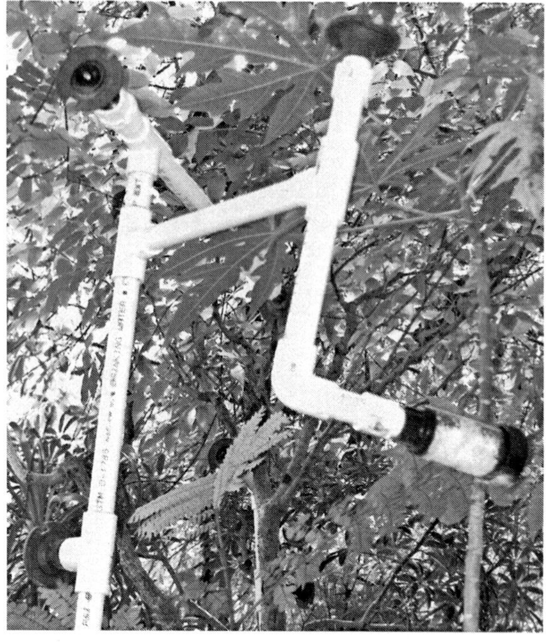

Multiple sprinkler heads from one supply line

Some people have installed automatic watering systems. These are usually PVC pipes and/or regular plumbing pipes attached to mechanisms that control the flow of water by time. They may be regular sprinklers or misters that go on at a specified time every day or every other day, or other intervals, for a predetermined period of time, such as 15 minutes or half an hour. They also have the ability to add fertilizer to the system and direct its application at predetermined times in the cycle of watering. In Chapter 12 we will look at a system of this type.

Hand sprayer attachment

Obtaining Sphagnum Moss

People often write to me asking where I get my sphagnum moss. When I started, I would buy the hobby bags available at nurseries or outlets, such as Home-Depot or Lowes. As my collection grew, so did my need for sphagnum moss. I learned that bales of this material were available but usually by special order only. Occasionally a good nursery would have bales available on a relatively frequent basis. It was much more economical to get the bales, rather than the hobby bags, and a nursery near me sometimes had bales in stock. More often I had to order them, but they never seemed to receive them, so I began to look elsewhere. And I found them on the internet. The material I found was a better quality than I had been getting at the nursery, and the shipping costs were competitive or better than the prices charged at the nursery. Plus it had the added advantage of coming in compressed bricks rather than the loose bags of eight cubic feet that I had been getting. This made storage easier, and as I said, the quality was better. When available, my order would take at least a week to be shipped to the nursery, but with the internet providers, my moss arrives in a few days at my house. I use one of the search engines (I use Google Product Search) to search for either "un-milled sphagnum moss," "sphagnum moss," or "long fibered sphagnum moss" (no quotation marks) and check out the offerings, being particularly aware of sites offering "sphagnum peat moss," as this is really just peat moss and not what you want. I have found a particular site that is quite efficient at getting my moss to me quickly, and it sells a Luster Leaf product that is top quality: http://www.amazon.com/Luster-Leaf-Long-Fiber-Sphagnum/dp/B001O85R6O product. People in areas outside of the United States will need to search for suppliers in their respective areas.

6

Bonsai Stands and Shelves

The concept behind most bonsai stands and shelves is basically a simple one. You need a base of support and a shelf to place your bonsai on. I use four inch by four inch pressure treated wood, cut to the length I want, for the supports. They are solid, are manufactured to last in outdoor conditions, and are relatively pleasing in appearance. If you desire, you can paint the supports whatever color you wish. Use an outdoor paint to avoid the problems that come with rain and sun exposure. On page 66 is a picture of a long shelf that I constructed for plants that need full sun.

I do not use nails to secure the parts to one another. If you have to replace a shelf plank, it is much easier to remove a screw rather than pry out a nail. I also believe that screw attachments are inherently stronger than nails due to their design of using an inclined plane, which provides more surface area for the friction that holds it all together. A drill with a reverse-direction adjustment makes the task of repair much easier. And after the effects of time, wind, and rain, eventually you will need to replace some parts of your shelves or stands.

You can make a single stand, consisting of a post topped off with a piece of planking that can be square, rectangular, or whatever shape you want. If you wish, you can put a border around it for esthetics, or perhaps to make it harder for squirrels to get to your plant. You can also have multiple levels attached to the post, allowing for multiple plants, perhaps spiraling around the post in a helix design.

The posts should have a sufficient portion (I like two feet) in the earth, with a base of support made of concrete. It is better to use more concrete than you think you might need, rather than too little. A deficiency of concrete may lead to the support giving way and falling or leaning. Take the time and effort to bury the post in a sufficient base of concrete to guarantee a solid support system.

The first shelves that I built were constructed after I had moved to Florida. In Philadelphia we had a deck with a plank edging that had enough room for most, if not all, of my bonsai. In Florida, I designed my own shelving system that has held up for the last 15 years, needing an occasional replacement of crossbeam support, and sometimes a buttressing of the crossbeams so that the shelves had a solid base to support them. I was able to add the buttressing crossbeams anytime I wished or needed them. Here is one of my first shelving structures.

A large multi-tiered shelf constructed to hold many bonsai

A simple shelf design using supports and planks for full sun exposure

My first shelving structure had the planks placed so they abutted their neighboring planks. I soon discovered that the closeness of the planks did not allow excess water, from rain or the hose, to get to the plants below. It made watering more difficult. I still have some of those shelves in place, but as I need to replace shelves that have been a victim of the weather, I now allow for a nice space between planks. On the bottom shelf planking, a closeness of the individual planks does no harm as there are no plants below that might benefit from the excess water. I used three planks on the bottom, two planks on the second shelf, and a single plank on the top shelf. If you are very tall, you can certainly add a fourth shelf, if so desired. The vertical spacing between the shelves should be enough to allow for various sized trees to fit comfortably. The top shelf, with no overhead restrictions, holds my tallest plants. At first I only used two support posts, which lead to a bellying and warping of the planks due to the weight if the bonsai. The next shelves I made had three support posts, which made the entire structure more secure.

You can coat your shelves with a sealer to extend their life, or paint them, which will also help keep them in good condition, but the paint will eventually need repainting. I find it easier to go with the natural look of the treated lumber. There are other materials that can be used, such as metal, plastic, or composite materials, that are durable and strong. The choice is yours.

A YouTube viewer asked about making a shelf that would allow for varying amounts of light to be received using roof structures that would block out some or most of the sun. You can do this by adding a roof structure that is solid to create a shade area; or a roof structure with openings, such as a lattice, that would allow more light through; or a semi-transparent material, allowing light in, but with a reduced intensity. You could place these differing roofs next to each other and thus have one shelf structure receiving varying amounts of light.

7

Making a Bonsai Using the New Method

For the first bonsai, I suggest you follow the following procedure and techniques to have a rewarding experience. I would also recommend that you view my first videos about this method that appear on YouTube before you start, so that you become familiar with the procedures and techniques. It is a three part series, and you should watch all three parts if possible. Here are the addresses of the three videos. Type the address into your internet browser, and it should take you to the video.

Bonsai New Easy Method #1 of 3 • http://www.youtube.com/watch?v=kPVaAXgRoKk
Bonsai New Easy Method #2 of 3 • http://www.youtube.com/watch?v=D7DhdiR7F4Q
Bonsai New Easy Method #3 of 3 • http://www.youtube.com/watch?v=FTqJToakbzA

Supplies

You will a need container for the sphagnum moss, sphagnum moss, pot, scissors, clippers, knife, hose with sprayer, edger, surface moss, and, of course, the specimen tree.

Container

For the first bonsai, I suggest and will use for our example, a pot. We could plant the tree on a slab of material, or use no material at all, and have the tree standing on a mound of sphagnum moss. These other methods of planting are covered in Chapter 00.

Sphagnum Moss

The dried sphagnum moss that you have obtained will first need to be soaked in water so the sphagnum moss can absorb the water, making it more pliable and readying it for planting of the tree. I use a mask to cover my nose and mouth so that I do not breathe in the particles that spread into the air as you take the sphagnum moss and place it in your

Dry sphagnum moss in a plastic pot ready for wetting

Spraying the sphagnum moss with water

container for soaking. For a small project such as this, an old plastic pot, about five to ten gallon size, will work just fine. Of course a bigger container will also work as well, but small containers can be a slight problem in properly wetting the sphagnum moss. If you have any open sores on your hands or arms, or have a reduced ability to fight diseases, it is highly suggested that you wear latex or vinyl gloves that will keep your hands dry. As mentioned previously, sporotrichosis is a possible infectious agent in the sphagnum moss, and care should be taken to protect yourself.

Take a good portion of the sphagnum moss and place it into your container. Using a fine spray, slowly wet the top surface of the moss. Keep your mask on during this part as particulate matter will be made airborne at this time. Once the top is wet, you can increase the flow of the spray, so that the deeper portions of the sphagnum moss are getting wet. Eventually you can have the hose running pretty heavily, and as you get the moss wet, you can use your free hand to squeeze and move the moss around in its container, so that the sphagnum moss has a good chance to soak up all the water it needs. Let it sit for a minute or two, and then add some more water. It should come out of the bottom of the pot, which is an indicator that the sphagnum moss has absorbed its maximum water content and is ready for planting.

Using a C-clamp to hold the spray nozzle

Water Supply

You will need a hose with a sprayer attached to the end that can be easily turned on and off. A regular plastic or brass nozzle is fine, as are the various multiple function sprayers that are available. I use a simple shut off nozzle with a control that I can work with one finger to turn it off or on and that can regulate the amount of spray by the position I select. I have, at times, used a C-clamp to hold the nozzle onto a work table so I have both hands free to work. I have become proficient enough so that I can now use one hand to hold the nozzle and one hand to hold the plant. It can certainly be done this way if you do not have access to a C-clamp.

Knife

A serrated knife, about 12 inches in length, will be needed to cut the root ball. I use a Ginsu Knife, as discussed and shown earlier.

Scissors

A comfortable pair of scissors, about six to eight inches long, will be necessary for cutting leaves and straggly roots.

Clippers

Clippers, with jaws big enough to cut the large branches and roots, will also be needed.

Chopstick and Edger

A chopstick of wood or plastic, and a wooded wedge, as discussed previously, will aid in finishing off your bonsai in a neat and clean manner.

Surface Covering

The surface of the sphagnum moss can be left as it is, or can be covered to make it look more appealing and older than it really is. You can use surface moss, which gives an appearance of grass. Gravel or small pebbles, either as a total covering or in concert with the surface moss, make a nice setting for your tree.

Technique

Picking Out a Specimen

The first thing we need to do is to pick out a suitable plant specimen to use. I decided to use a Parson's juniper for this project, as it can be picked out for a nice trunk shape, and the small leaves make it

A parson's juniper, our subject specimen

ideal for bonsai. I went to a local hardware store that has a good sized nursery section. I looked at each of the Parson's junipers that they had. In looking at them, I used my fingers to move away the foliage so that I could see the trunk and look for one that I liked. I got it down to the three that I liked and then finally decided on the one I eventually chose. I liked the trunk shape and also the branches. This is something you will develop an eye for as you do more bonsai plantings. I also chose this species because it is what people usually think of as a bonsai. It has an oriental look about it and makes for a great first choice as a bonsai, as it is hardy and will grow well in sphagnum moss.

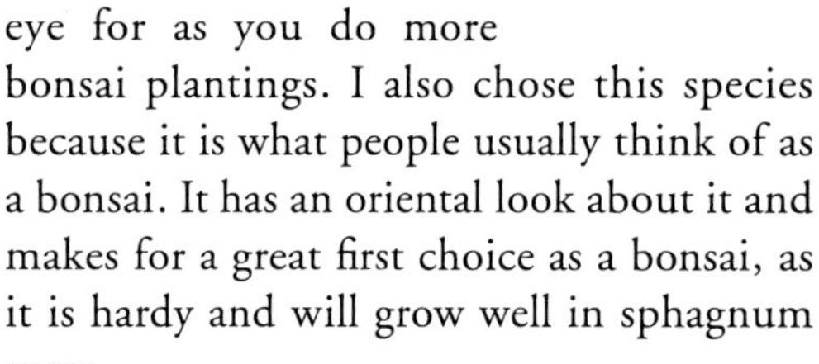

Moving the foliage to get a better view of the trunk and branch structure

Roots coming out of the container bottom that need to be cut

Taking the Specimen Out of the Pot It Came In

You should get your sphagnum moss wetted and ready for use as described above. To get your specimen out of your pot, gently place your fingers around the trunk and pull slightly on the plant. Turning the plant upside down sometimes makes this step easier. If it separates easily from the container it is in, just continue pulling until it is out of the pot. Place it on your work table or lazy susan. If it is not so easy to pull out of the pot, turn it over to see if there are roots coming out of the drainage hole and if

Grasping the plant for removal from its pot

that is what is impeding its easy removal. If there are roots, take your scissors, or clippers if thick, and cut off the roots coming out of the container. Now try to remove the plant again. If it comes out easily now, you are ready for the next step. If it is still stuck in the pot, place the container on the ground (the containers are usually plastic) and gently roll the container against the ground. You want to try to slightly alter the shape of the container from round to slightly oval as you roll it back and forth to break up any adhesions that may be present from the roots attaching to the side walls of the container. Then try again to remove the plant. If it still does not come out easily, take your clippers and cut the container from the top edge to the drainage hole and separate the tree's root ball from the container. A plant from a good nursery will usually separate easily from its container. Plants that have been growing too long will be more troublesome to remove.

The specimen, partially out of its pot

Cleaning the Roots

If you have your hose held down by a C-Clamp, or if you are working with one hand holding the trunk of the tree, begin to spray the root ball with a light spray. As the root ball becomes saturated, the soil and other materials (usually bark or wood chips) will begin to loosen and fall away from the roots. Start to increase the flow of the spray and you can make it fairly strong and wash away the original growth medium. You do not want to leave any of the old medium, so take your time and do it thoroughly, as leftover material can be a source of bacteria or fungus

Cleaning the roots by heavy spraying

that may attack the roots. Sometimes you can't get it all, and you can leave some pieces in there, but try to get at least 95 percent of the previous growth medium separated from the root ball. Once this is done, place the tree and roots in the pot you have chosen and get a feel for where you would like it to be situated in the pot and its orientation. You can have it in the middle, off centered, or at the edge. It is your choice.

After cleaning the roots with a hose

Pick up your tree by the trunk and, using your scissors, cut off about a third of the roots, going straight across the bottom of the root ball. This is often a scary part for beginners, but it will all be fine if you follow through with the techniques presented below. (Sometimes before the tree has been planted in the sphagnum moss, I work on it to remove excess foliage that I see I will not want. It is easier to trim it at this time than when planted, and it makes it easier to handle. Keep the roots wet with periodic showers of water as you trim the excess foliage.)

Cutting off the excess roots with scissors

Placing of the Sphagnum Moss

Take a pad of the wet sphagnum moss, about enough to fill the bottom third of your pot, and place it there, spreading it out evenly. Turn your tree upside down, holding it by the trunk. Now you want to take smaller chunks of the sphagnum moss and place it inside the root structure, trying to get maximum contact between the roots and the sphagnum moss. Do this as best you can. It is okay to have roots lying on top of your new root ball, as they will be covered by sphagnum moss as we continue. Take the new root ball of wet sphagnum moss and roots and turn the tree over and place the root ball on top of the sphagnum moss inside the pot. Position your tree where you want it, paying attention to the trunk shape and how it goes along with the shape of the pot and the position you place it in. Holding your tree with one hand on the trunk so it doesn't fall, use your other hand to take a clump of sphagnum moss and place it on the side nearest you, pressing it against the exposed roots and on top of the root ball. Press fairly hard, so that you see the water squeezing out of the top. Holding everything secure, turn the plant around and place another clump of sphagnum moss on the opposite side and press it firmly down. Your plant may be able to stand on its own at this point. If not, continue to hold the trunk as you place clumps at

After cutting the roots

A pad of sphagnum moss in the pot bottom

the sides and ends, pressing it down firmly. Your plant should be standing on its own by now. If not, keep taking the sphagnum moss and adding it to the pot, all the time pushing down fairly hard until you feel a solid packing below your finger tips. Keep turning the tree around and placing more and more sphagnum moss into the pot. Use your fingers to feel for hollow spots and fill these up with sphagnum moss. Don't be afraid to press really hard, as the roots, even if they break, will heal quickly. The better the contact, the better your tree will do. When the entire pot is solid with sphagnum moss you can sit back and take a look. If it is not positioned as you want it, you can remove it and start over, or you can take out some of the sphagnum moss and turn or move the tree to where you want it. If it is too far down in the pot and you want the base of the trunk higher, pull the plant out of the pot and put some more sphagnum moss in the bottom. Then place the root ball on top and push down hard until it is seated firmly. The hardest part is over. Congratulations!

Sphagnum moss packed into pot

Tree supported by packed sphagnum moss

Trimming

Trimming a bonsai is similar to giving someone a haircut. The thing to keep in mind is that if you make what you consider to be a mistake, things will grow back, just like hair does. It is only a temporary setback, and sometimes it can turn into a positive result.

Opposite, top: **The root ball stuffed with sphagnum moss.** ***Bottom:*** **Root ball and sphagnum moss placed onto a pad inside the pot.**

Covering a branch with my hand to visualize the result of pruning

Because one of our goals in the sphagnum moss method is fast growth, we will see results of trimming surprisingly fast. The subject of this particular exercise, the Parson's juniper, is a good specimen to start with as some simple tricks will make your bonsai look great in a short time.

You need to be able to visualize how you want your bonsai to appear when it is done. But along the way, you may change your mind and take a slightly different path than what you expected. So it was with the plant I chose to use to demonstrate the making of your first bonsai.

Cutting off the unwanted branch with clippers

The first thing I do is to clean up the bottom growth by trimming away all unwanted growth that blocks the view of the trunk. Using scissors and clippers, I prune away the growth that is blocking my view of the structure of the plant. Often the middle of the tree is filled with foliage, and the removal of some of this gives you a better feel as to what you want as the end result. Once I can see a little bit better, I move on to the higher structures, clearing them as I feel necessary. You need to look at your tree from all sides. In the traditional method, there is usually a front and a back to the tree. It is designed for a specific viewpoint, and often if the tree is seen from a different angle, it does not look as appealing as the designed view. If that is what you wish to do, that is fine. Personally, I like my trees to be as they usually are in nature, with an appearance that can be viewed from many angles and give a pleasing picture. It is a matter of personal taste, and your decision is as valid as anyone else's in regard to tree appearance.

I then begin to look for the major branch structure that appeals to me. With my hand or by bending them away, I start to hide the branches that I visualize being cut and try to see how the tree will look with that branch removed. If I decide to cut it off, I will use my clippers to cut it close to the trunk, as I usually prefer not to have portions of old branches protruding from the trunk. Sometimes I want to leave them, as that adds character to the tree. Using special techniques (jin or shari, for example), which will be discussed later, these partial branches can be given the appearance of age or natural damage that is often appealing.

The trunk after removal of the branch

Clipping another branch blocking the view

After clearing out unwanted lower and interior foliage

As your tree begins to change shape, often your design changes in response to the pruning you have done. Such was the case with the sample specimen I worked on here. It ended up being different from what I had first visualized. For me that is part of the unexpected fun of creating bonsai.

After this initial pruning your bonsai starts to get closer to the final product of your imagination. There is a simple trick to make your juniper have an oriental look about it. That is to cut off any of the foliage that is growing downward from the branches. By doing this simple task, you will give your branches an upwards windswept look that is quite appealing. I also look for foliage that is too tall for the branch and prune it down carefully, trying to cut the leaf stem, rather than the leaves themselves. Cutting the leaves will usually result in browning of that section, but this can easily be repaired, when noticed, by trimming the leaf stem without cutting the leaves themselves. I look for things such as branches that are directly opposite each other, as I find I like the appearance of branches that are displaced along the main branch, rather than opposite pairs. It is totally up to you to create your bonsai as you see fit.

Hiding with my hand a vertical branch I may want to cut off

A branch with downward growing foliage

The upward windswept look after pruning the downward growing foliage

The bonsai in its final stages, without surface moss

There is no absolute right or wrong, and people who claim that their way is the only, and ultimately correct, way are losing sight of the experience that bonsai creation should have for everyone. As you do more bonsai, you may find that your tastes change. It is a flowing and flexible art that has room for all sorts of experimentation.

I continue to trim away unwanted foliage until I find a configuration of leaves, branches, and trunk that appeals to me. It is often better to stop sooner rather than later, as you can always come back and make further cuts after studying your work. It happened many times in the creation of my juniper that I used here as an example. When I thought I had finished, I found one last leaf that just didn't look right, so I cut it off and felt at that point I was really done with my pruning, for now.

Surface Covering

Once the plant has been pruned, I move onto what I want the surface of the sphagnum moss to look like. I find the most pleasing appearance is provided by the use of surface moss. Surface moss will be discussed in greater detail in a later chapter. But for now, you need to know that the moss we frequently see in shady, moist places is a plant known as a bryophyte. This moss has no root structure. It gets its water from absorption on its surface of dew or rain or heavy humidity. With a miniature tree, it looks like a grassy field. I love the way it looks, but where I live I have a problem with squirrels. They love to dig in my plants looking for, or burying, seeds or nuts. I often find strange plants growing from my bonsai because of squirrel intervention. Sometimes it might be due to bird droppings that have a seed in them. But the squirrels dig up my surface moss, and they do not replace it. So I often spend a lot of time making my surfaces look wonderful only to have them destroyed by my friends, the squirrels. It is just the way it is when we share space in the outdoors. So I usually do not use surface moss for two reasons — the squirrels and the difficulty in finding a good supply here in Florida. If you live in an area rich in surface moss, you can easily replace any moss disturbed by our animal friends. I am always on the lookout for moss and carry a spatula in my trunk should I unexpectedly come across a patch or two. I often go moss hunting in areas I hope will have the wanted growth.

Moss can grow on many different substrates. Rocks, trees, soil, sand, and just about anything else can be home for this luxurious looking growth. Moss growing on rocks, walls, and trees is difficult to remove in sheets and has little use for bonsai enthusiasts. The moss I find and use is usually growing on soil or sand and sometimes clay. There is a baseball field near my home that has a warning track around the outfield that has a clay surface. At certain times of the year, I am able to find surface moss there before the groundskeepers come and destroy it. Around my house I mostly find surface moss on sand. I collect it using a spatula or putty knife with a wide blade, and shave it off the surface, including the substrate it rests upon. I use flat trays to hold the moss. If you are lucky enough to find an excess of moss either on soil, sand or clay, you can layer the surface moss with like sides facing like sides. That is, the green surface should be placed on top of the other green surface, and the substrate surface should be placed against the other substrate surface. This will allow you to carry multiple tiers of the surface moss.

The procedure for preparation of the moss is the same no matter what the substrate is. I hold a piece of the moss in one hand, as I use a fine spray of water to wash away the substrate. The substrate washes away easily, and it is better to leave a little substrate attached to the moss, because if you wash away too much, the surface moss will break apart as it has no roots to anchor it in place. Most attached substrate material will wash through the sphagnum moss with repeated watering and exit through the drainage hole in the bottom of your pot. Much of the surface moss I find around my house is riddled with weeds. Usually artillery fern, clover, or dollar weed are the culprits. Once the surface moss is wet, you can gently pull out the weeds. There will usually be some breakup of the surface moss no matter how delicate your touch, but this is not a problem. Smaller patches of moss can be placed adjacent to other moss, and they will grow together for a solid appearance.

I place the wet surface moss on the top of the sphagnum moss, substrate side down, starting at the trunk and working my way towards the edge of the pot. You can do it any way you please. The trick is to push it down firmly, with pressure being put on all areas in contact with the sphagnum moss, and press until you see water coming up through the surface moss. When you see water coming through the surface moss, you know you have good contact between the surface moss and the sphagnum moss, which is essential to avoid separation of the two mosses and subsequent dying of the surface moss. When you reach the end of the pot and have covered the entire surface, or however much you wish to cover (if you are adding gravel, pebbles or rocks, these areas will not have surface moss), you will need a way too neaten the appearance of your bonsai. I use a wedge of wood to neaten the appearance of the edges. Besides using just a straight-edged piece of wood, I have also taken wooden spoons and cut off the ends for curved edges of pots, as discussed in the chapter about tools. Chopsticks are also good for edging, especially in oddly shaped pots or corners. You just push down gently until the edge of the surface moss is inside the edge of the pot, then move down the edge until the entire edge is clear of overhanging moss and gives a tidy appearance. Once this is done, a light and gentle spray of the sides of the pot will finish off your work, and you can sit back and gaze at your accomplishment.

Edging using a wooden wedge tool

If you want to add rocks to your bonsai setting, just push a hole into the sphagnum moss and place your rock securely into it, using more sphagnum moss to secure it in place. Add surface moss to fill around the perimeter of the rock. Some people like the look of a gravel or pebble surface, either fully or made to look like a pathway beside the tree. If you lack enough surface moss to complete coverage of your sphagnum moss, this is a good way to fill in undone areas. The trick to keeping the gravel or pebbles in place is to use a clear-drying wood glue, such as Elmer's Glue, and quickly drip it over the entire surface of gravel or small pebbles (larger pebbles will stay in place from gravity if pushed partially into the sphagnum moss). Don't be afraid of using a lot of it, as it will dry clear and present no obstacle to watering. It will not harm the roots, and the end result will usually help retain water in the sphagnum moss.

Some people like to add miniature figurines of people or structures, such as buildings or bridges, to their bonsai surface. The idea is to keep things in proportion with the tree size. Various sized figurines are usually available at bonsai nurseries or on the internet.

Once your bonsai is complete, you need to remember that the tree and its roots have gone through an ordeal. It is best to let your tree recover for a week or so in an area of shade and avoid full sun. The roots need to adjust, and full sun can cause too much transpiration from the leaves, causing the tree to wither and die. Once you see new growth coming out near the areas you have pruned, you can slowly increase the amount of direct sun it receives until it has adapted to the environment.

8

Special Techniques

Controlling Leaf Size

Proportion is one of the aspects of bonsai that can help make a pleasing appearance. We have taken a specimen tree and made it to appear to be a dwarf version of the tree we see in nature. We use surface moss to give an appearance of tiny grass blades and small rocks that look like boulders. Sometimes small figurines help give an impression of a miniature scene. Small things, in order to appear truly as tiny replicas of the real thing, need to be in proportion. That is why we frequently choose subject trees that have naturally small leaves, so the picture we create fits into our expected view of a world made diminutive. There is also a simple but effective technique to make leaves that would be larger naturally, grow stunted and much smaller than a leaf from a full-sized tree of that type. It is a sort of selective pruning that if practiced on a regular basis will give you miniature leaves. All you need to do is prune away the biggest leaves you see. If you keep doing this repeatedly, the tree will eventually be trained to have only small leaves. It is an effective way to promote tiny leaves where larger ones are expected. Some people will take a tree in its growing season and almost totally defoliate it of all leaves. The tree responds by growing replacement leaves that start out small. By selectively pruning any leaf that gets too big, you will have a tree with leaves in better proportion to the tree structure you have created. I prefer to work on the leaves as they grow, rather than take such a radical step as taking off all of the leaves. In the long run it works just as well as the total removal method but is not nearly as scary, and you always have foliage to look at.

Directional Pruning

This is the method by which you can shape your tree without the use of wiring to bend and manipulate branches and trunks into shapes you find pleasing. Wiring will be discussed in short while. By cutting branches and having a good idea as to where and how the new offshoots will grow, you can produce denser growth that will make fuller canopies of foliage. This will help give your bonsai a more pleasing look and stop the formation of leggy, long branched plants.

Look at trees in the wild from a distance. They have tightly formed clumps of leaves and lack long extensions of branches that can occur on your bonsai if it is not pruned. The tip of the branch is where most new growth occurs. When these ends are allowed to grow, they produce a chemical that inhibits lateral growth along the branch and thus encourages it to grow in an extended manner as it searches upwards for light. Along the branch you will see tiny nodes that appear as small bumps. These are adventitious growth nodes, ready to spring into action if the branch is damaged by wind or animals. It is the mechanism by which plants recover from injury. If you cut off the tip, the distal growth is halted, and the adventitious nodes burst into action, producing side shoots that will become densely packed and help produce a natural looking tree. Often at the end, two or more new shoots will appear, and this also helps keep the lengthening of the branch at a minimum, while promoting the growth of the fuller and thicker foliage that you want. This is similar to the roots, which also will grow collateral root structures in response to pruning. By using sphagnum moss as a growth medium, where the roots do so well and grow so freely, this is a beneficial effect that will help keep your plant healthy. Leaf pruning allows for an increased amount of surface area that promotes expanded photosynthesis. You can cut off the growing tips with scissors or by pinching the bud with your fingernails and removing it. Either method is fine.

If a branch has naturally split and has two branches growing from its end, the direction of one may be more desired in the shaping of your tree than the other. Branches that cut back across the plant can have an unpleasant appearance, as can branches that extend upwards rather than laterally. By cutting off the branch segment that is going in the wrong direction, you will have changed the shape of the tree and encouraged thicker growth on the surviving branch. Or in the case of the juniper from the last chapter, the pruning of all leaves that grow downwards on a branch gives it an appearance of being swept upwards. You can also do this in reverse and get trees with a downward growth of leaves, if that is the shape you desire. This technique is known as directional pruning. It is an effective and easy method of shaping your tree. Newly transplanted trees should not be overpruned, as they may not recover from the drastic changes and lack of good root structure. It is always best to err on the side of caution, as you can always cut off more at a later time, when the tree has adapted to its new environment.

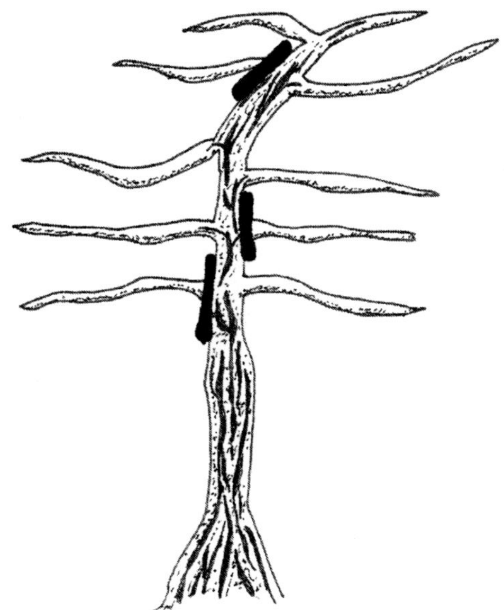

Trunk with opposite positioned branches ready for pruning

You can also practice a method of slightly bending branches to the shape you want them to take. By repeated and frequent bending you can direct the branches to go in a direction you want. Of course, overbending can easily cause breakage and a deformity to the structure you are trying to create.

The structure of branches coming out of the trunk can also be modified by directional pruning to give the appearance you wish your bonsai to have. Branches that are opposite each other along the trunk

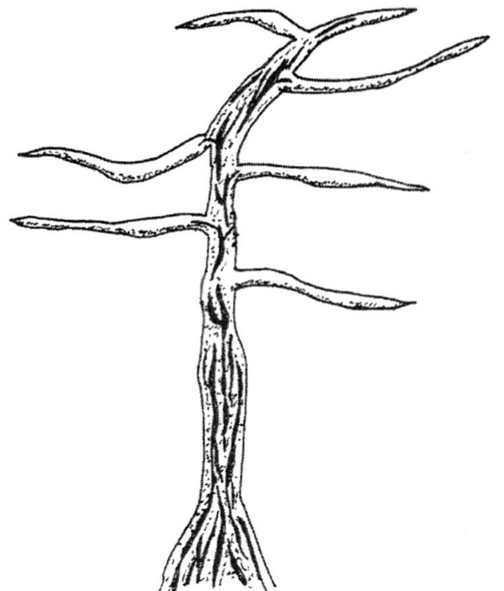

Trunk shape after pruning

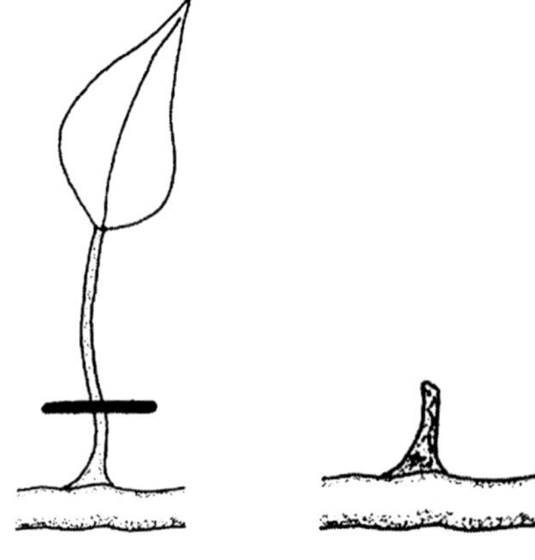

Left: A deciduous leaf before pruning. *Right:* The stump of the cut stem of a deciduous leaf

are often removed in order to produce an asymmetric growth pattern.

When pruning simple leaves of deciduous trees, it is best to leave a portion of the leaf stem on the tree. After a few days, the stump will either fall off on its own, or by brushing your hand over the site, the stump will be removed leaving a natural appearing scar.

The technique is slightly different when cutting conifer leaves. If cutting scaly leaves, as a juniper, try to cut between the scales using small scissors. This may not be possible due to the closeness of the scales, so do the best you can. On trees with needles, such as pines, you can trim the individual needles to the length you want, but don't cut the sheaths that cover the stems of the needles as they come off of the branch.

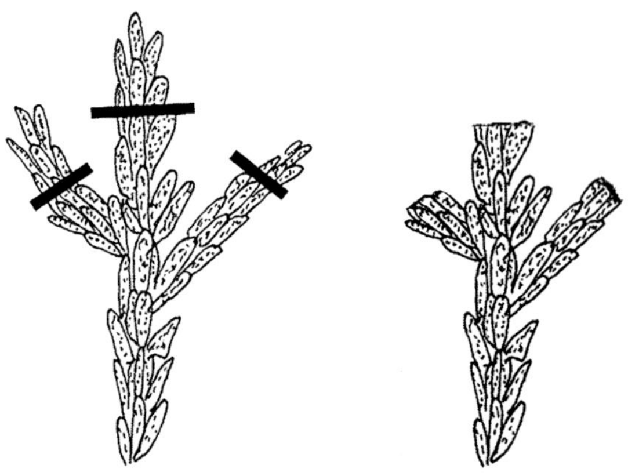

Left: Trimming a juniper leaf. *Right:* The result after trimming a juniper leaf

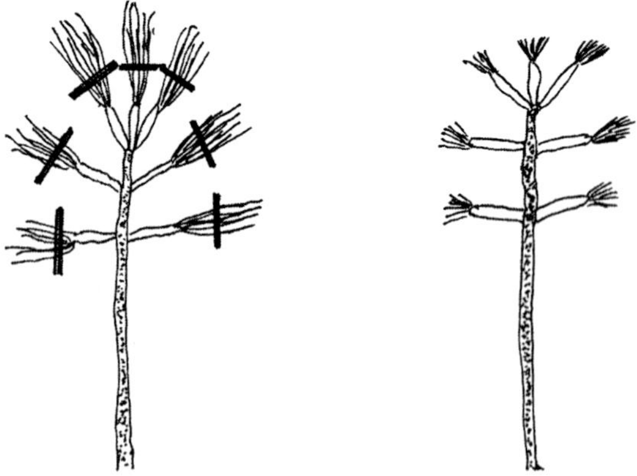

Left: Trimming pine needles, making sure you don't trim the sheaths. *Right:* The shortened needles after pruning

Wiring

Wiring is a tried and true method of shaping trees that has been in use for

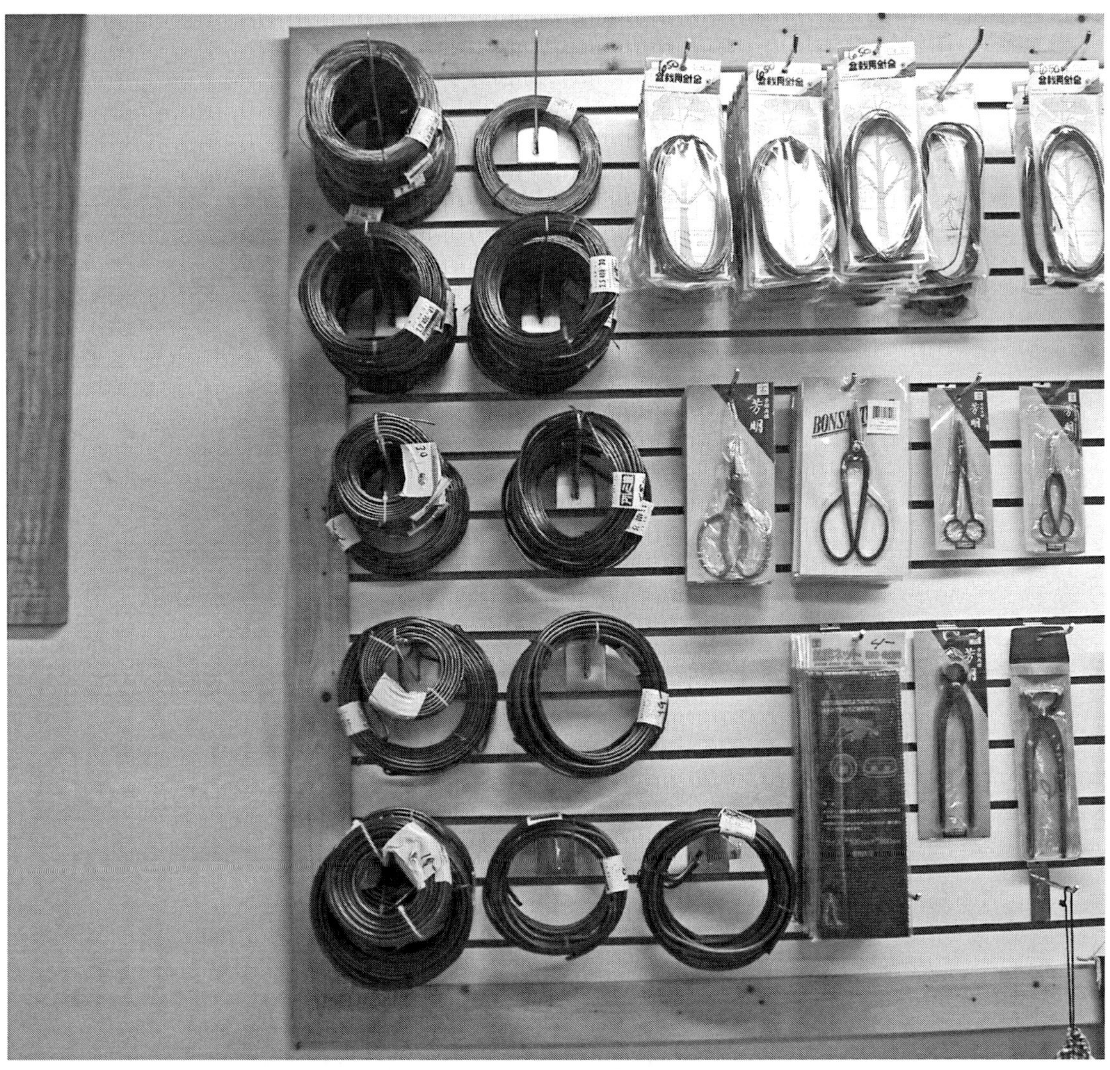

Many sizes of wire as seen at Wigert's Bonsai Nursery

a long time in the traditional method. It works well and, if done properly, will result in beautiful confirmations of shape that are very pleasing to the eye. But in the traditional method, trees are grown slowly, while in the sphagnum moss method, the trees are encouraged to grow fast by frequent fertilization. The danger with wiring sphagnum moss trees is that sometimes they grow too fast, and if you have multiple trees, you may lose sight of wiring locations. When you do rediscover them, often the branch may be scarred as it grows around the wire, leaving a rut or trench along the branch. I have had this happen on numerous occasions, and I have found that I can shape trees just as easily using directional pruning techniques.

There are many sizes of bonsai wire available in bonsai nurseries. The thinner wire is used for the slender branches, and the thick heavy wire can be used for trunk bending. These wires have been annealed, with low heat, to make them more malleable and less likely to cause damage than wire that has not been annealed and is stiffer. The thinner the branch,

A single strand of wire shaping branches, anchored on the trunk

Left: **Multiple strands of wire on a trunk.** ***Right:*** **Wires and wire anchors; all three at Wigert's Bonsai Nursery**

the more flexible it usually is, and the more you can bend it. Trunks need to be bent slowly so as not to break. Sometimes padding is used around the branches to prevent rut and trench formation from the wire. Multiple wires around a branch are also used to spread out the forces acting on the branch. I would urge you to try wiring, as it is an interesting art unto itself, and the methods and tricks of the traditional bonsai masters can easily be incorporated into the sphagnum moss method to produce an esthetically pleasing bonsai.

Ropes and Strings

String exerting tension to shape branch

The use of ropes and strings to alter the shapes of branches is similar to the wiring methods but not nearly as dangerous for the trees. Using padding to avoid scarring of the trees is a useful, though not as exacting a method as wiring. You can create pull on the rope by tying it to the pot, branches, or trunk. You can also use weights to have gravity exert its influence. Tying to the pot is the better method, in that you can control to shape more exactly, and are not subject to wind created problems. Tying to the pot helps if the pot must be moved, as tying to the stand may create problems if a fast move is necessary, such as when a hurricane is approaching. Use an appropriate sized thickness of rope for the size of the branch you are bending, and be careful not to overbend and break the branch.

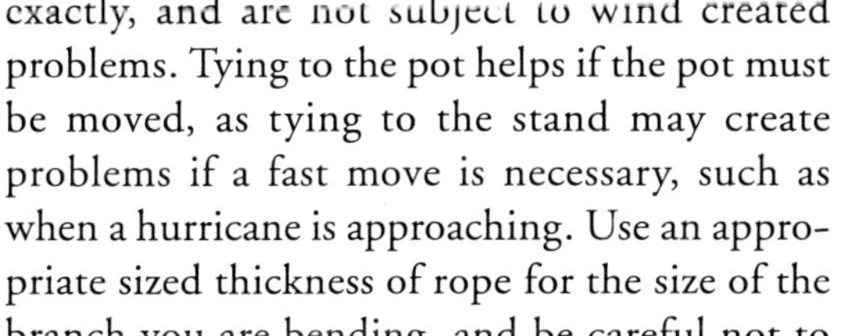

Where and How to Plant?

Bonsai planted over a rock at Wigert's Bonsai Nursery

A pot is the most common manner of holding bonsai. Pots can be all shapes and sizes, colors and textures. The pot can be ostentatious in its own right, or plain so that the eye of the viewer focuses on the tree rather than the pot. It is the artist's choice, and if he or she wants to change the pot later, the sphagnum moss method allows for ease of conversion.

Planting trees on rocks is a popular method.

Some of the roots will be exposed, and it is important to have roots long enough to go over the rock and extend into the sphagnum moss deeply enough to establish themselves. Over time, the roots will conform to the rock's surface and make an interesting scene.

Bonsai and rock planting

Planting your trees along side of rocks is another very popular manner in which to make a miniature scene (pun-ching). I used to be able to get individual rocks at pet stores, where the rocks were weighed and priced by the pound. Lately it seems as if the pet stores only sell packs of rocks, and you have to buy the whole bag, which may include rocks that you don't want. So now I go to local quarries where I can pick out and buy individual rocks. I try to buy sandstone rocks, which often come in various colors and patterns. Igneous or metamorphic rocks can have an alkaline nature, but they are also fine to use. I have used various types of rocks in plantings with no problems, but the safest rock type would be the sandstones.

There are other ways that bonsai can be planted. You can mound the sphagnum moss and plant the tree on a slab. The slab may be any material, as long as it is basically inert and will cause no damage to the plant when the roots reach it. For instance, a limestone slab may be injurious to the tree because of its alkaline nature and contact of the roots. Often on larger plantings of this sort it is advisable to wrap string around the mound to hold it in place until the roots expand enough to hold the sphagnum moss on their own. Then the string can be removed, and the mound will retain its shape. Trees fashioned in this manner can be kept on a slab, giving it a flat bottom, and then later removed from the slab and placed on a shelf or stand.

Planting with Surface Moss

The use of surface moss can be one of the most effective methods of giving your bonsai a pleasing natural appearance. Surface moss is in the bryophyte family of plants and can usually be obtained in shady, moist areas. It usually grows in sheets, which can be removed relatively easily using a metal spatula or putty knife, as described earlier. The trick with the

Surface moss on sphagnum moss

sphagnum moss method is to push down on the surface moss so that water comes up through it from the wet sphagnum moss below. That helps in making good contact between the two types of moss, which is essential for the surface moss to survive and not dry out and die. You can use small pieces and by placing them close to one another, allow for them to fill in the empty spaces between over time.

You can also purchase or make a powder of surface moss. Place dried out surface moss, or purchased powder moss, in a blender with some water, and then blend it into a mixture. Using that mixture, water the sphagnum moss; the surface moss in the mixture will eventually grow on the surface of the sphagnum moss. Make sure it receives enough water, by regular watering or misting, and is started in a shady area. Moss coverings in bright, hot sunlight may wither and die, so if your tree does well in partial or full shade, it is likely the surface moss will do well in that situation.

Surface Gravel

You can find nice gravel, either natural or colored, in pet stores. This can be used as an entire covering for your plant, or in combination with surface moss and/or rocks. You lay the gravel in the location you have chosen and then cover it with a wood glue, such as Elmer's, or leave it loose.

Jin, Sharimiki, Sabamiki

Jin, sharimiki, and sabamiki are techniques used to make your bonsai look older by making it look like has survived some natural disaster, such as breakage or lightning strikes.

Jin is the artificial aging of branches, sharimiki of trunks, and sabamiki is the hollowing out of trunks.

A branch that has been actually damaged by trimming errors can be made into an interesting feature of your bonsai. These are areas usually seen on conifers, as the deciduous trees usually heal the wounds, and often the branch is dropped later. If you have branches that are being clipped off for the overall design of the tree, you may want to leave portions of them to be turned into jin, making an aged appearance.

You will need a sharp blade of some sort, such as a penknife or box-cutter. The bark is carefully stripped away from the branch from the trunk outwards. You will need to remove the outer bark, the inner bark, and the cambium layers to get to the heartwood of the branch. You can use wood carving tools to give an interesting surface to the jin, including longitudinal grooves, depressions, or twisting topography. Or you can leave it smooth. Once you have the shape as you like it, a flame can be used carefully to burn off any fibers that remain, or sand it down with an emery cloth. Be careful not to overheat the jin when using a flame. Then you need to carefully use a brush and paint on lime sulfur, a chemical that can be obtained at most bonsai nurseries. This is a caustic material so make sure you wear goggles to protect your eyes and gloves to protect your hands. If you get some on your skin, wash it off immediately with water and even vinegar to counteract the effects of the alkaline material. The lime sulfur will whiten the dead wood and also protect it. Usually by the next day, the lime sulfur has dried and the process is complete. Wash off any residual material with water. If you wish additional whitening, repeat the procedure.

In sharimiki (or shari as it is often referred to), the same procedure is done to a portion of the trunk in a longitudinal manner. Never cut a band around the trunk; this will kill your tree as it stops the necessary nutrients and water from travelling from the roots to the foliage. Keep the stripping of the trunk above the ground line. You can use chisels or woodcarving tools to make it more natural looking. Then using the lime sulfur, as described above, makes this portion white.

Sabamiki is the hollowing out of a trunk. You can cut out the hollow portion using chisels or woodcarving tools. If you use a slow speed and are careful, power tools can be used, but the marks left are usually unnatural looking and will need to be sanded. Again, use the lime sulfur on the exposed area to make a whitened appearance and to protect the dead wood. Often the edge of the cut will produce a rollover that gives it a natural appearance. This same effect can also be produced in sharimiki.

Grafting

Grafting is usually not seen in bonsai, though it can be a method that has its benefits. When growing citrus trees that you wish to have fruit, often a grafted tree is the quickest way to achieve this. They can also be made by using cuttings of trees that have produced fruit. Ficus trees can have branches

Fruited lemon bonsai made from a cutting

grow into one another by contact over a period of time. I often take my ficus and twist branches around each other to produce a grafted site, as they do naturally, especially in varieties such as banyan trees. It can take a few years until the branches mold into one another, so patience is necessary.

Forests

You can have single trees, trees in pairs or triplets, or other small multiples. But one of the more interesting bonsai configurations is that of forests. Forest bonsai are many small trees grown to give an appearance of a forest in miniature. They have a special appeal and will often be your visitors' favorite. The result can be a striking landscape scene if rocks and/or figurines are added (pun-ching) or just a simple forest (yose-ue). Once you have the forest, you can develop it into a landscape scene. We will discuss three methods for growing forest bonsai.

Jade plant used for cuttings for forest

The first method is that of growing your forest by seeds. If you take the seeds from a relatively fast-growing tree species, such as mimosa or mahogany, they can make lovely forests. You just get a pot of appropriate size to hold many small trees, fill it with sphagnum moss, and plant the seeds. Plant more seeds than you may wish for your final forest, as some will not germinate, and others may be runts, or less desirable because of shape. You can always cull the trees you don't want, and that is easier than trying to plant more seeds later and hoping they catch up. It is best to start them in the early spring so they get a season of growth before winter arrives. The individual trees need to be cared for as any single tree that you might grow from a seed. As they gain in stature, they will start to encroach upon one another and trimming can be a little more difficult than working on a single tree, but you will probably find it more rewarding. If you keep pruning the larger leaves as they grow, eventually you will have many small leaves that are more in proportion with the individual trees in your forest.

Another method of forest growth is to take many cuttings from a tree whose cuttings grow easily, like Fukien tea, jade, or schefflera. All you need do is take the cuttings from new or young shoots (as they will grow easier than old shoots) and after a heavy pruning of the leaves on the stalk, plant them into the sphagnum moss where you want them to grow, and then take care of them as you would any other cutting. (Keep them in the shade at first until they become established, then gradually accustom them to the proper light conditions.) Once again, overplant the cuttings so that ones that do not grow can be culled.

The third method involves taking a specimen plant that has many branches coming from one side of the trunk. You then cut off all of the branches on the opposite side. The tree is then taken out of its pot and laid on its side. You can now use wire, if you like, to help straighten out the upright branches to the direction you wish, or you can let them

Jade cuttings, leaves trimmed and ready for planting

grow on their own. Because of the sphagnum moss and the way it keeps its shape when removed from its pot, you can then tie the tree down to an understructure, such as a wood plank or shelf, to keep it from rolling off of its support. If you want you can also lay it down in its pot, with the plant on its side. Then tie the tree and the pot so it is secure. You can also trim the upright branches so that the tree starts to grow additional branches along the trunk. Once the new branches show signs of growth and have adopted to the tree's new position, you can remove the top portion of the root ball (top, meaning the side that is adjacent to the remaining branches, leaving the root ball that was under the branches that have been removed, still attached to the tree). You can do this in stages to make sure the tree does not go into shock and so that it has enough roots to support the foliage. With strong growing trees, such as Fukien teas or scheffleras, there is less risk in cutting the root ball in this way. Once your plant is doing well, you can transplant the entire tree into a larger pot that will accommodate it, burying the trunk and root ball and leaving the branches extending upwards from the surface. The trunk will eventually grow roots under the branches, and you will have a nice forest growing.

A specimen with many branches extending perpendicular

All branches on the opposite and lateral sides trimmed off

The tree is taken out of its pot, the top of the root ball is cut away, and the tree is replanted. Left on its side, and secured, the tree adjusts to the new pot after a few months.

9

Finishing Touches

Surface Moss

One of the tools of the bonsai artist is surface moss. The little miniature scenes that we construct are replicas of the natural world around us. The goal is to have the scene fool the eye, so that it looks as if an actual outdoor scene, with a tree or trees, that has been magically shrunken in a scaled proportion. A great part of the illusion that is created is the surface of the grounds surrounding the tree. Some people use gravel or stones to create a rocky surface. I have used both, but prefer using a layer of surface moss. It is the green velvety carpet that we see near places of moisture in nature, or where our sprinkler-system world dampens areas on a regular basis, and the sun does not get an opportunity to dry roast it. A nice piece of moss can make a tremendous difference in the appearance of a bonsai. It adds a matured and tailored look to the tree in a pot.

Moss Anatomy

Moss belongs to the plant kingdom and is known scientifically as a *bryophyte,* which means they are nonvascular plants, lacking tubules to carry water and nutrients to various parts of the plant. The higher forms of vegetative life have veins and capillaries to perform the vital function of water and nutrient transportation. Moss forms masses that lie relatively flat, contouring to the top of the surface immediately below them. These clumps and spots of moss are usually found in areas of dampness or out of direct sunlight for most of the day. These are small plants, being about a half inch to four inches tall, depending on the species, of which there are about 12,000 known and extant.

They consist of a series of simple leaves running the length of a filamentous strand that projects perpendicularly from the surface. They have no flowers or seeds. They reproduce by spores that are located in capsules held above the moss by longer stems. The mosses are related to the liverworts and hornworts. Most have easily differentiated stems and leaves. The leaves are not segmented, pinnate, or deeply lobulated. The leaves may often appear as elongated spears, flattened top to bottom. Sometimes they have more of a thickness to them along the elongations. They connect to one another by means of rhizoids, a system of hair-like structures, almost root-like, intertangled, and helping form the mat-like nature of moss.

Mosses have an interesting sex life. Most animals and more complex plants have a system in which the body of the creature or plant has a full set of chromosomes. For example, humans have 46 chromosomes in each of their non-sex cells (diploid), while the sex cells, the sperm and egg, each carry half of that (haploid), or 23 chromosomes. When sperm fertilizes the egg in humans the chromosome number increases to the needed 46, or 23 pairs. In mosses, the plant we see and describe as "moss" has half its full number of chromosomes, while the spores it produces and then launches has a full set of chromosomes. The spores are short-lived and are controlled in production by the moss. The sperm are produced in the antheridial head in a structure called the antheridium. There are multiple antheridia in the antheridial head. It is a reverse situation from most species on the planet. The female portion of moss has a structure called the archegonial head, containing the venter, which contains the eggs.

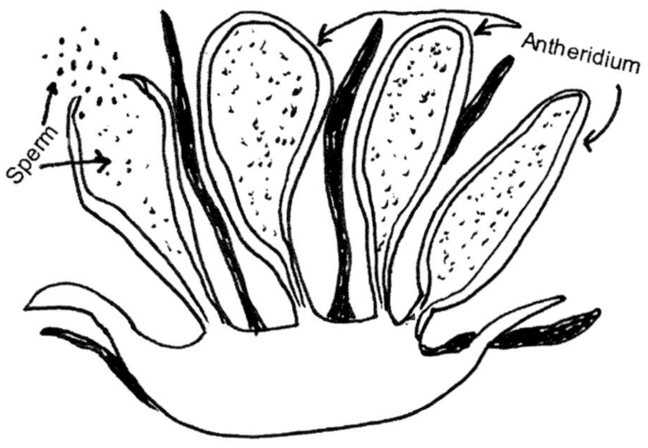

Male structure of the sperm producing antheridial head

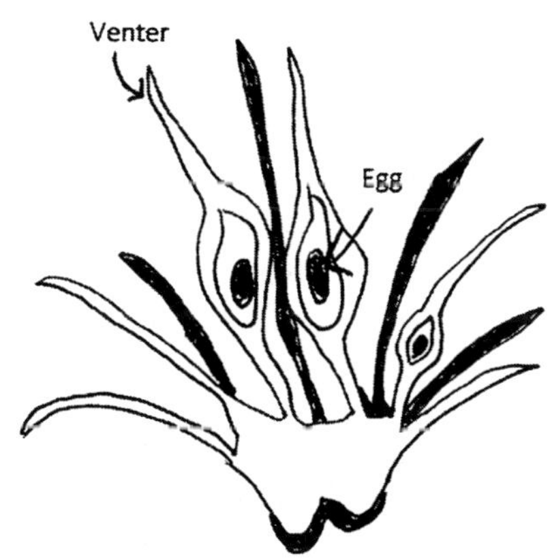

Female structure of the egg producing archegonial head

When ready, the moss sends up gametophytes, which are slender stalks holding the antheridial heads and the spores, soon to be released and spread. The gametophytes also hold the archegonial heads, with the eggs ready to be fertilized. The gametophytes have nonvascular leaves and stems, and a rhizoid base anchoring the plant. The difference between roots and rhizoids is that roots are multicellular while rhizoids are unicellular. Roots in more developed plants contain vascular components called phloem and xylem that transport water. Rhizoids in mosses lack this vascular tissue. The antheridium releases sperm that swim to the venter. The sperm are biflagellate (having two whip-like flagellae for propulsion) transporting them to where fertilization occurs and the area in which early embryos develop. The moss produces a sporophyte containing the spores, which are eventually released starting the process over again. If you watch your moss, you will see these phase changes occur. Moss can also reproduce

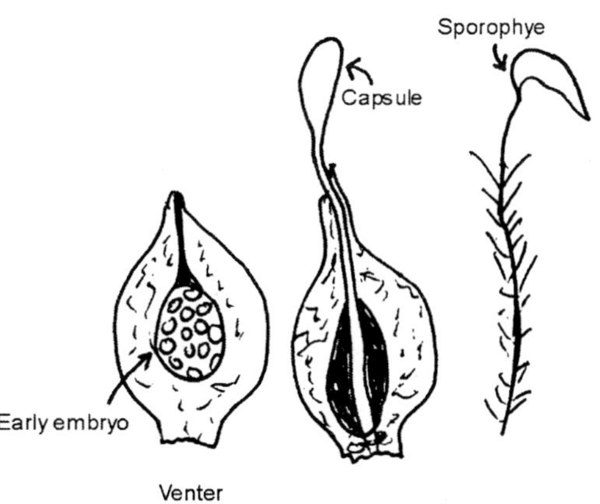

Gametophyte structure showing the sexual heads, avascular leaves and rhizoids

asexually by forming gemmae, which are green structures that form on leaves and stems and then break off and grow, thus eliminating the need for sexual fertilization.

Using Surface Moss

Once you have collected your moss and stored it in a protected area, there will come a time when you will wish to use it. The many things to which moss can cling each present their own problems in the use of the moss. Moss grows on soil, sand, bark, rocks, wood chips or bark chips, gravel, weeds, asphalt, wood, or just about anything, so it seems.

The aim is to gently separate the moss from the substrate it is growing on and attached to. If it is soil or sand, a fine spray from a hose, or soaking it in a basin of water and gently using your fingers, will remove most if not all of the soil or sand substrate. If the moss has grown on wood chips or bark chips, you should gently rinse out any soil or sand associated with the chips and the chips themselves. You will need to pick out, with fingers or forceps, as many of the chips as you can. But when you do this procedure, it is very common to damage and break apart the pad of moss you are holding. You can then piece it together when you apply it to the sphagnum moss. Moss that grows on wood planks or rocks is pretty much useless, as you end up scraping it off and you lose the pad effect. But this moss from hard surfaces is useful for another method of moss propagation. If you want to make a spray mixture of ground-up moss and water, then these hard, flat surfaces are ideal. Just scrape off the moss and collect it in a jar or other container. Mixed in a blender, it can then be spread onto the surface where in time it should grow into a nice uniform covering.

Gravel needs to be picked out as best as possible. It may cause breakdown of the moss clumps. Weeds are often present growing in the midst of the moss fields, and often their roots entangle the moss undersurface. Try to wash the weeds out with a fine stream of water, and then slowly try to extract the roots by slowly pulling on one end until free of the moss (the bigger and thicker end should be pulled out to do the least damage to the moss). Try to get out the most offensive and biggest of the weeds. There will often be other very tiny weeds growing in the moss pad. These should be removed with forceps when the moss is wet or damp. Extract them slowly, and sometimes it helps to have a finger next to the site to prevent the accidental pulling of the moss with the weed. Moss taken near roadways may have pieces of asphalt incorporated into them. I suggest not using any part of the moss that has asphalt because of the potentially damaging nature of the chemicals; they may be toxic and severely damage the moss or plant.

Once you have cleaned the moss as well as you can (most times you cannot get it all out and some of this extraneous material goes along for the ride), you are ready to continue. I have never found incomplete cleaning to be a problem. Just do the best job you can and move on to the next step, which is placing the surface moss on the sphagnum moss. Once you pick the location for the piece you wish to place, just press it firmly against the moss, pressing the entire surface area of the piece against the corresponding area of sphagnum moss below it until you see water coming through the moss and over the entire moss surface. This means you have made good contact and that is very important in helping the surface moss get established. If it is just lying on the sphagnum moss, it will dry up and the edges will curl, and it will die. So just give it a good push, look for water coming up through the surface moss, and move on to the next piece. You can easily edit the moss by tucking it in or tearing it so that the edges meet nicely, or you can even overlap it a bit. I like to start around the trunk and work away towards the edge of the pot.

Some people like a nice flat plane of moss, resembling a well-kept lawn. Other people like ridges and ruts, mounds and other changes of relief, that present a more accurate representation of the topography making up the world around us. If you want to make a rut, or valley, just push with your fingers held together and rigid, and make a slow stabbing motion into the surface moss, pushing down into the sphagnum moss. You will create a depression that you can extend and curve, and slowly have rise up into a mound. For surface depressions smaller than your fingers, a chopstick or wooden dowel can be employed. To make a mound, just cup your hands and push the surface moss and sphagnum moss into a lump. You can always add sphagnum moss under the surface moss to make a mound. Then add more surface moss to make up for the breakaway areas as the surface moss was pushed up the mound. You can add gravel or small rocks to make interesting surface areas, such as pathways, to accompany your tree. You can add sand also if you want a waterfront type of view. Rocks, as discussed earlier, can be a pleasing addition.

I find squirrels to be my most dangerous and persistent adversary when it comes to moss, be it surface or sphagnum. They like to dig through my surface moss into the sphagnum moss in search of seeds or to hide seeds. Other than that, moss is usually unmolested.

Moss from areas other than where you raise your bonsai may not do well in your locale. There are, as mentioned previously, probably more than 12,000 species of moss. Many look alike, and many have similar life necessities and responses to stimuli. But many can look alike, yet have great differences in tolerance to the local conditions into which they are introduced and end up dying. I had found lovely mats of a verdant surface moss inhabiting the space next to a driveway in Rochester, New York (I lived in Philadelphia, 255 miles away by air). They were beautiful, thick, full mats that lifted easily, and there was a lot of it. I took as much as was reasonable and brought it back to Philadelphia, as protected and moist as possible. It arrived in great shape. It made my plants look wonderful. But it didn't take and eventually ended up sloughing off. It is best to find surface moss in your area to increase the chances of it becoming an essential and important part of your bonsai artwork. It immediately gives a bonsai an air of age and beauty. With time, it gives it an air of antiquity and an elegance that defines the bonsai's specialness and unique character.

I have seen traditional bonsai artists use surface moss as full mats, green and lush, or as spotty, hit or miss patches of scrawny and straggling tundra-like land, coldish and forbidding. It looks great either way, when done with a feeling for what one wishes to express and convey. Remember, it is your art. It is your style you are developing. If you truly like your creation and see beauty and interesting things in it, then most likely most other people will see it as a thing of workmanship and toil, patience and love. There will always be the negative people who seem to only enjoy life by taking potshots at those who try. They sit and do nothing, having few accomplishments, but are just so mean spirited they need to build their egos by attempting to knock down yours. How you handle this is your call. Be prepared for that possible eventuality.

Topography

As discussed in the previous section, the surface of the planting can be smooth if you like. Often a more natural look is achieved by making furrows, dips, or other surface depressions or humps. The sphagnum moss method allows for easy, quick, and effective changes in topography. Using one's fingers or instruments, such as chopsticks, you can make depressions or furrows in a few seconds. If you want humps or mounds, just add an appropriate amount of sphagnum moss and shape it to the desired height, first removing the surface moss if it has already been placed, and then recovering it after the change.

Weeding

Removing weeds from your bonsai will not only make it look better, but help protect the plant. It is easier to remove weeds after a thorough watering of the plant. Bigger weeds can be gently removed with your fingers, while tiny newly starting weeds are often best pulled out by means of forceps. Remove them slowly, and if you pull out some of the surface moss during the extraction, just remove that portion from the weed and place it back where it came from.

Figurines and Ornaments

If making a miniature scene, add your figurines and/or ornaments if you wish. They often have small posts attached to the bottom to use in placing them into the growth medium. Gently push them in, and they will move any roots in their way without breaking them.

Edge Trimming

Using flat and straight wooden wedges or wooden spoons with curved edges, gently push down on the surface moss where the surface moss meets the pot edge until that edge is buried. I take wooden curved spoons and cut off their ends to give them a flat bottom, which works nicely with curved pots. Chopsticks can also be used on irregular shaped pots where there is not enough room for a wedge or spoon. You can also use chopsticks to make the meeting of rocks and surface moss less shaggy looking.

Traditional bonsai at Wigert's Bonsai Nursery

Surinam cherry bonsai with red fruit

C-2

Dried sphagnum moss

Root ball packed with sphagnum moss removed from pot, showing knife for trimming roots

Artillery fern showing flowers and seeds

Planting on a rock slab at Wigert's Bonsai Nursery

C-4

Hobby bag sitting atop bale of sphagnum moss

Shaded bonsai shelves of the author

Shelves for full sun exposure

Surface moss growing on a wood plank

C-6

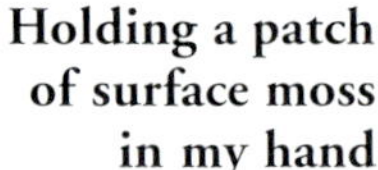

Holding a patch of surface moss in my hand

Placement of the surface moss at the base of the trunk and working out toward the edge of the pot

Surface moss complete, awaiting finishing touches

The finished bonsai

Moss patch in Iceland (courtesy of Bernard Shore, M.D.)

Moss field on lava flow in Iceland (courtesy of Bernard Shore, M.D.)

Miniature figurines at Wigert's Bonsai Nursery

Strangler fig roots growing over sculpture as depicted on Cambodian currency

A banyan bonsai defoliated about 97 percent

Banyan with new tiny leaf growth a few days after defoliation

Applying wood glue to gravel surface

Surface after wood glue dries

Jade cuttings planted for small forest

Jin at Wigert's Bonsai Nursery

C-13

Sharimiki and samamiki at Wigert's Bonsai Nursery

C-14

One of Erik Wigert's striking bonsai examples showing a breathtaking sharimiki

Erik and Andrea Wigert at their bonsai nursery

Pine forest at Wigert's Bonsai Nursery

Rows upon rows of beautiful bonsai specimens at Wigert's Nursery

Part of the selection of pots and figurines at Wigert's Nursery

10

Maintenance

Pruning

To keep your plant healthy and growing in the manner that you have envisioned, you will need to periodically prune your plant. Leaves that are dying, yellowed, insect eaten, or too large should be removed as soon as you notice them. The energy that the tree uses to try to save these structures can be used for increasing the growth of the foliage you want. By removing large leaves on a continual basis you will encourage the formation of smaller leaves that will be more in proportion to the tree conformation and size (this technique was discussed previously). Foliage that is being attacked by insects or fungus can be aided by the use of insecticides and fungicides. I use a mixed combination of Malthione and copper fungicide, sprayed periodically, to control these pests and diseases.

Dead or damaged branches should also be removed upon discovery. Using clippers of the correct size, cut off the unwanted portions. Small branches usually need no protection on the cut end, as they will heal quickly and naturally as they do in nature after breakage from wind, rock slides, or animals. If it is a bigger branch with a larger diameter, you may want to apply some pruning sealer. Spray the sealer into a plastic or paper cup and apply it to the affected area using a cotton swab. I usually do not do this and have run into no, or very few, problems in pruning branches.

Surface Moss Spread onto Trunks

Often your surface moss might start climbing up the trunk of your tree. It is best to gently remove this with something, such as a popsicle stick, so as not to damage the bark of the tree. Scrape it downwards until it is at the level of the growth medium. If you like how it looks, it is okay to leave it on the bark.

Inspection of Sphagnum Moss

This is one of the most important maintenance procedures you should perform. It is much easier using the sphagnum moss method compared to the traditional method. If you notice that the tree is not growing well, gently pull the plant from its pot. First look at the sphagnum moss and see what color and consistency it has. If it is dark and not as stringy as when planted, the sphagnum moss may be decomposing into peat moss. If this is the case, you will need to remove the old sphagnum moss using a hose and replace it with fresh sphagnum moss. When replacing the old with new sphagnum moss make sure you have as much contact between the roots and the sphagnum moss as possible. When you repot, firmly place the root ball back into its container, adding sphagnum moss to fill in any hollows. You can remove any surface moss before doing this and replace it afterwards, making solid contact between the surface moss and the sphagnum moss.

If you take the tree out of its pot and you see a root bound plant, just take your serrated knife and cut off about a quarter of an inch of the roots, place a wad of new sphagnum moss in the bottom of your pot and firmly place the plant back into its pot.

Over- or underwatering will also be noticed during inspections, and corrections should be implemented immediately. When you have sphagnum moss that is very dry, simply give the plant a good watering. If the sphagnum moss is oversaturated with water, put it in a location where rain cannot get to it and let it dry.

You may find ants or other invertebrates inhabiting the sphagnum moss. For ants I sprinkle a fire ant insecticide on the surface and water thoroughly, carrying the insecticide into the sphagnum moss. This sends the ants packing, though they may move to another one of your plants, which may then have to be treated in the same manner. Other pests, such as worms or grubs, can be treated by various grub worm treatments available at nurseries, greenhouses, or hardware stores that carry plants. Use them as directed.

11

Wigert's Bonsai Nursery

Finding a bonsai nursery is like finding lost treasure. Nurseries specializing in bonsai are few and far between, so when I happened upon Wigert's Bonsai Nursery, in North Ft. Myers, Florida, it was like a dream come true. It is a 50-minute drive from my house, and I always look forward to going there. If you are anywhere near, you should most definitely stop in for a visit. I urge people to plan a day trip to visit with the Wigerts if at all possible. Erik Wigert is a bonsai master, and his wife, Andrea Wigert, is a knowledgeable and pleasant person who goes out of her way to make you feel comfortable.

Wigert's Bonsai Nursery entrance

A large selection of specimen bonsai at Wigert's Nursery

One of the classrooms at Wigert's Nursery

Some of the tools and wires at Wigert's Nursery

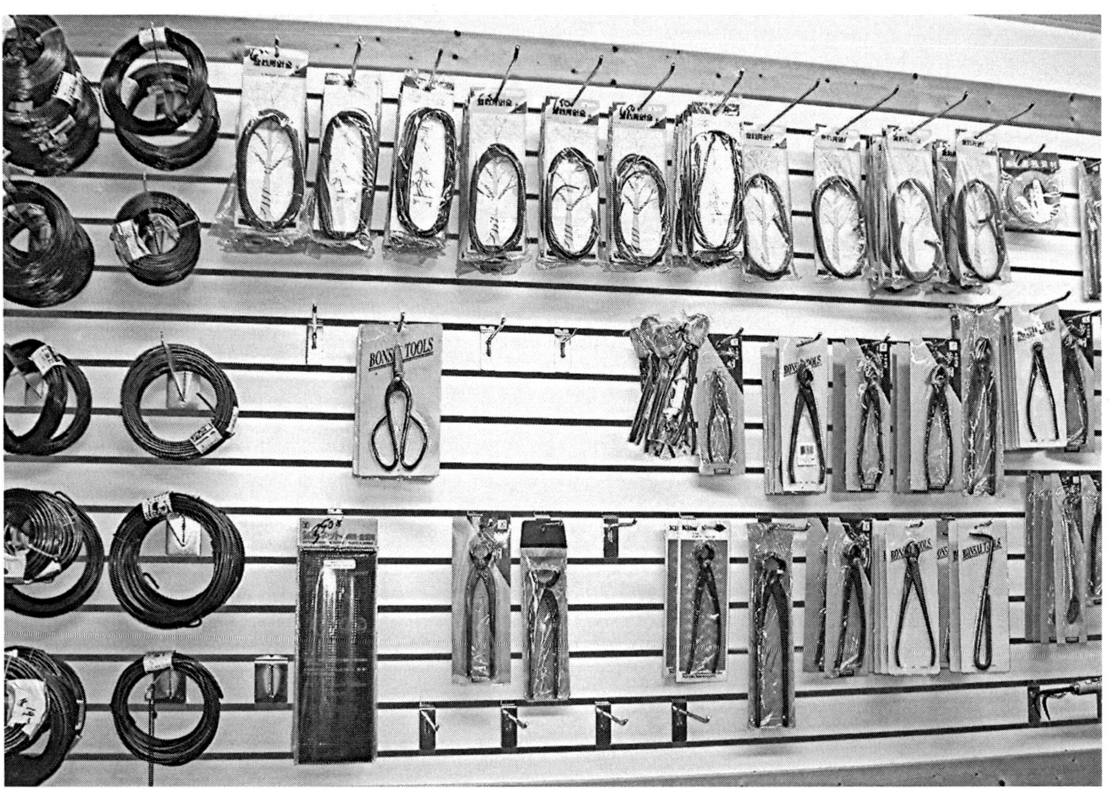

Tools of all kinds and wire of all sizes for the choosing at Wigert's Nursery

The nursery inhabits five acres and is not far from Interstate 75, which runs up the Gulf of Mexico side of Florida. By 2010 Erik has been in the bonsai field for only about ten years, but like his trees, he is experienced and possesses a talent far beyond his years. Erik was born in 1976 in Waterman, Illinois, and moved to Pine Island, Florida, at the tender age of one year old. His family had a mango grove, and his contact and experience with plants and trees have served him well. He started out as a vet tech and one day went to a meeting of a bonsai club in Ft. Myers. There he met the mentor who helped him develop his bonsai skills. He went to Puerto Rico where he studied under Pedro Morales, a well-known bonsai master. Reading many books and studying on his own, he has become a force of his own in the world of bonsai. His traditional bonsai are breathtaking and always give me a thrill when I see them. Erik was named winner for the Best Tropical Bonsai at the First U.S. National Bonsai Exhibit in Rochester, New York, in 2008. He has also had his trees showcased at Epcot Center, Walt Disney World, in 2005, 2006, 2007, 2008, 2009, and 2010. This is quite an accomplishment for a young man. Erik also teaches many bonsai classes (beginner, intermediate, and advanced) at their nursery, and he presents workshops on bonsai both nationally and internationally. He also travels to give demonstrations around the area and throughout Florida. His favorite trees for bonsai are bougainvillea and unusual species from Puerto Rico. Raising and caring for bonsai, along with his travel, is a full-time job for Erik, seven days a week. Erik says that he fertilizes four to five times a year and is forever trimming his multitude of plants.

Andrea was born in Brazil in 1979 and came to Miami, Florida, at nine years of age. The two of them met at the Morikami Museum (dedicated to Japanese garden settings and bonsai), when Erik was doing a show and Andrea's family was also doing a show. They have been married for three years. Her parents had an involvement in plants all of her life and now have a nursery in Florida.

The nursery has many different varieties of trees, in differing sizes, available for purchase. They are arranged in a large display area with thousands of specimens on shelves. The trees in this area receive full sun, and they also have an area in a screened structure that receives reduced sunlight for those plants not accustomed to full sun. The Wigerts have a workshop studio where Erik instructs people in the art of bonsai. They also have a shop carrying tools, pots, figurines, fertilizers, wiring, and other items.

It is best to call if you are planning a visit and wish to speak with Erik, as he is often away giving lectures and workshops. Their address and telephone number are:

Wigert's Mango Grove and Bonsai Nursery
2930 South Road
North Ft. Myers, FL 33917
Telephone: 239-543-2234
Website address: http://www.wigertsbonsai.com/

12

Automatic Water and Fertilization and Semi-Automatic Water System

Automatic System

Water and fertilization of your bonsai is an important task. For people going on vacations, of poor health who need to avoid the hot summer sun, or who just want it done for them, an automatic watering and fertilization system is a great solution. If you only have a few plants, watering by hand is preferred, unless you will not be home or need an automatic system to help you because of other concerns or situations. Lawrence Harold, a master plumber

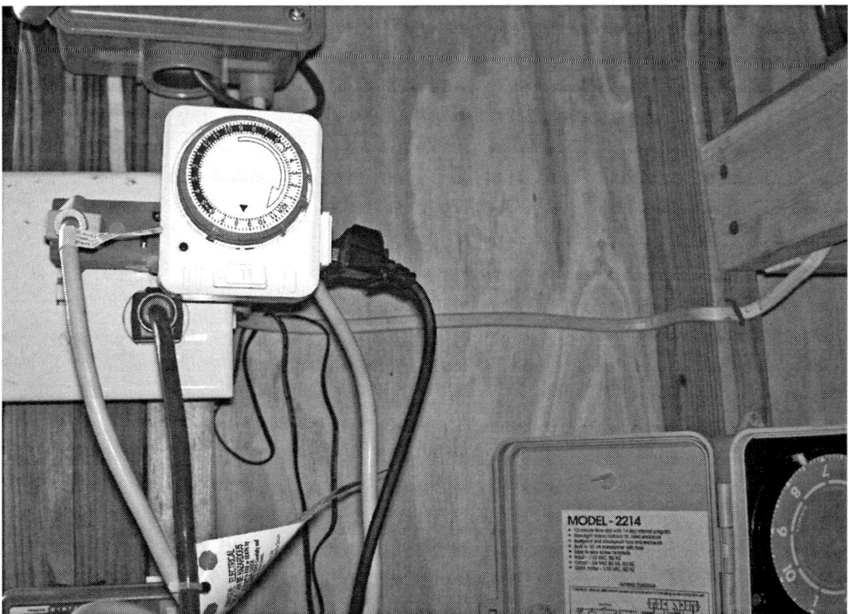

Timers control the propagation misters. The inexpensive white timer above is set to turn on for 15 minutes at 7 A.M., 11 A.M., 1 P.M., 4 P.M. The timer to the right, model-2214, was bought at a greenhouse supply company. It turns on for 30 seconds every 10 minutes. The misters come on at least once at 7, 11, 1, 4 o'clock.

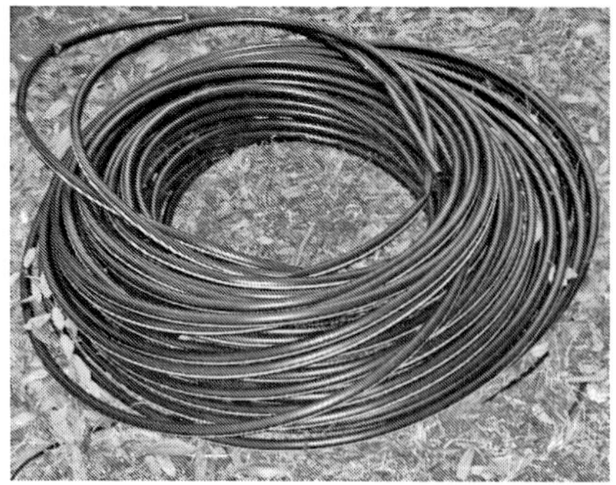

A thousand foot roll of half inch black poly pipe

Main supply water valve

Water powered fertilizer injector pump, set at .4 percent ratio

A series of electric 24 volt three-quarter inch solenoid valves. The main water line is three-quarter inch white PVC above. Each valve is directly wired to three programmable controllers. When the valve opens water or fertilizer is pumped to the trees. The half inch black poly lines below go to different zones.

A close-up of the half inch poly with drip emitters attached. Each emitter is for one tree irrigation line. The eighth inch tubing runs to the tree stake.

and plumbing instructor, has devised such a system, as he has many bonsai spread over a large area. He enjoys the consistency of his system and the ability to have it work for him when he is away on vacation. He supplied the captions to the author's photographs in this chapter.

The main water supply comes onto the property, then there is an offshoot where first controllers are used to start and stop the flow of water to the propagation misting area. The propagation misting pipeway is just an offshoot, while the main water flow continues towards the plants. At the misting station Mr. Harold has various sprinkler heads that release the pressurized water in various fashions from a fine mist to a more robust sprinkling, adjusted

A spaghetti of black poly tubing, the white two inch PVC is a mixing chamber for the liquid fertilizer

A special propagation misting nozzle

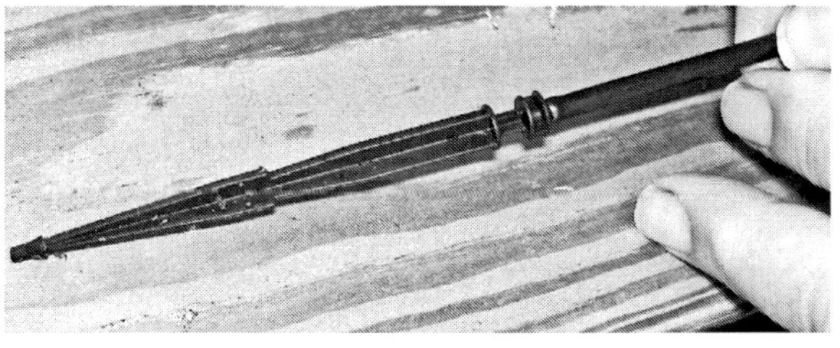

A close-up of the eighth inch poly tubing attached to the tree stake

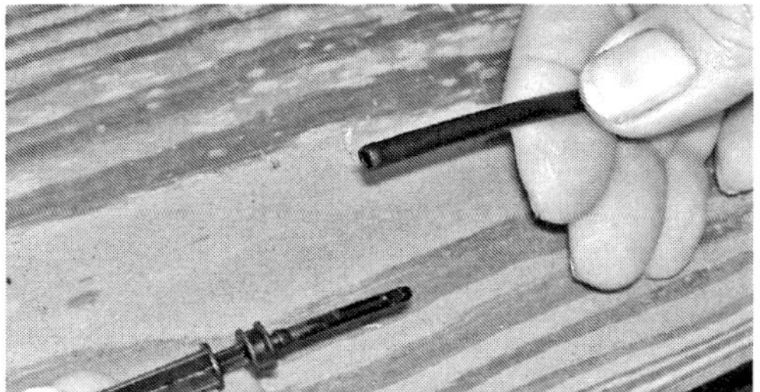

The tube disconnected from the stake

The propagation area under 80 percent shade-cloth

A row of bonsai, with an eighth inch poly tree stake in each pot

Galvanized #9 wire staples to hold down half inch poly pipe. This is very important if you use a lawnmower.

Tree stakes in each pot

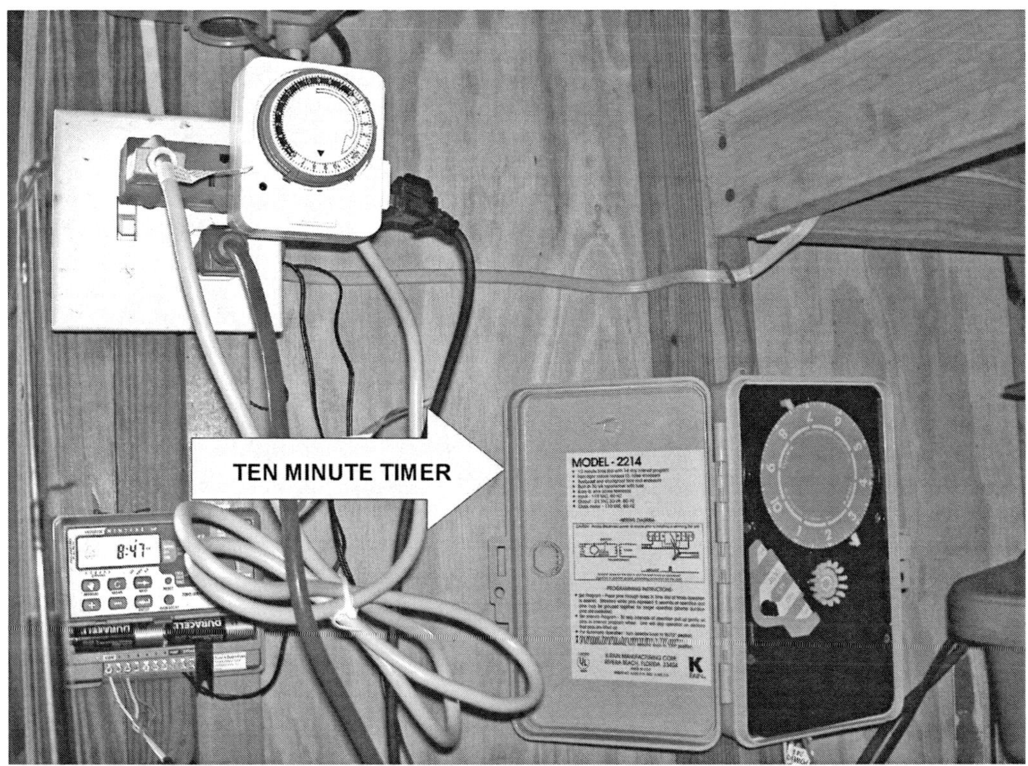

A ten minute timer for the propagation zone. It makes one clock revolution every ten minutes when activated.

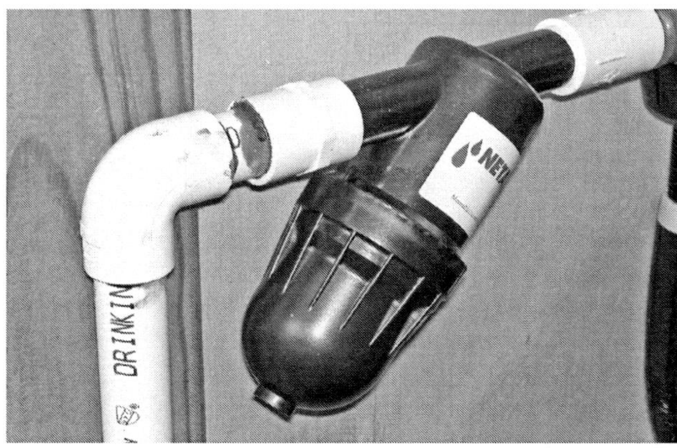

A water strainer

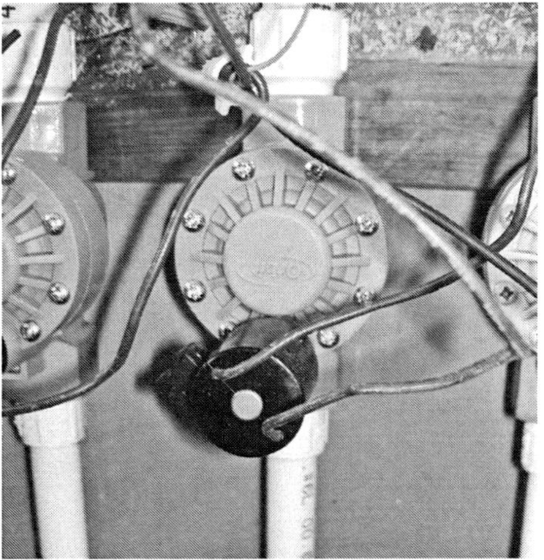

A single solenoid valve in a bank of six. Each is a separate zone. One goes to plants on bench #1 and one to plants planted beside the south house wall, and one to plants on bench #2 and one to other plants. Each valve is controlled by a timer.

to his desires. At the misting station he uses two sets of timers. The ten-minute timer actually controls the application of water to the misting site. This allows for ten minutes total of misting, which is broken down into 30-second periods of actual misting once during this ten-minute period. The ten-minute timer

A tree stake in sphagnum moss

Pipe hangers on water supply

A hose connected to the water supply (a well), showing other water outlets connected to other hoses, or a sprinkler system

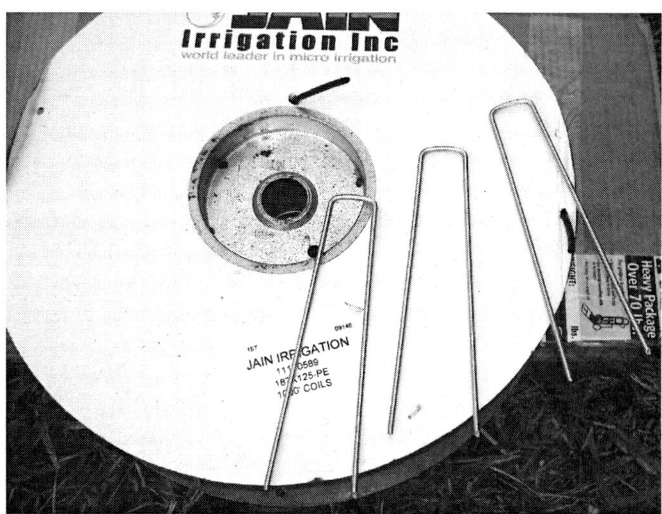

A 1000 foot roll of eighth inch poly tubing with three #9 ground staples

Half gallon per hour emitters

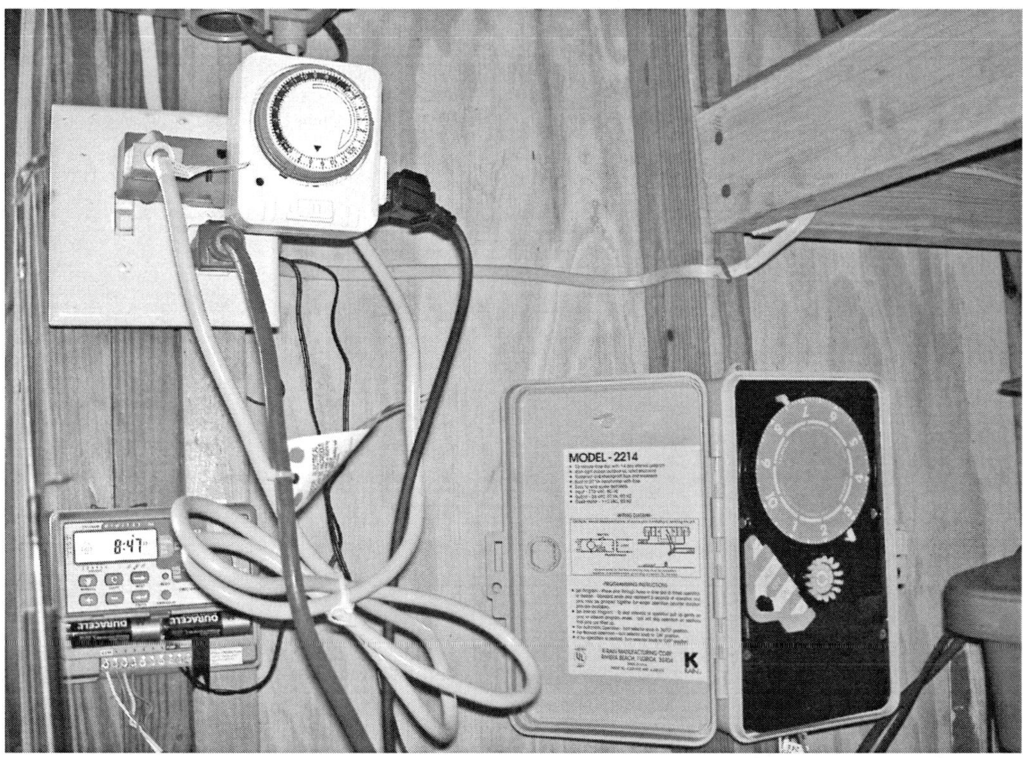

Three different timers/controllers: the current watering schedule is 9 A.M. Monday through Saturday, three minutes of water irrigation. On Sundays at 10 A.M. fertilizer goes out for four minutes.

Semi-automated watering system at work

Full-sun shelves with PVC pipes and sprinkler heads

works for 30 minutes so there are three 30-second mistings in one half hour. The ten-minute timer has a controlling timer that turns the ten-minute timer on and off. He uses a simple 24-hour timer to regulate the ten-minute timer to go for thirty minutes a period for as many periods as he wants on each day.

The hose connected to the main bonsai shelves

The water continues on its way, and before it gets to the plants, a fertilizer mixture is injected into the water system after it has passed the mister section. As the water flows through a fertilizer injection pump, it adds fertilizer to the water at a 4 percent ratio. The fertilizer injection pump is controlled to add fertilizer to the water heading to the plants by three programmable controllers that regulate a series of solenoid valves allowing the fertilized water to go to various zones of use. The amount of fertilizer received by the plants is controlled by a timing mechanism.

Lawrence Harold can have the water without fertilizer flowing to his plants on a steady basis, and then have the fertilizer system kick in when he wants to provide fertilizer to his plants and shut-off when not needed. He has half-gallon-per-hour emitters controlling the amount of water delivered to the plants. His misting station is independent of the fertilizing management and acts on an independent timing system.

Semi-Automatic System

There is a relatively easy way to help water your bonsai for those taking care of a number of plants. This is not an automatic system as described above. This is a way to help you water without lugging a hose or water can around. It is based on using your hose to hook up to a system of pipes and sprinkler heads. The water is delivered either by the manual start of the water flow by a valve, or it can also be controlled by using an automatic lawn-sprinkling system, but it will not deliver fertilizer to your bonsai. This is a system I have set up to help me water my plants, and it makes things quite a bit easier.

I have a couple of hoses connected to outlets at my well, and I use another sprinkler system that was used for a garden area that now goes to my full-sun shelves. I used PVC piping and created a structure that uses variously spaced sprinkler heads to water all the plants. On my three main bonsai stands under my oak tree, I also use the same type of PVC sprinkler system.

13

Cold Weather Care

If you live where the winters are cold you will need to take special precautions to protect your bonsai. The outdoor trees that naturally survive in these climates do so because their roots extend well underground where they are protected from the severe temperatures and the wind. A bonsai left outside to fend for itself is in a pot, above ground, and will feel the full effects of the change in weather. The pot will freeze completely, as will the roots inside that pot. The wind will have a drying effect on the sphagnum moss or soil, creating additional problems. Bonsai need protection from these extremes. If you have a greenhouse, that will usually be protection enough against the elements. The lighting will naturally shorten as the season progresses to the winter solstice. (In the Northern Hemisphere this is the day with the shortest amount of light, usually around December 20 or 21. The summer solstice occurs around June 20 or 21, and is the day with the greatest sunlight available. These are reversed in the Southern Hemisphere.) Because the trees get the correct light exposure at the correct times, there will not be unseasonal growth for trees that need a rest period. Trees are sensitive to the amount of daily light they receive and use that as a signal to start (spring) or slow (fall) their growth patterns. They do not do this based on temperature.

If you do not have a greenhouse, there are other methods of protecting your trees. If you have a deck where you can keep your trees, you can construct a winter covering extending from your railings, propped up by center posts, and enclosing the area. Also enclose any opening through the rails. This will help stop the wind and some of the cold from getting to your plants. If the temperatures become extremely cold, it would be prudent to bring your trees inside for the cold periods, storing them in a basement or other chilly area of the house. If in a basement, remember that they will need some light, so a periodic exposure to light of six to eight hours a day by light bulbs is a good idea. When indoors see that they are not directly exposed to the hot air from heater vents. Also examine their growth medium to see that it does not dry out and damage the roots.

When I lived in the North, I used to have an outdoor shed that I lined with shelves. I put my bonsai in there where cracks in the construction and a window allowed light to penetrate. I watered them periodically inside the shed, not allowing them to dry out.

You can also make a cold weather storage area called a cold frame. You will need to dig a rectilinear hole (so that you can reach all of the plants) in the ground (before it freezes) about 24 to 36 inches deep. Line it with exterior plywood along the sides, but not on the bottom. The plywood should extend about 6 to 18 inches above the surface, depending on the maximum height of the plants that you wish to inhabit the cold frame. If you have smaller bonsai, then make the above-ground plywood sufficient for your plants without overextending it. Put a four to six inch layer of gravel in the bottom. Then put your bonsai into this recess and spread hay, straw, or mulch between and over them, up to the bottom branches. You will need to construct a cover that can be opened easily and will let light in. You should water your plants in the morning and avoid late day watering in case the overnight temperatures cause the water to freeze, which can crack your pots. There are cold frame kits available from local gardening suppliers and on the internet.

For those of you in the tropics or sub-tropics, winters are usually mild enough to leave your bonsai out all year. But occasionally, cold spells will be upon you requiring a quick response to save your plants. You need to pay attention to the weather forecasters as to how long an overnight drop in temperatures will last. Here in Florida we occasionally get temperature drops into the mid to high 20s (F). When the temperature will only be that low for three to four hours, your plants may be able to survive outside. If it is for a more extended period, you will need to protect your plants. I bring my temperature-sensitive plants inside the two outdoor sheds that I have, packing them in closely. Certain plants that I have do poorly if exposed to temperatures that fall below 40 or 50 degrees (F). These go into the sheds or my garage when the temperatures fall below their tolerance threshold. When left outside during temperature drops, sprinkling the foliage with water in the evening will sometimes fend off the cold weather extremes. If it is a relatively short period of expected cold, say three to five days, then I bring my sensitive plants into the house itself (mainly our bathroom). You may find lizards and insects that come along for the ride.

Trees that normally grow in cold weather should not be fertilized if you live in a cold climate and are allowing your trees to go through the cold as they normally would do, just protecting the roots from freezing as discussed above. You don't want to initiate early growth by fertilization. If you live in the tropics, where you will only be experiencing relatively mild cold periods, you would use it is a different strategy of fertilization. Because we want our plants to grow to their maximum ability, continue to fertilize your trees but at a reduced schedule. I only fertilize my bonsai once a month during our short winters. The shortening of sunlight during the days as we approach the winter solstice is a signal to our trees to slow down their growth somewhat. Weekly fertilization is not a necessity. If your plants are in a heated and well-lit greenhouse, where the growth is pretty much as it is in summer, then seven to ten day fertilization schedules can be maintained.

14

Propagation

Seeds

There are multiple methods of propagating plants. One of the best known of these methods is the simple planting of seeds. It is the easiest to perform. But the results are often disappointing. One of the problem areas with the seed method is that of time. It takes a long time for most trees to grow to a size that is appropriate for bonsai. The growing process can take years for your seedling to reach a reasonable size. I have planted many seeds of trees, and on average, I would say, it takes three to seven years to produce a plant worthy of being called a bonsai, if not longer. In addition, you cannot foresee what the plant will turn into. Yet some of my favorite bonsai have been grown by this method, by using trees that have a fairly fast maturation rate. The fertilization method of the sphagnum moss method is also a contributing factor in encouraging thicker and thus older looking trunks in a shorter time.

Sometimes you are unable to obtain specimens of trees that you would like to have. Seeds are often the only way to obtain certain trees (in the United States) that are native to faraway lands. One of my favorite trees is the baobob tree of Africa. I have rarely seen a specimen tree available in the United States, though I am certain you can easily obtain them in Africa or Australia. I purchased seeds on an online auction site, and after they had sprouted and I had grown them in pots (not as bonsai, but as full size tree seedlings), I planted them around my house. They grew well, and I was happy to see them adjusting nicely to the Florida weather patterns. They were about four feet tall when I transplanted them from their pots to the grounds outside. They did well in the new locations. Eventually we ran into one of the cold spells we get on a periodic basis here in Florida, when the temperature dipped into the mid-twenty-degree (F) range, and though I covered them to protect them, they died. About three years ago I found an internet site that sold baobob seedlings. I ordered six of them. I planted two as bonsai and four as outside trees. I still have the two bonsai, but only three outdoor trees remain, one having been lost to the recent cold winter. If their root structures can expand enough, perhaps one day I will have full-grown baobob trees on our property. The bonsai baobob I can protect by bringing them indoors when the weather conditions merit special care.

Another one of my favorites is mimosa trees. I received seeds from a friend in California about 12 years ago and still have that tree as a bonsai. I recently purchased 50 mimosa seeds on the internet and made a forest planting. I have also obtained cotton seeds, which grow quite easily and produce lovely flowers and bolls of cotton. So seeds have their place in bonsai, and you should consider them. But many seeds are difficult to germinate, and with some trees the germination time can be measured in years. Some seeds need to be scored, cut, soaked, or frozen. I received Texas ebony seeds during a visit to a cactus nursery in Arizona and was directed to freeze them for two weeks before planting. I planted about ten seeds, but only two sprouted. One of the two died, but I later found two seedlings on the internet and I now have three Texas ebony bonsai. I used to periodically purchase banyan tree seeds, which are tiny and need special care. They need a moist environment and need to be covered with a plastic wrap to germinate them. I was unsuccessful in germinating any of them. Seeds allow you to grow many varieties of trees that you might not get otherwise, but many have inherent problems. It is definitely worth the try, and I urge you to take a seed and plant it. I find sphagnum moss a great medium for seed germination. Before I knew about sphagnum moss, I planted the seed from a lemon that I had eaten. I still have that tree, and it is the oldest tree in my collection.

Cuttings

Cuttings are one of the fastest and most rewarding methods of plant propagation. Some plants are very easy to grow from cuttings and some are very difficult. One species that I find exceptionally easy to grow from cuttings is the Fukien tea. These trees grow easily in sphagnum moss, and they tend to have leggy offshoots that need frequent pruning. All you need to do is cut off an overly long branch and make a cutting. Making cuttings is a simple procedure. Make your cut clean and perpendicular to the direction of growth. If you are working with a plant that produces suckers, which are offshoots growing near the base of the trunk, these make excellent cuttings. Look for branches that have new growth and are expanding in size. Cut off the piece you wish for your cutting, or a piece left over from a trimming. Then you need to reduce the foliage along the cutting. Cut away all of the foliage from the bottom of the cutting that will go into the sphagnum moss. This should be about one to three inches. Then cut off 90 to 95 percent of the foliage left on the cutting. You can leave tiny new leaves in place and cut remaining bigger leaves so there is only a small portion left. Because the cutting has no roots yet, the more of the foliage you cut off, the less the cutting will have to struggle to get water to the remaining greenery. You need some foliage to allow for the chlorophyll to absorb sunlight and make nutrients for the cutting. Keep the sphagnum moss well watered, but not overwatered, and keep the cuttings in the shade. Once you see new growth on the cutting, you can slowly expose it to more light as it establishes itself in its growth medium. Do not transplant the cutting until it has had sufficient time to develop into a healthy and vital plant. This time varies from species to species, but usually six months is a sufficient amount of time. You can group cuttings together to get a forest bonsai, or plant a few close together to get a grafted trunk, or perhaps for a multiple trunk setting. Avoid insecticides as much as possible during the first three to five weeks of growth, and likewise avoid fertilizing those three to five weeks to avoid root burn.

Cuttings can also be made from thick branches. This will allow your bonsai to have a thick trunk almost immediately. But it may be harder to get a thickened and older portion of the tree to root. It is best to get as many of these cuttings as is practical so that if only one or a few out of the batch grows, you will have some that can become bonsai. Some people like to use rooting hormone to start cuttings. This is a powder that is readily available in nurseries and garden shops. All you need to do is wet the portion that will be inserted into the growth medium, dip that portion into the rooting hormone, and then plant the cutting. People who use soil for their cuttings use this material frequently in cutting propagation. I never use it in sphagnum-moss cutting propagation because I have found it totally unnecessary. The sphagnum moss seems to have an ability to work well with cuttings and enhance their survival rate. I have tested rooting hormone in sphagnum moss and found no difference in the yield of successful plants to those that had no rooting hormone. It will certainly do no harm to use rooting hormone if you so desire.

Cuttings are wonderful way to obtain bonsai that are fruit bearing. A seed planting of a citrus tree can take up to 20 to 30 years, if ever, to produce bonsai fruit. But if you take a cutting from an area of a citrus tree that already has produced fruit, then your cutting will most likely also bear fruit.

Ground and Air Layering

Air layering is an interesting technique for tree propagation. It is a good way to get a trunk that is thick and old. The idea is to damage the bark and force the tree to grow new roots, at which point the segment can be separated from the parent tree and replanted. The best time for layering is the spring when plants are ready to grow and expand. With a thick branch, this branch becomes the new, desirable trunk. There are two methods of layering: ground layering and air layering.

Ground layering is performed using low branches that can reach the ground easily and are somewhat supple. It is very similar to what happens naturally to a branch that is near the ground so that when it is damaged or bent, soil covers that portion. Often the tree will produce roots in that site. In ground layering, this process is simulated and helped along by tried and true methods. When you have a branch that is long enough and flexible enough to be pushed underground with its tip emerging from the soil, that branch is a good candidate for ground layering. All you need do is make a few slits into the bark that is closest to the ground, running along the length of the branch portion to be buried. Cover this portion with rooting hormone and then wrap sphagnum moss in a heap around that portion. Then bury the sphagnum moss enclosed portion of the branch under the ground and water it. Keep it moist, but not overly so, for the next three months. You can secure it in place using U-clamps driven into the soil. Then you can carefully dig around the branch portion with your fingers so as not to damage any roots that have grown. If you find a decent number of roots present, you can raise that branch out of the ground and saw off its base, leaving a small portion of the branch that is unrooted as the base. Then plant this rooted cutting in sphagnum moss and care for it as you normally would. This is the same method that growers who use soil as their growth medium have used with great success for years.

Air layering is similar but with necessary differences. In air layering, you are taking a branch that is above ground and attempting to get roots to grow out of the branch where they wouldn't normally grow. You need to find a nice thick branch and cut two rings around the circumference of the branch at an approximate distance from each other as twice the diameter of the branch. Then you need to strip the portion of bark between these two cuts you have made all around the branch. It is essential that you also remove the cambium layer, which is usually greenish and soft, and get down to the hardwood of the branch. Then you take a good sized clump of wet sphagnum moss and wrap it around the damaged bark area, keeping good contact with the damaged area. Then wrap the sphagnum moss and the underlying branch tightly with a plastic wrap, such as Saran Wrap or a plastic bag. Using a clear plastic tape, tightly secure the plastic wrap around the branch at both ends. Make a small hole at the top of this plastic enclosure to allow for easy watering. The sun will tend to cause evaporation of the water of the sphagnum moss so it is essential that you check the site frequently and water it as necessary, making sure not to overwater it as the excess water will lie on the bottom of the plastic enclosure and cause rotting. A good site to make the ring stripping is just below an old leaf bud as there are usually many adventitious buds that can develop into roots. Examine the plastic bag or wrapping frequently to see if there is root growth. Once root growth has started, allow it to develop to the point where you will feel comfortable transplanting it to sphagnum moss.

You can also use a slightly different technique in the air layering method to injure the bark. This is the tourniquet method. Take the desired section of bark to be damaged and encircle it with thick wire, tightening it severely around the branch. This will stop the flow of nutrients to the bark area you wish damaged and have the same effect as cutting the bark around the branch.

15

Pot Drainage

Perhaps the most important consideration in using the sphagnum moss method is that of proper container drainage. Because of sphagnum moss's special ability to hold the water that it needs and to allow the excess to drain off, drainage is very important. A proper drainage outlet will eliminate water from staying in the bottom of the pot or container, possibly causing root rot. If you have a small drainage hole, it can easily be blocked by debris that acts as a plug, preventing the excess water from escaping. With many soil based plants, screening is placed over the drainage holes to keep soil from dripping out onto tables or patios and giving an unkempt look to the area around the plant. Because sphagnum moss drains clear, this problem doesn't exist with this method. So you should never use screens with sphagnum moss as they will tend to clog drainage holes. Make sure when you are transplanting a specimen or cutting to a different pot that you wash out the new pot with a strong spray from a hose to remove any soil that may have accumulated in the pot. This will enable you to see the bottom of the pot clearly and determine if an old screening piece is there. Sometimes they are difficult to see. If you find one, remove it.

If you have your tree situated on a slab of some material, in general you do not have to worry about drainage, as the excess water will pass over the unrestrained sides. But if your slab is curved in a in a slightly bowl-shaped manner, water may accumulate in the lowest point of the concavity. It will be necessary to provide drainage so excess water can drain out harmlessly.

If you are using a pot of metal or plastic, it is best to drill out a larger drainage hole if the one that is present is too small or there is no drainage hole. Rather than try to drill one large hole, it is safer to drill many smaller holes in a circular formation, and then drill away the connecting bridges between the smaller holes, or break them apart carefully until you have a sufficiently sized drainage hole.

If your pot is made out of wood, the same method of drilling many smaller holes rather than one big hole is encouraged. You can then chisel out the connecting bridges between the drilled holes. If you think that drilling a large number of small holes over most of the bottom surface is sufficient, you may be risking your plant. The smaller holes often become clogged easily, and even though you have a lot of them, many, if not all, of them can easily be obstructed, thwarting your idea of more is better. Actually, larger is better. You can have fewer drainage holes as long as they are larger drainage holes.

Ceramic saucer with wood drilling support block

Ceramic saucer placed on top of wood block

Making first drill hole in ceramic saucer

Holes drilled around area to be punched out

After the site has been chiseled away

Terra cotta pots and saucers and ceramic pots and saucers make great bonsai containers. It is important to increase the size of the manufactured holes in these containers. The method for creating bigger holes in terra cotta is relatively simple. Take a basin that is larger than the pot or saucer whose drainage hole you wish to enlarge and allow the terra cotta container to soak completely submerged in water for approximately 24 hours. When ready for drilling, take the terra cotta out of its water bath and dry it with a towel lightly. Take the bowel or saucer and place it upside down on a piece of wood, or multiple pieces of wood, that provide a solid and steady base that lifts the edge of the pot or saucer above the table level you are working on. When you drill, this allows the pressure to be focused on the area you wish instead of being distributed around the edge, as pressure around the edge may cause the pot or saucer to split or break. When you drill, drill slowly. Using a glass or ceramic drill bit, make a series of small holes in an approximate circle around the area you have chosen for the drainage site. Try to keep the holes close together, so the bridges between the holes are minimal. Once you have all the holes drilled, gently hammer the bridges using a sharp chisel. They will break away and soon you will have an opening that is sufficient. Be careful as the chiseled edges can be sharp, and you may want to sand or grind them down to dull the edges.

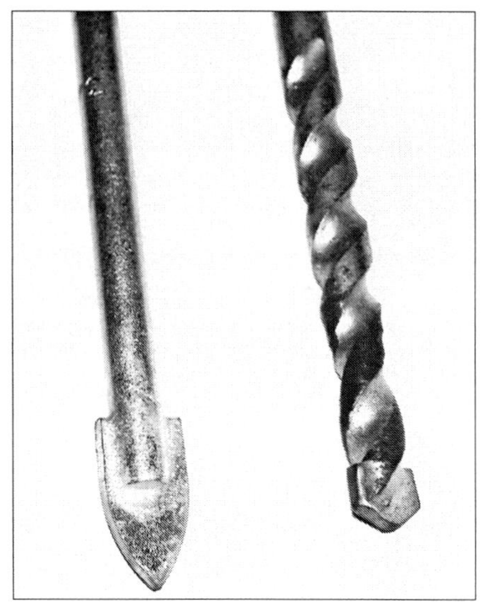

Glass drill bit (left) and masonry drill bit

Making holes in ceramic pots is similar to the procedure for terra cotta containers, but has its differences. Because ceramic pots usually have a glazed coating, they are impervious to water, so there is no need to soak them in water overnight as you do with terra cotta. You will need a glass-cutting drill bit, as a masonry drill bit that can work with terra cotta will not work with ceramics. A glass-cutting drill bit can work well with either ceramics or terra cotta. The procedure is the same in drilling multiple small holes in a circular pattern in the area or areas you want for large drainage holes. The more large drainage holes you make in ceramic pots, the weaker the bottom structure becomes and you risk breakage. I recommend having one large drainage hole in ceramic pots, whereas with terra cotta, because of the water softening the material, there is slightly less chance of breakage. With the ceramics, use a wood support on the upside-down pot, as with the terra cotta containers. But be careful of the heat factor. Terra cotta containers, because they have water incorporated into them from the overnight soaking, will not get as hot from the revolutions of the drill causing friction. With the ceramic pots, the hardness of the surface and the lack of neighboring water to cool the drill bit will cause the drill bit and the ceramic material to become extremely hot. You can easily burn yourself if you touch the drill bit or the pot before it has cooled off. If you drill too much in the one area, the friction can create enough heat so that the pot is unevenly heated, causing it to crack, the way an ice cube cracks when warm water is dropped onto its frozen surface.

16

Directional Pruning

Pruning the various parts of your bonsai is a very important aspect of bonsai creation and care. This chapter will attempt to show by diagrams some of the concepts mentioned earlier in this book so you can have that information in one place, rather than spread throughout the book.

The first concept we will discuss is simple leaf pruning. We will look at two types of compound leaves: pinnately and bipinnately. Pruning branches along a trunk is a very important step in shaping a bonsai.

Pruning of the roots is an important aspect of caring for bonsai. The roots will develop secondary and tertiary roots after pruning that increase the absorptive surface area of the roots, greatly enhancing the bonsai's chances of survival. This measure also increases the tree's growth potential by allowing for greater pruning of the foliage to enable denser and more vibrant foliage.

Scaly leaves and pine needles, common on conifers, can also be pruned. When pruning pine needles be careful not to prune the sheaths near the base of the needle, as this can result in the death of the needle.

Pruning a branch can greatly alter its shape by cutting off side branches and leaves. To create an upward windswept look, simply prune branches hanging down. To create a downward windswept look, simply reverse the process. Trees can also be pruned and planted to establish a bonsai forest, as shown previously. Take specimen tree and prune as discussed above; then after it has established itself growing on its side, plant the entire tree under a bed of sphagnum moss. The old side branches will appear as the individual trees of a forest.

Aerial roots that extend down from side branches and root into the ground below can be spectacular features of full-sized trees, such as banyans. Likewise, they greatly add to the look of aging and structure of bonsai. Let one of your bonsai grow a side branch without trimming it for a while so that its length will allow it to be bent to the ground with a few inches to spare. Bend the side branch where it contacts the ground in a U-shape, making small cuts on the outer, lower curve of the "U" and plant this as shown in the diagrams below. Allow it to root for about four to six months, secured in place by a U-staple; once rooted, cut off the protruding piece for a nice looking aerial root.

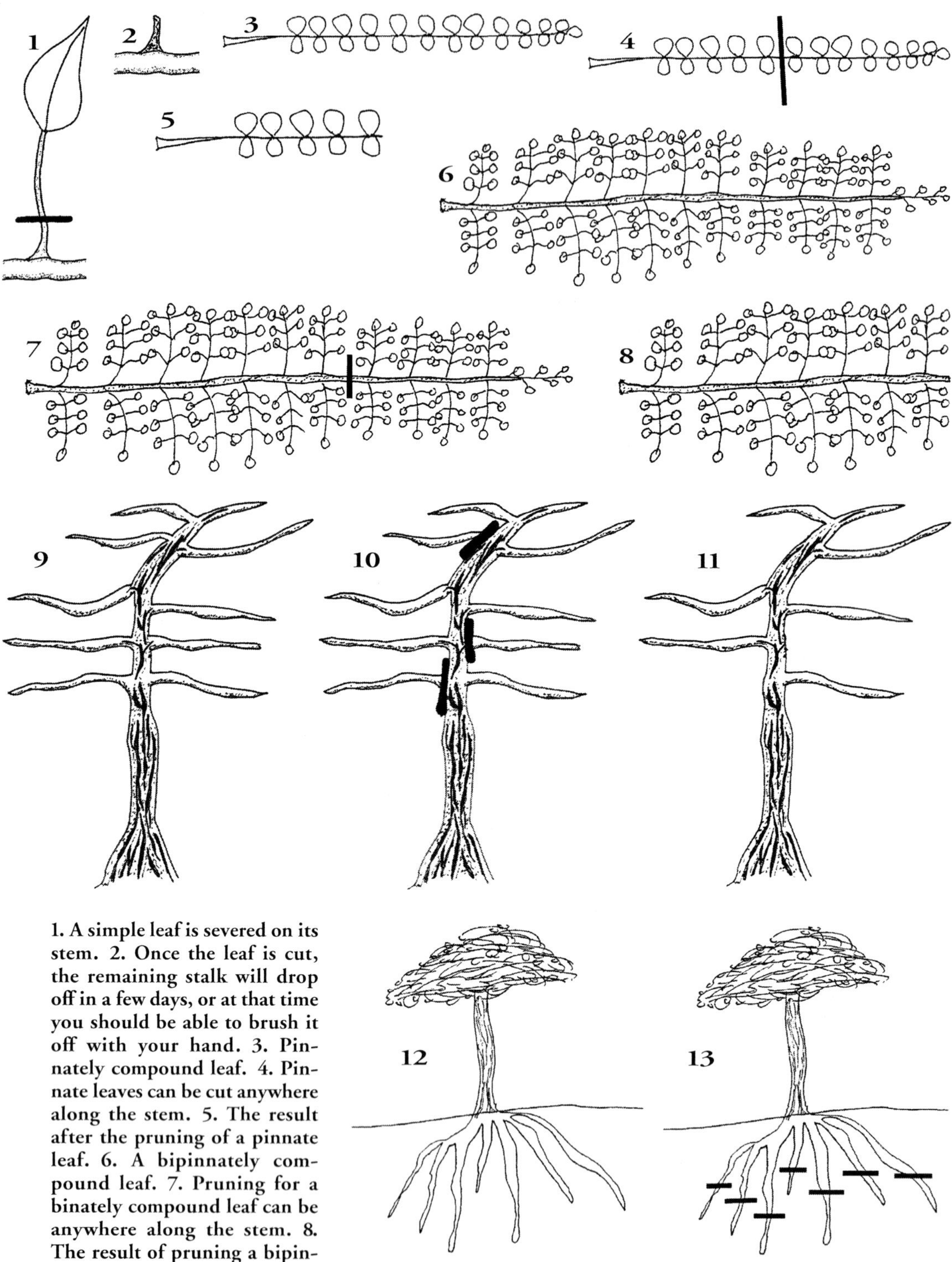

1. A simple leaf is severed on its stem. 2. Once the leaf is cut, the remaining stalk will drop off in a few days, or at that time you should be able to brush it off with your hand. 3. Pinnately compound leaf. 4. Pinnate leaves can be cut anywhere along the stem. 5. The result after the pruning of a pinnate leaf. 6. A bipinnately compound leaf. 7. Pruning for a binately compound leaf can be anywhere along the stem. 8. The result of pruning a bipinnate leaf. 9. A trunk shape ready for branch pruning. 10. Projected cuts of unwanted branches along the trunk. 11. Anticipated result of pruning the unwanted branches of the bonsai trunk. 12. A typical underground root structure of a tree. 13. Location of cuts to be made after the soil or sphagnum moss has been removed.

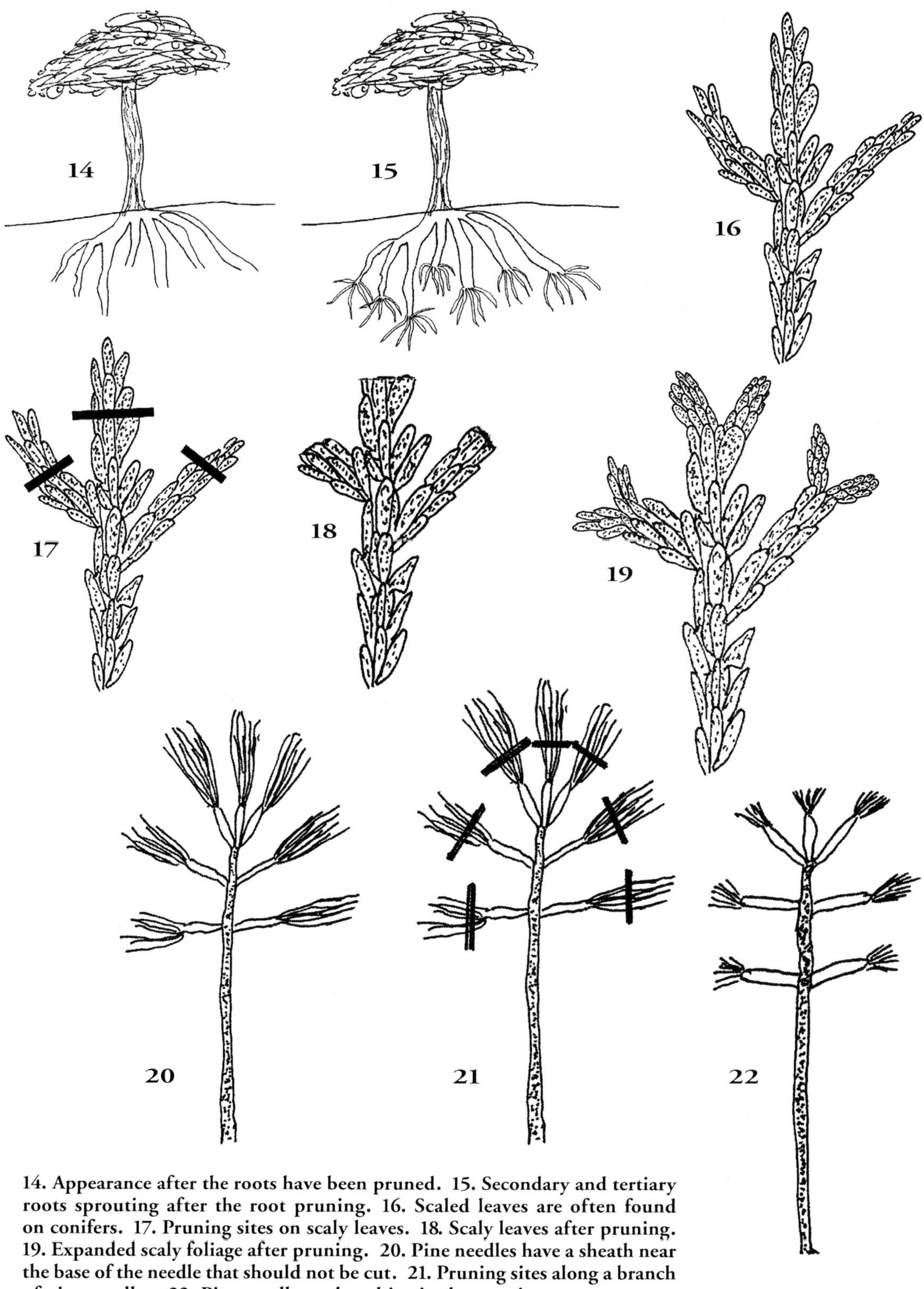

14. Appearance after the roots have been pruned. 15. Secondary and tertiary roots sprouting after the root pruning. 16. Scaled leaves are often found on conifers. 17. Pruning sites on scaly leaves. 18. Scaly leaves after pruning. 19. Expanded scaly foliage after pruning. 20. Pine needles have a sheath near the base of the needle that should not be cut. 21. Pruning sites along a branch of pine needles. 22. Pine needles reduced in size by pruning.

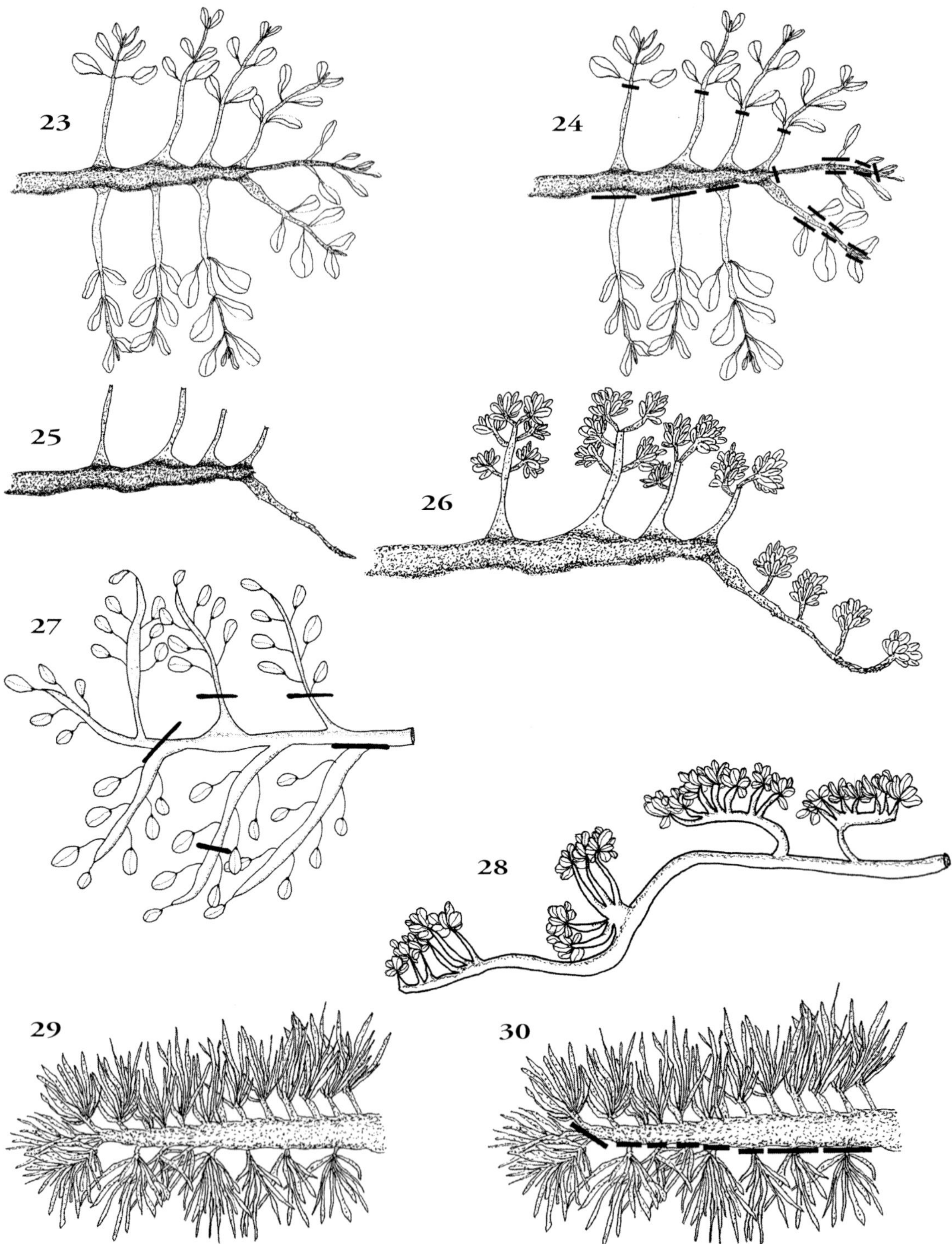

23. A branch that you wish to change in shape and leaf density. 24. The location of planned pruning sites. 25. The branch after pruning. 26. New growth along the newly shaped branch. 27. A branch showing pruning sites. 28. New shape of pruned branch. 29. This branch can be trimmed to give it an upwards windswept look. 30. Trim along the bottom as shown.

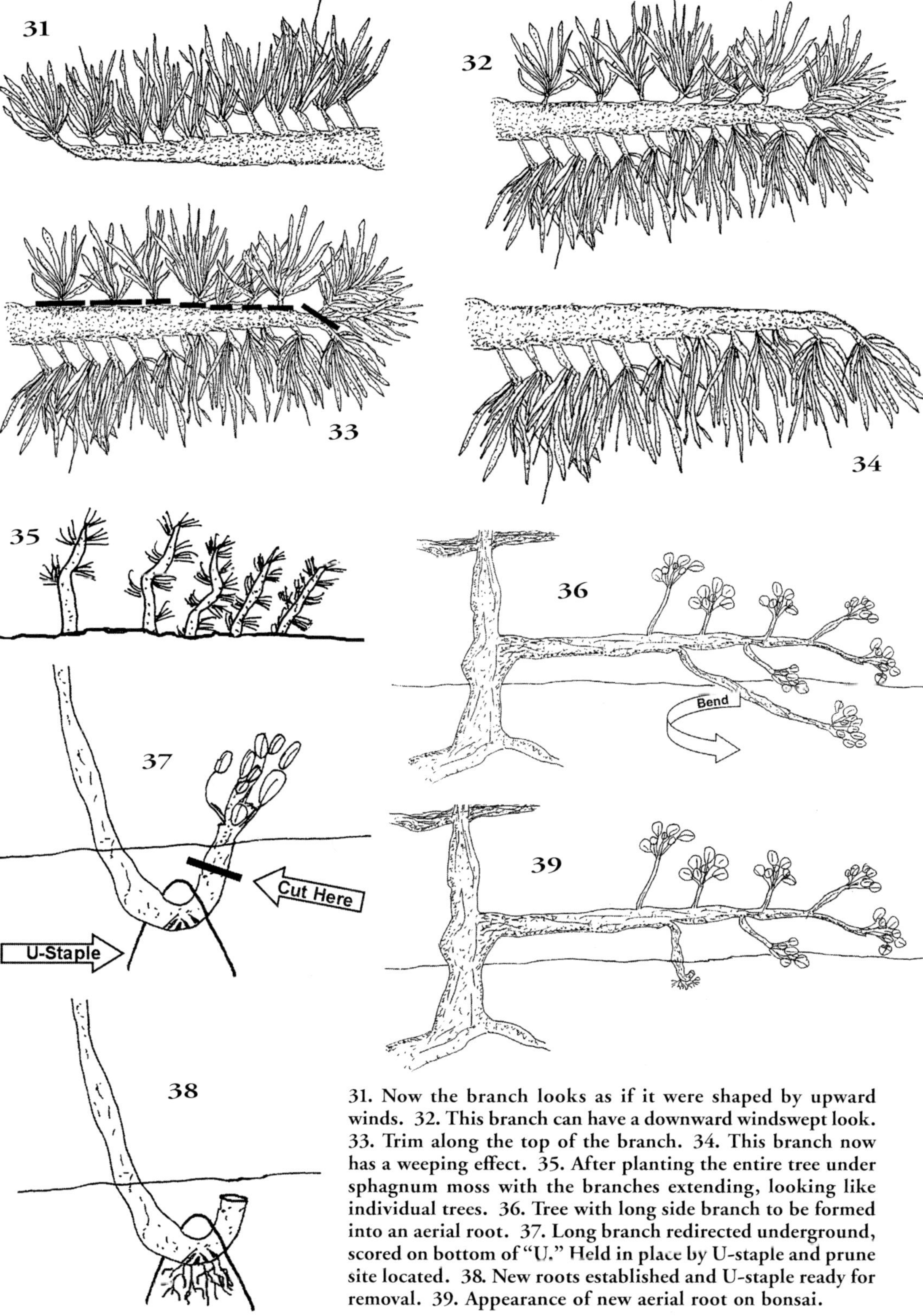

31. Now the branch looks as if it were shaped by upward winds. 32. This branch can have a downward windswept look. 33. Trim along the top of the branch. 34. This branch now has a weeping effect. 35. After planting the entire tree under sphagnum moss with the branches extending, looking like individual trees. 36. Tree with long side branch to be formed into an aerial root. 37. Long branch redirected underground, scored on bottom of "U." Held in place by U-staple and prune site located. 38. New roots established and U-staple ready for removal. 39. Appearance of new aerial root on bonsai.

17

Planting a Specimen from the Wild

The original bonsai were located in crevasses between rocks where, because of the constricted size of their natural container, and lack of fertilization and ground water, their growth was restricted. They were prized as tiny replicas of mature trees, and many lives were lost as people climbed steep and dangerous cliffs to recover these natural works of art. As bonsai cultivation developed and people realized the same effects could be obtained by using small containers, directional pruning, and wiring, the dangerous scaling of mountains diminished. People saw plants they envisioned as bonsai as small seedlings growing out of the ground or even older plants that because of light restrictions had also remained dwarfed. The method of extracting these is not difficult, but patience is needed.

A sharp shovel that can cut through roots is essential. When you find a specimen that has been approved for removal by the owner of the land, you can begin. The first stage is the cutting of the roots by slicing the earth with the shovel in a circular pattern around the plant, allowing for the root ball that you are sculpting to have sufficient roots to support

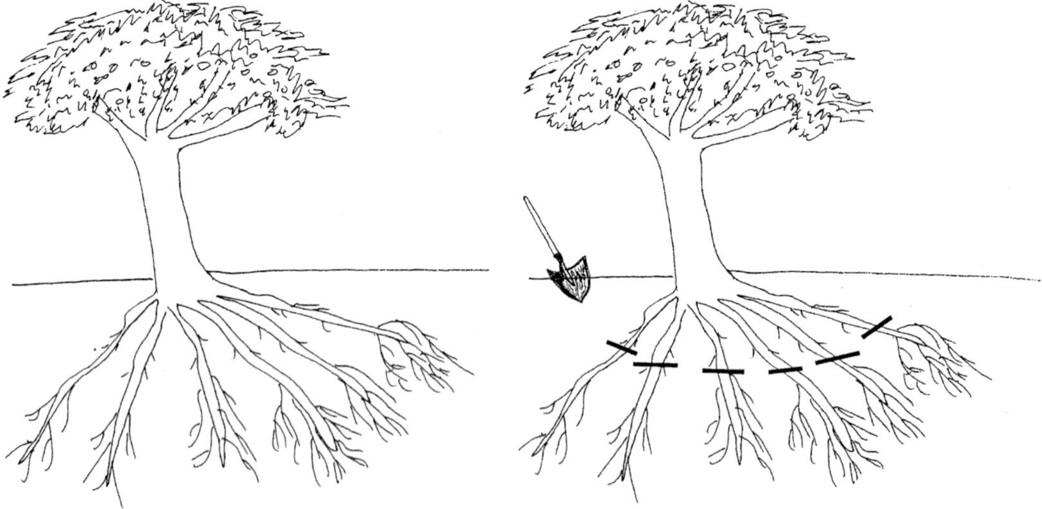

Left: **A tree and its roots in the wild to be made into a bonsai.** ***Right:*** **Cutting the roots with a sharp shovel and leaving the plant in the ground.**

the upper structures of foliage. Do not attempt to undercut the root ball at this time and just make vertical or near vertical cuts with your sharp shovel.

The tree should be trimmed of a portion of the top foliage that approximates in your mind the amount of root material that has been separated from the tree. You may want to mark the tree with a plastic band or rag for later identification. You need to leave the tree where it is for the next four to six months to allow it to adjust to the shock and its reduced root structure. When ready, gently extract the tree and its new roots from the site. There may be older roots that were under the tree that were not pruned previously, and it is a good idea to have a set of long-handled loppers to cut each uncut root as you extract the tree. If there is a taproot, cut that also. Take your tree and wrap the root ball in burlap and wet it down for the trip home. Find a spot and plant the tree and root ball into the soil and again allow a period of two to four months for the tree to recover from the shock. When ready, remove your tree from its temporary home and transplant it into its new growth medium of sphagnum moss, where again you will let the tree adjust to its new environment. Certain fast growing and hardy trees will be able to have shorter periods of adjustment but being overly cautious does no harm.

Have fun with your bonsai!

Appendix A: YouTube Videos About the Sphagnum Moss Method

To view these following video subjects, type in the internet addresses next to the titles into your web browser. For additional videos posted since publication of this book, do a search for bonsai9723 on youtube.com.

Bonsai New Easy Method #1 of 3 • http://www.youtube.com/watch?v=kPVaAXgRoKk
Bonsai New Easy Method #2 of 3 • http://www.youtube.com/watch?v=D7DhdiR7F4Q
Bonsai New Easy Method #3 of 3 • http://www.youtube.com/watch?v=FTqJToakbzA
Bonsai New Easy Method #4: Repotting, Fertilizing • http://www.youtube.com/watch?v=0OmfNN1br_Y
Bonsai New Easy Method #5: Trim a Serrisa • http://www.youtube.com/watch?v=sXJvkf8MuoA
Bonsai New Easy Method #6: Trimming Tree • http://www.youtube.com/watch?v=0JkAvtmJL40
Bonsai New Easy Method #7: Fulien Tea Replant and Prune • http://www.youtube.com/watch?v=NgOEP8ktyj8
Bonsai New Easy Method #8: Bamboo Bonsai • http://www.youtube.com/watch?v=PM2uyMLvg7A
Bonsai New Easy Method #9: Pony Tail Palm Replant and Trim • http://www.youtube.com/watch?v=mVnNZG0oGTM
Bonsai New Easy Method #10: Schefflera (Umbrella Tree) • http://www.youtube.com/watch?v=J6YPlZI3WVs
Bonsai New Easy Method #11: Updating Trees, Etc. • http://www.youtube.com/watch?v=S_oZcO7HsUA
Bonsai New Easy Method #12: Warning—Sphagnum Moss • http://www.youtube.com/watch?v=K7xIlOXuY0o
Bonsai New Easy Method #13: Ficus Pruning • http://www.youtube.com/watch?v=97yhxzV8baI
Bonsai New Easy Method #14: Wiring to Shape • http://www.youtube.com/watch?v=d4qqaYJWhhU
Bonsai New Easy Method #15: Bougainvillea Trim and Repot • http://www.youtube.com/watch?v=QEoHScju7wo
Bonsai New Easy Method #16: Sea Grape Trim; Weed Removal • http://www.youtube.com/watch?v=7AYuC3NpLmE
Bonsai New Easy Method #17: Small Schefflera Repot and Trim • http://www.youtube.com/watch?v=AIlM6Xqe68g
Bonsai New Easy Method #18: Big, Little, Old, New, Leaf-Ming • http://www.youtube.com/watch?v=EIlgTDJtRto
Bonsai New Easy Method #19: Moss, Gravel Surfacing • http://www.youtube.com/watch?v=C7L6vVAUkxs
Bonsai New Easy Method #20: Major Trim Ficus (?) Banyan (?) • http://www.youtube.com/watch?v=Pr48b4PQnVo

Bonsai New Easy Method #21A: Major Trim Juniper Project (Part 1) • http://www.youtube.com/watch?v=WeB2p8l5reQ
Bonsai New Easy Method #21B: Major Trim Juniper Project (Part 2) • http://www.youtube.com/watch?v=8kEGRIzjOhQ
Bonsai New Easy Method #22A: Pots & Banyan (Part 1) • http://www.youtube.com/watch?v=xupvi UmcssM
Bonsai New Easy Method #22B: Pots & Banyan (Part 2) • http://www.youtube.com/watch?v=pwWv 47zBLss
Bonsai New Easy Method #22C: Pots & Banyan (Part 3) • http://www.youtube.com/watch?v=ZvCMe 4lcGuk
Bonsai New Easy Method #22D: Fine Points 1 Banyan (Part 4) • http://www.youtube.com/watch?v=wfH_GlOChXA
Bonsai New Easy Method #22E: Fine Points 2 Banyan (Part 5) • http://www.youtube.com/watch?v=ot WEjUlHqlA)
Bonsai New Easy Method #23: Revisit Plants • http://www.youtube.com/watch?v=yUNKXNw8uMw
Bonsai New Easy Method #24: Lemon Tree • http://www.youtube.com/watch?v=XbSYjH6pBkA
Bonsai New Easy Method #25: Sea Grape Leaf Size • http://www.youtube.com/watch?v=er2JFeUK_ig
Bonsai New Easy Method #26: Questions & Answers • http://www.youtube.com/watch?v=8nfkoggh-Iw
Bonsai New Easy Method #27: Air Layering • http://www.youtube.com/watch?v=ZmlyUmwI9bE
Bonsai New Easy Method #28A: Ginko Trim (Part 1) • http://www.youtube.com/watch?v=-dgcHGj AFvs
Bonsai New Easy Method #28B: Ginko Trim (Part 2) • http://www.youtube.com/watch?v=zlYQBjvj SsI
Bonsai New Easy Method #29: Exposed Root Chinese Elm • http://www.youtube.com/watch?v=cb DRFMDC9hA
Bonsai New Easy Method #30A: Mahogany Tree (Part 1) • http://www.youtube.com/watch?v=OyHT gnqO0sM
Bonsai New Easy Method #30B: Mahogany Tree (Part 2) • http://www.youtube.com/watch?v=kW43 honC0pQ
Bonsai New Easy Method #31: Banyan Update • http://www.youtube.com/watch?v=3ZGrKIEu7JI
Bonsai New Easy Method #32: Revisit Trees from Before • http://www.youtube.com/watch?v=YF8HE-j4-lk
Bonsai New Easy Method #33: Jade Bonsai • http://www.youtube.com/watch?v=pGxR2j6BaE4
Bonsai New Easy Method #34: Banyan Revisit • http://www.youtube.com/watch?v=UBh66URSlR8
Bonsai New Easy Method #35: Wiring Revisited • http://www.youtube.com/watch?v=ZlctcRIqw5A
Bonsai New Easy Method #36: Texas Ebony • http://www.youtube.com/watch?v=6ybYp3FdUR0
Bonsai New Easy Method #37: Pittosporum Bonsai • http://www.youtube.com/watch?v=OqQVcZv BRZQ
Bonsai New Easy Method #38: Banyan (No. 2) Potting • http://www.youtube.com/watch?v=4LjCgi2 RauE
Bonsai New Easy Method #39: Banyan of 6-22-08 Revisited • http://www.youtube.com/watch?v=rl Pu-JQm45c
Bonsai New Easy Method #40: Baobob Tree • http://www.youtube.com/watch?v=W7KxQq02QgA
Bonsai New Easy Method #41: Slime Mold Attacks Banyan Moss • http://www.youtube.com/watch?v=Pe8dW6iyRr8
Bonsai New Easy Method #42: Revisit Lemon, Juniper, Jade, Etc. • http://www.youtube.com/watch?v=RFFayMfg51A
Bonsai New Easy Method #43: Slime Mold on Banyan Update • http://www.youtube.com/watch?v=HJLW2NlCkDQ
Bonsai New Easy Method #44: Air Layering Follow-Up • http://www.youtube.com/watch?v=xWtrN 8nKlFA
Bonsai New Easy Method #45: Poinsettia Super Trim • http://www.youtube.com/watch?v=T4Nsd-t D6KY
Bonsai New Easy Method #46: Cuttings — What Happened • http://www.youtube.com/watch?v=V-PMOclNUSo
Bonsai New Easy Method #47: Banyan (1) Revisited • http://www.youtube.com/watch?v=twbqK9ylcaE

Bonsai New Easy Method #48: Hurricane Preparations • http://www.youtube.com/watch?v=RT35d2q5YXM
Bonsai New Easy Method #49: Hurricane Faye — Day Later • http://www.youtube.com/watch?v=5olAc_TJdps
Bonsai New Easy Method #50: Hurricane Postscript • http://www.youtube.com/watch?v=brdkQm9xGdQ
Bonsai New Easy Method #51A: Mahogany on Granite Slab (Part 1) • http://www.youtube.com/watch?v=1bvWu7tD7UY
Bonsai New Easy Method #51B: Mahogany on Granite Slab (Part 2) • http://www.youtube.com/watch?v=aYBO-uL3_5k
Bonsai New Easy Method #51C: Mahogany on Granite Slab (Part 3) • http://www.youtube.com/watch?v=EbMepfpoKsc
Bonsai New Easy Method #51D: Mahogany on Granite Slab (Part 4) • http://www.youtube.com/watch?v=8sQovmtf8wk
Bonsai New Easy Method #51E: Mahogany on Granite Slab (Part 5) • http://www.youtube.com/watch?v=__2mfLTUrZQ
Bonsai New Easy Method #51F: Mahogany on Granite Slab (Part 6) • http://www.youtube.com/watch?v=xN_PAHSkULs
Bonsai New Easy Method #52: Surinam Cherry Repot, Trim, Reposition Trunk • http://www.youtube.com/watch?v=mbXIj7sObKY
Bonsai New Easy Method #53: Watering Techniques • http://www.youtube.com/watch?v=d4bEYTPAHSI
Bonsai New Easy Method #54: Banyan (No. 1) Maintainence • http://www.youtube.com/watch?v=FhJMJmsuqgY
Bonsai New Easy Method #55A: Cotton Plant; Revisit Poinsettias, Grapes (Part 1) • http://www.youtube.com/watch?v=LnbW7T3zTJ4
Bonsai New Easy Method #55B: Cotton Plant; Revisit Poinsettias, Grapes (Part 2) • http://www.youtube.com/watch?v=N49RfSGwYsg
Bonsai New Easy Method #56: Fruits and Flowering Bonsai • http://www.youtube.com/watch?v=kRJ3eiNJ0GU
Bonsai New Easy Method #57: Long Leaf Ficus • http://www.youtube.com/watch?v=IxWun6qxFCw
Bonsai New Easy Method #58: Papaya Tree • http://www.youtube.com/watch?v=SoGv5QDsCfM
Bonsai New Easy Method #59: Juniper (First Episode) — My 100th YouTube Video • http://wwwyoutube.com/watch?v=rdVpD640D5k
Bonsai New Easy Method #60: Cabbage Palm • http://www.youtube.com/watch?v=xdbZ9jSR9lI
Bonsai New Easy Method #61: Chinese Elm Replant and Major Trim • http://www.youtube.com/watch?v=0Dq42fcVQF8
Bonsai New Easy Method #62: Banyan #2 Clean and Trim • http://www.youtube.com/watch?v=vzBDx4uJpbU
Bonsai New Easy Method #63: Making a Gift Bonsai • http://www.youtube.com/watch?v=VWN0W6J45EA
Bonsai New Easy Method #64: Wintertime for Bonsai • http://www.youtube.com/watch?v=GpTFY1Nprdw
Bonsai New Easy Method #65: Bamboo Forest — Revisit and Trim • http://www.youtube.com/watch?v=Sooof0A-lSQ
Bonsai New Easy Method #66: Bare Chinese Elm Revisited, Etc. • http://www.youtube.com/watch?v=FnPPWlb9zlM
Bonsai New Easy Method #67: Coconut Palm Bonsai • http://www.youtube.com/watch?v=MgQ9uSgbcWI
Bonsai New Easy Method #68: Lemon Picked from Bonsai • http://www.youtube.com/watch?v=GaseJDKlfgE
Bonsai New Easy Method #69: Bonsai Lemon Gets Flowers and Cotton Bolls Burst • http://www.youtube.com/watch?v=mTTBurL-6ao
Bonsai New Easy Method #70: Freeze Hits Florida • http://www.youtube.com/watch?v=7YE69JVcifg
Bonsai New Easy Method #71: Jade Repot, Trim, Start New Cutting • http://www.youtube.com/watch?v=vXBKJ3C_rOs

Bonsai New Easy Method #72: Coffee Beans, Cotton, Lemon, Flowers, Etc. • http://www.youtube.com/watch?v=lkd8SebUU6A
Bonsai New Easy Method #73: Jin, Shari, Germination in Shagnum Moss • http://www.youtube.com/watch?v=ryNBC9wnSAA
Bonsai New Easy Method #74: Jade Tree Revisit • http://www.youtube.com/watch?v=tUPxRYp8_G8
Bonsai New Easy Method #75: Coffee Fruit Harvest • http://www.youtube.com/watch?v=AgWn2RLCCY
Bonsai New Easy Method #76A: Coffee Tree Severe Trim and Repot (Part 1) • http://www.youtube.com/watch?v=U2zbTY3D734
Bonsai New Easy Method #76B: Coffee Tree Severe Trim and Repot (Part 2) • http://www.youtube.com/watch?v=2-EfDi7MpQg
Bonsai New Easy Method #77: Making Outside Wood Bonsai Stands • http://www.youtube.com/watch?v=HjlEfmJIQvY
Bonsai New Easy Method #78: Watering Sprinkler System for Outside Bonsai • http://www.youtube.com/watch?v=lTcbsKa3xCU
Bonsai New Easy Method #79: Replacing Old, Spent Shagnum Moss • http://www.youtube.com/watch?v=Bf5WhrIsb8o
Bonsai New Easy Method #80: Springtime Bonsai Happenings • http://www.youtube.com/watch?v=wmIdqfH86AM
Bonsai New Easy Method #81: Springtime • http://www.youtube.com/watch?v=Oouhkg3eHM8
Bonsai New Easy Method #82: Been Away • http://www.youtube.com/watch?v=dd3FjNcld6U
Bonsai New Easy Method #83: Pony Tail Palm Planting • http://www.youtube.com/watch?v=LoTgRXEvcAs
Bonsai New Easy Method #84A: Strangler Fig Refurbished (Part 1) • http://www.youtube.com/watch?v=LpfL5PBFBrQ
Bonsai New Easy Method #84B: Strangler Fig Refurbished (Part 2) • http://www.youtube.com/watch?v=rhVCi76QIA4
Bonsai New Easy Method #85: Jade Tree Miniature Worked On • http://www.youtube.com/watch?v=6oilM-JdPhI
Bonsai New Easy Method #86: Checking Out Various Bonsai • http://www.youtube.com/watch?v=njdbAqEbGfA
Bonsai New Easy Method #87: Fig Tree (and Velvet Ant Cameo) • http://www.youtube.com/watch?v=X_7TbS1RuVU
Bonsai New Easy Method #88: Papayas — Bonsai and in Ground • http://www.youtube.com/watch?v=iSR88ANvzfo
Bonsai New Easy Method #89: White Hibiscus Bonsai • http://www.youtube.com/watch?v=8jbEGwK9jDo
Bonsai New Easy Method #90A: Favorite Trees and Fukien Major Trim (Part 1) • http://www.youtube.com/watch?v=kcKTvJ0fXg8
Bonsai New Easy Method #90B: Favorite Trees and Fukien Major Trim (Part 2) • http://www.youtube.com/watch?v=kcKTvJ0fXg8
Bonsai New Easy Method #91: Checking Out the Bonsai, Etc. • http://www.youtube.com/watch?v=l77WfknNxA4
Bonsai New Easy Method #92: Little Banyan Problem Diagnosed and Treated • http://www.youtube.com/watch?v=phhQXnDqiAI
Bonsai New Easy Method #93A: Visiting the Wigert's Bonsa Nursery (Part 1) • http://www.youtube.com/watch?v=s45oEk0Z0PM
Bonsai New Easy Method #93B: Visiting the Wigert's Bonsa Nursery (Part 2) • http://www.youtube.com/watch?v=me03U0nE0oE
Bonsai New Easy Method #94: Buddha Belly Plant Transplant • http://www.youtube.com/watch?v=Z5tZiVQkfqA
Bonsai New Easy Method #95: Bullhorn Acacia Tree Repotting • http://www.youtube.com/watch?v=wCbJqorr8Vk
Bonsai New Easy Method #96: Making Simple Bonsai Pots • http://www.youtube.com/watch?v=wCbJqorr8Vk
Bonsai New Easy Method #97: Bald Cypress Potting and Trim • http://www.youtube.com/watch?v=4GheKZtUhHQ

Bonsai New Easy Method #98: Checking the Little Banyan for Progress • http://www.youtube.com/watch?v=TKtJv5HBC04
Bonsai New Easy Method #99: Tamarind Tree Repotting • http://www.youtube.com/watch?v=Oe_JszbE_Z8
Bonsai New Easy Method #100: Southern Mimosa and Acacia Repottings • http://www.youtube.com/watch?v=y5t7MgqGPkI
Bonsai New Easy Method #101: Operculicarya Decaryi — An Odd Succulent Repot as Bonsai • http://www.youtube.com/watch?v=W_2_QRLUKLM
Bonsai New Easy Method #102: Trying to Save the Southern Mimosa • http://www.youtube.com/watch?v=PhOg9_8H2R0
Bonsai New Easy Method #103: Ming Tree Forest Trim • http://www.youtube.com/watch?v=24zXpTDuOUg
Bonsai New Easy Method #104: Little Banyan Tree Leave Size Control • http://www.youtube.com/watch?v=o7k62KFlvMU
Bonsai New Easy Method #105: Surface Moss — Acacia and Bald Cypress • http://www.youtube.com/watch?v=8c9D7XBj-L4
Bonsai New Easy Method #106: Overgrown Fukien Tea Gets Major Trim • http://www.youtube.com/watch?v=qg0_ArkFDlo
Bonsai New Easy Method #107: Revisit Juniper from First Video • http://www.youtube.com/watch?v=6XWW0Wr0P3A
Bonsai New Easy Method #108: Revisit to Specimens Transplanted to Sphagnum Moss • http://www.youtube.com/watch?v=jLC3IrpVqgU
Bonsai New Easy Method #109: Bamboo Forest Planted by Seed • http://www.youtube.com/watch?v=7kUP2AMjKO4
Bonsai New Easy Method #110: Look at Bonsai Soil Specimens' Progress After Transplant • http://www.youtube.com/watch?v=fHA-z8XqDww
Bonsai New Easy Method #111: Tamarind Tree Trim • http://www.youtube.com/watch?v=JE1GXTHa_HQ
Bonsai New Easy Method #112: Picking a Nursery Specimen • http://www.youtube.com/watch?v=bHxhdmLzQbs
Bonsai New Easy Method #113: Barbados Cherry Repot & Trim • http://www.youtube.com/watch?v=_m8cTF0dtbA
Bonsai New Easy Method #114: Rabbit's Foot Acacia (Bell Mimosa) Repot and Trim • http://www.youtube.com/watch?v=HUEmsiUq58c
Bonsai New Easy Method #115: Buying Sphagnum Moss on the Internet • http://www.youtube.com/watch?v=NOrU4QFzuLo
Bonsai New Easy Method #116: When Sphagnum Moss Gets Old and Decomposes — Lemon Tree • http://www.youtube.com/watch?v=wpQlX3vbigE
Bonsai New Easy Method #117: Escambron Repot and Trim • http://www.youtube.com/watch?v=6YEWLtUZp6A
Bonsai New Easy Method #118: Update on Southern Mimosa • http://www.youtube.com/watch?v=NrZI9D0zAJM
Bonsai New Easy Method #119A: Ficus Transplant and Trim — Special Circumstances (Part 1) • http://www.youtube.com/watch?v=-Dpt2T3AC1I
Bonsai New Easy Method #119B: Ficus Transplant and Trim — Special Circumstances (PART 2) • http://www.youtube.com/watch?v=l57ZaDxNL0E)
Bonsai New Easy Method #120: Green Sphagnum Moss — An Answer? • http://www.youtube.com/watch?v=Sv2fUcgs-KQ
Bonsai New Easy Method #121: Boxwood Tree — Repot And Extreme Trim • http://www.youtube.com/watch?v=YdPOxRCnDUE
Bonsai New Easy Method #122: Cold Weather Bonsai Care • http://www.youtube.com/watch?v=3AqbyvfQDMQ
Bonsai New Easy Method #123: Revisit to Specimens Transplanted from Soil • http://www.youtube.com/watch?v=6V8wNWMRb3o
Bonsai New Easy Method #124: Southern Mimosa Revisit • http://www.youtube.com/watch?v=y5DDeV5AnxI
Bonsai New Easy Method #125: Northern Mimosa Rescue • http://www.youtube.com/watch?v=2ddRd6MVdZE

Bonsai New Easy Method #126: Chinese Elms Gift Bonsai • http://www.youtube.com/watch?v=7sYkWjQRRW8
Bonsai New Easy Method #127: Soil Versus Sphagnum Moss Experiment • http://www.youtube.com/watch?v=j0aWf4-1VMU
Bonsai New Easy Method #128: A Visit to Dutch and Donna's Bonsai Heaven • http://www.youtube.com/watch?v=nsxVX6svSmg
Bonsai New Easy Method #129: Bougainvillea Repot and Woodwork • http://www.youtube.com/watch?v=bkou-rYgkUU
Bonsai New Easy Method #130: Fukien Tea — Major Trim and Repot of My Favorite • http://www.youtube.com/watch?v=z-7e6pC6LeE
Bonsai New Easy Method #131: Ming Tree Group Planting with Large Rocks • http://www.youtube.com/watch?v=OvGR5QBvV3M
Bonsai New Easy Method #132: Soil Versus Sphagnum Moss Experiment — Early Results • http://www.youtube.com/watch?v=ly8MSPtp41Y
Bonsai New Easy Method #133: Tiny Leaf Fukien Tea Transplant • http://www.youtube.com/watch?v=baunsbSpnX4
Bonsai New Easy Method #134: Ant and Root Problems in a Bamboo Bonsai • http://www.youtube.com/watch?v=vYCRmtA9QZA
Bonsai New Easy Method #135: Repairing Bonsai Shelves • http://www.youtube.com/watch?v=-Pa4nDvhcJE
Bonsai New Easy Method #136: Surface Moss — Growing Your Own • http://www.youtube.com/watch?v=VrVQOs6LZiI
Bonsai New Easy Method #137: Brazilian Rain Tree Trimming • http://www.youtube.com/watch?v=c-cy6OQ2rPE
Bonsai New Easy Method #138: Kabuki (?) Pine Replant and Trim • http://www.youtube.com/watch?v=j-7ypgCFDfE
Bonsai New Easy Method #139: Black Olive Tree Repot and Trim • http://www.youtube.com/watch?v=XYhlezDmYoM
Bonsai New Easy Method #140: Tamarind Tree Trim • http://www.youtube.com/watch?v=6VXrQX-uOCQ
Bonsai New Easy Method #141: Easy Repot of 25-Year-Old Lemon Bonsai • http://www.youtube.com/watch?v=dTQYRL__kLE
Bonsai New Easy Method #142: Ming Tree Repot • http://www.youtube.com/watch?v=KuDp2dYf_Ug
Bonsai New Easy Method #143: Latest on Some Trees and Making Ceramic Bonsai Pots • http://www.youtube.com/watch?v=Pr5bRkMgQWA
Bonsai New Easy Method #144: Giant Bonsai Repot — Bismarck Palm • http://www.youtube.com/watch?v=aP8NCTAN5CU
Bonsai New Easy Method #145: Ring-Necked Snake on the Lanai, Bonsai Video News • http://www.youtube.com/watch?v=NrPGfPWFh6E
Bonsai New Easy Method #146: Dedication Bonsai • http://www.youtube.com/watch?v=qKMVkMMxqvk
Bonsai New Easy Method #147A: Making Bonsai Pots (Part 1) • http://www.youtube.com/watch?v=GIFkhlfV2Es
Bonsai New Easy Method #147B: Making Bonsai Pots (Part 2) • http://www.youtube.com/watch?v=XGOS1YrVAVY
Bonsai New Easy Method #147C: Making Bonsai Pots (Part 3) • http://www.youtube.com/watch?v=l8m8mrJxXMM
Bonsai New Easy Method #147D: Making Bonsai Pots (Part 4) • http://www.youtube.com/watch?v=HayoxizHMwE
Bonsai New Easy Method #147E: Making Bonsai Pots (Part 5) • http://www.youtube.com/watch?v=CAyzs34pSMU
Bonsai New Easy Method #147F: Making Bonsai Pots (Part 6) • http://www.youtube.com/watch?v=C8smk6YK3kQ
Bonsai New Easy Method #147G: Making Bonsai Pots (Part 7) • http://www.youtube.com/watch?v=M_W4_xOKzfg
Bonsai New Easy Method #148: Postscript — Making Bonsai Pots • http://www.youtube.com/watch?v=jJAC9c9pSns

Bonsai New Easy Method #149: Back with Bonsai — Winter Problems • http://www.youtube.com/watch?v=RAHqh3u2UtY

Bonsai New Easy Method #150: Hard Winter Effects • http://www.youtube.com/watch?v=Kdklg_hPxN0

Bonsai New Easy Method #151: Escambron Potting • http://www.youtube.com/watch?v=s8shLGq0C6c

Bonsai New Easy Method #152: In the Spring There Will Be Growth (Peter Sellers in *Being There*) • http://www.youtube.com/watch?v=AMHI8Ag_v6E

Bonsai New Easy Method #153: Repotting a Loose Plant • http://www.youtube.com/watch?v=LgAIsVtzDjQ

Bonsai New Easy Method #154: Bullhorn Acacia Trim and Cuttings • http://www.youtube.com/watch?v=GbmbTVmOiAc

Bonsai New Easy Method #155: Ming Trees • http://www.youtube.com/watch?v=a4hcqIQ7qbY

Bonsai New Easy Method #156: Trimming a Chinese Elm, Tamarind, & Fukien Tea • http://www.youtube.com/watch?v=gHPcTGsSHjQ

Bonsai New Easy Method #157: Bougainvillea Repot, Trim, Cutting, Planting • http://www.youtube.com/watch?v=uMU2a48kcrs

Bonsai New Easy Method #158: Trying to Save My Coffee Tree Bonsai • http://www.youtube.com/watch?v=-QxS3I-7eBI

Bonsai New Easy Method #159: Gmelinia Phillipenensis — Parrot's Beak Repot and Trim • http://www.youtube.com/watch?v=RjU2jmXyG5g

Bonsai New Easy Method #160: Escambron Examination, Repot, Major Trim, and Cuttings • http://www.youtube.com/watch?v=ztOi1iL1baY

Bonsai New Easy Method #161: Olive Tree Transplant onto Rock • http://www.youtube.com/watch?v=5rGBalh_w_4

Bonsai New Easy Method #162: Part 1 — New Bonsai Shelf, Trimmings, and Cuttings • http://www.youtube.com/watch?v=uigJ_XMWdkw

Bonsai New Easy Method #162: Part 2 — New Bonsai Stand, Pruning, Cuttings • http://www.youtube.com/watch?v=__ndM91bj4I

Bonsai New Easy Method #163: Poinciana Tree Replant and Radical Cutting • http://www.youtube.com/watch?v=AW5d7VeS2q8

Bonsai New Easy Method #164: Big Bull Horn Acacia Is Transplanted to Sphagnum Moss • http://www.youtube.com/watch?v=-n3yvwwyJPg

Bonsai New Easy Method #165: Repot and Major Trim of Lemon Tree • http://www.youtube.com/watch?v=EdxA_0Ye-Ac

Bonsai New Easy Method #166: Big Schefflera Repot and Trim • http://www.youtube.com/watch?v=xqtvZ2emjM4

Bonsai New Easy Method #167: Update on Bonsai and YouTube Email • http://www.youtube.com/watch?v=Lmhc9jS3Ewo

Bonsai New Easy Method #168: Reduced Leaf Size by Major Trim of Banyan • http://www.youtube.com/watch?v=9OjXFfbw9K4

Bonsai New Easy Method #169: Making Large Drainage Hole in Ceramic Pot • http://www.youtube.com/watch?v=U4fGnp4xxVQ

Bonsai New Easy Method #170: Memorial Bonsai — Green Island Ficus • http://www.youtube.com/watch?v=uvgL2bQkH1E

Bonsai New Easy Method #171: Update on Banyan Leaf Size and Kiwi Memorial Bonsai • http://www.youtube.com/watch?v=iHJJ6la3dYs

Bonsai New Easy Method #172: Juiper from First Episode Trimmed • http://www.youtube.com/watch?v=KoeexhrwH-o

Bonsai New Easy Method #173: New Book About the Sphagnum Moss Method • http://www.youtube.com/watch?v=N0b4p9bGxN07

Bonsai New Easy Method #174: Forest Plantings • http://www.youtube.com/watch?v=7IVW1hotiIk

Bonsai New Easy Method #175: Part A — Jin and Sharimiki — Age by Whitening • http://www.youtube.com/watch?v=etFLCNTwR5s

Bonsai New Easy Method #175: Part B — Jin and Sharimiki Continued • http://www.youtube.com/watch?v=MpDEOzl2YJk

Bonsai New Easy Method #176: Fertilize by Dunking; Bonsai Hoarding • http://www.youtube.com/watch?v=PWYZRQqG1Xg

Bonsai New Easy Method #177: Guest Video from Nate • http://www.youtube.com/watch?v=psdDo4cjSfk
Bonsai New Easy Method #178: Mame Bonsai • http://www.youtube.com/watch?v=xG_DvnI7Sbk
Bonsai New Easy Method #179: Desert Rose Bonsai • http://www.youtube.com/watch?v=dB4M2NZw6V0
Bonsai New Easy Method #180: Making an Aerial Root from a Branch • http://www.youtube.com/watch?v=TIdSOsuvrqQ
Bonsai New Easy Method #181: Fukien Tea Forrest & Desert Rose Update • http://www.youtube.com/watch?v=_Zn-oQ3fvM4
Bonsai New Easy Method #182: Surface Moss • http://www.youtube.com/watch?v=4ovGPQ_r5dM
Bonsai New Easy Method #183: Chinese Elm — Major, Major Repot and Trim • http://www.youtube.com/watch?v=J1Tp6qSleXw
Bonsai New Easy Method #184: Sago Palm Bonsai • http://www.youtube.com/watch?v=3o5zDDm2LWQ
Bonsai New Easy Method #185: Ming Bonsai Made from Outdoor Plant • http://www.youtube.com/watch?v=WKZl4z-aMG4
Bonsai New Easy Method #186: Part A — Bonsai Revisited • http://www.youtube.com/watch?v=PBr294ZuR2I
Bonsai New Easy Method #186: Part B — Bonsai Revisited • http://www.youtube.com/watch?v=lGZf-bMe8WpY
Bonsai New Easy Method #187: Bougainvillea Pre-Winter Pruning • http://www.youtube.com/watch?v=eGZxtX5c2wA
Bonsai New Easy Method #188: Bonsai Book Pre-Publication Ordering Information • http://www.youtube.com/watch?v=btPQy44p5Xg
Bonsai New Easy Method #189: Guest Video from Mauritius • http://www.youtube.com/watch?v=dzhS_FbC-zM
Bonsai New Easy Method #190: Preparing Auction Bonsai and Ficus Fig • http://www.youtube.com/watch?v=3iUNmIyo7mo
Bonsai New Easy Method #191: Strangler Fig Trim, Surface Moss, Rocks • http://www.youtube.com/watch?v=H1BEFLQdGdo
Bonsai New Easy Method #192: Effects of Florida Freeze • http://www.youtube.com/watch?v=SMSqqpJFNCY
Bonsai New Easy Method #193: Bottlecap Bonsai • http://www.youtube.com/watch?v=BDZ7FX_p07s
Bonsai New Easy Method #194: Guest Video — Jade Bottlecap Bonsai • http://www.youtube.com/watch?v=qp0aYdl-EPY
Bonsai New Easy Method #195: Sweet Acacia Planning & Pruning • http://www.youtube.com/watch?v=CR_WU2SQMt4
Bonsai New Easy Method #196: After the Winter — Bonsai Survival • http://www.youtube.com/watch?v=qEp-yReAKVk
Bonsai New Easy Method #197: Spring Sruce-Up • http://www.youtube.com/watch?v=ia7kBVXjty8

Appendix B: Bonsai Clubs, Societies, and Nurseries

North America

• *United States* •

Bonsai Societies—

ALABAMA

BIRMINGHAM

Alabama Bonsai Society. Meets at Birmingham Botanical Gardens Auditorium, 2612 Lane Park Road, Birmingham, Alabama, the second Monday each month at 7:00 P.M. Contact: Oscar Ethridge, president, Tel: (205) 414-3900.

DECATUR/HUNTSVILLE

The Living Art Bonsai Society. Meets the first Tuesday of the month at the Huntsville Botanical Gardens on Bob Wallace in Huntsville, AL, at 7:00 P.M. Contact: Roy McCorkle, Tel: (256) 777-0617. Email: WRM@PCLnet.net.

MOBILE

Azalea City Bonsai Society. Meets at Mobile Botanical Garden in Langan Park, first Tuesday, 7:30 P.M. Shows spring and fall of each year. Host of regional show every third year. Contact: Joe B. Day, Tel: (251) 344-5873. Email: acbsbonsai@aol.com.

ALASKA

NORTH POLE

Borealis Bonsai Club. Meets at 2653 Tenakee Way, North Pole, Alaska. Six meetings a year (May-October), first Saturday of each month, from 2:00 to 4:00 P.M. Contact founders Kevin and Lorri Heneveld at Borealis Bonsai & Landscaping, P.O. Box 57262, North Pole, AK 99705. Tel: (907) 488-5786.

ARIZONA

PAYSON

Bonsai of Payson. Meets at 905 N. Hillcrest, Payson, first Monday, 7:00 P.M. Larry Mueller, 905 N. Hillcrest, Payson, AZ. Tel: (602) 474-3370.

PHOENIX

Phoenix Bonsai Society. Meets at Valley Garden Center, 1809 N. 15th Ave., first three Tuesdays, September through May, 7:30 P.M. Elsie Andrade, 2026 W. Northview, Phoenix, AZ 85021. Tel: (602) 995-3870.

SCOTTSDALE

Bonsai of Scottsdale. Meets at Via Linda Senior Center, 10440 E Via Linda near Shea Blvd., first and third Saturdays of the month at 1:30 P.M. Contact Fairlee Winfield, Tel: (480) 860-9348.

TUCSON

Southern Arizona Bonsai Enthusiasts. Meets every third Saturday, 10:30 A.M., at Desert Gardens Cumberland Presbyterian Church, 10851 E. Old Spanish Trail. Contact: Doris Cavanaugh, Tel: (520) 290-0522, Email: doris.c@worldnet.att.net or Loveda Petrie, Tel: (520) 886-2446, Email: veda27@earthlink.net.

Tucson Bonsai Society, Inc. Meets every third Sunday, 11:00 A.M. to 3:30 P.M., at Tucson Botanical Garden, 2150 N. Alvernon Way. Contact: Gregory A. Baumgartner, Tel: (520) 762-1572.

ARKANSAS

HOT SPRINGS

Bonsai Club of Hot Springs. Meets the first Thursday of each month at 6 P.M. at the Arkansas School of Math and Science, 200 Whittington, in Hot springs. Contact: James Harwood, 1110 N Hwy 7, Hot Springs, AR 71909. Tel: (501) 624-7779. Email: *jharwood@cablelynx.com.*

LITTLE ROCK

Bonsai Society of Central Arkansas. Meeting

time and place to be announced. Contact: Cindy Cones, Tel: (501) 455-0007, Email: *conesc@sbc global.net.*

California

ALAMEDA

Bay Island Bonsai. Meets the first Tuesday of each month at 7:30 P.M., at the First Congregational Church located at 1912 Central Ave., Alameda CA. Contact: Boon Manankitivipart.

ANAHEIM

Kofu Bonsai Kai. Meets in Anaheim at United Methodist Church, 1000 South State College Blvd., Anaheim, 7:00 P.M., third Saturday evening. Website: www.prepgraphics.com/kofu.html.

Orange Empire Bonsai Society. Meets the fourth Sunday of each month at 1:00 P.M. at the O.C. Buddhist Church, 909 S. Dale St., just north of Ball Road in West Anaheim. Contact: Ken Schlothan, Email: ocbonsai@gmail.com.

ARCADIA

Santa Anita Bonsai Society. Meets at 301 N. Baldwin Ave., Arcadia, second Saturday of each month except July, August, and December, 7:30 P.M. Contact: Jim Barrett, Tel: (818)445-4529.

Shohin Bonsai Society. Meets at Los Angeles Arboretum, 301 N. Baldwin Ave., Arcadia, second Wednesday, except July and August, 7:30 P.M. Marty Hagbery, Tel: (818) 332-8381. Edith Izant, 1021 Sierra Vista Dr., La Habra, CA 90631. Tel: (310) 691-3450.

ARCATA

Humboldt Bonsai Society. Meets at homes of members at varied dates. Karen Haas, PO Box 816, Trinidad, CA 95570. Tel: (707) 677-0636.

CASTRO VALLEY

Yamato Bonsai Club. Meets at the Castro Valley Women's Club, 18330 Redwood Road, Castro Valley, CA, every third Thursday of each month at 7:30 P.M. Website: yamatobonsaiclub.org. Email: lubedardjr@yahoo.com.

CHICO

Chico Bonsai Society. Meets at Pleasant Valley Recreation Center, 2320 North Ave., fourth Sunday, except July and August, 1:00 P.M. Contact: Pat Gilmore, Tel: (530) 343-3447. Website: http://www.chicobonsai.org.

CRESCENT CITY

Seacrest Bonsai Club. Meets at various locations, second Monday, October through May, 7:00 P.M. Ted Weber, 288 W. 5th St., Crescent City, CA 95531. Tel: (707) 464-4949.

FRESNO

Fresno Bonsai Society. Meets at Fresno City College on the second Friday of every month, except we are off for the months June, July and August. Any questions contact Steve DaSilva. Email: tree kutter@hotmail.com.

GARDENA

California Bonsai Society. Meets at 7:00 P.M. on first Friday at Ken Nakaoka Community Center, 1700 W. 162nd Street, Gardena, CA. Roy Nagatoshi: Tel: (818)362-5476.

Dai Ichi Bonsai Kai. Meets at Ken Nakaoka Community Center, 1670 W. 162nd St., third Friday, 7:00 P.M. Contact: Andrea Wagner, Tel: (310) 370-5492. Email: rickandrea@earthlink.net. Website: http://www.gsbf-bonsai.org/daiichibonsaikai.

HANFORD

Hanford Bonsai Society, Inc. Meets at Kings County Civic Center Agriculture Building, 680 N. Campus Dr., Suite F (of the Ag Center), third Thursday at 7:00 P.M. Contact: Bob Hilvers, Tel: (559) 732-9286.

LA CANADA (FLINTRIDGE)

Descanso Bonsai Society. Meets at Descanso Gardens, La Canada Flintridge, CA, third Tuesday, 7:00 P.M. Contact: Jim Barrett, 480 Oxford Dr, Arcadia, CA 91007. Tel: (818) 445-4529. Email: lizlikes@aol.com. Website: www.descanso-bonsai.com.

MODESTO

Modesto Bonsai Club. Meets the third Saturday of each month except December from 10:00 A.M. to 2.00 P.M. at the Blue Oak Nursery, 784 Albers Rd., near Hwy 132, Modesto. Mailing address is PO Box 578518, Modesto, CA 95357-8518. Contact: Jerry Jumper, Tel: (209) 667-6701. Website: http://www.modestobonsaiclub.com.

NAPA

Napa Valley Bonsai Club. Meets at 1500 Jefferson, third Monday, 7:15 P.M. Penny Pawl, PO Box 2220, Napa, CA 94558. Tel: (707) 224-8983. Email: papl142@juno.com.

OAKLAND

East Bay Bonsai Society. Meets at Lakeside Garden Center, 666 Bellevue, Oakland, second Wednesday, 7:30 P.M. Max Cooperstein, PO Box 1575, El Cerrito, CA 94530.

PALO ALTO

Kusamura Bonsai Club. Meets at First Congregational Church, Louis & Embarcadero, second Friday, 7:00 P.M. Website: http://www.geocities.com/kusamura. Bonsai contact: Sandy Planting, Tel: (650) 323-6955.

RIVERSIDE

Inland Empire Bonsai Society. Meets at Botanic Gardens Conference Room, UC Riverside, second Sunday except July and August at 1:00 to 4:00 P.M. Mrs. Knox, 3349 Dwight Ave., Riverside, CA, 92507. Tel: (909) 682-6623.

Sacramento

American Bonsai Assoc. of Sacramento. Meets the fourth Tuesday each month at 7:00 P.M. at the Sacramento Garden and Arts Center, 3330 McKinley Blvd. Contact: Simon Lau, Tel: (530) 622-9681. Email: NHCatLady@aol.com. Website: http://www.bonsaisacramento.org.

Satsuki Aikokai Sacramento. Meets at the Shepard Garden Center, 3330 McKinley Blvd, third Monday each month at 7:00 P.M. Betty Pitts, 2701 Corabel Lane, #55, Sacramento, CA 95821. Contact: Ronn Pigram, Tel: (916) 428-8505, Email: satsukiaikokaisac@sbcglobal.net.

San Diego

San Diego Bonsai Club. Meets at Casa del Prado Bldg., Room 101, Balboa Park, second Sunday, 11:00 A.M. Tel: (619) 699-8776. Website: www.sandiego bonsaiclub.com.

San Francisco

Bonsai Society of San Francisco. Meets at Hall of Flowers, 9th Ave. and Lincoln Way, second Thursday, 8:00 P.M. Mia Amato: Tel: (415) 285-6807. Spring exhibit. Website: http://www.bssf.org.

San Jose

Kusamura Bonsai Club. Meets every third Friday of the month at St. Mark's Episcopal Church, 600 Colorado Ave., Palo Alto, in the Parish Hall. Meetings are at 7:00 P.M. Contact: Jerry Carpenter, Email: jcsfl090@earthlink.net. Website: http://www.gsbf-bonsai.org/kusAMura/.

The Midori Bonsai Club. Meets the first and third Thursday of the month year round at 7:30 P.M. at St. Edwards Episcopal Church at Union Ave. and Hwy 85. Contact John Thompson (JT), Tel: (408)371-7737.

San Mateo

Bay Area Shohin. Meets at several locations in the greater San Francisco Bay area, Sunday, except July, August and December, 1:30 P.M. Bill Sullivan, 117 Jefferson Dr., Tiburon, CA 94920. Tel: (415) 388-5854.

Hillsborough Bonsai Society. Meets at San Mateo Garden Center, 605 Parkside Way, third Friday, 7:30 P.M. Barbara Bokeland, Tel: (415) 348-2835.

Sei Boku Bonsai Kai. Meets at 605 Parkside Way, fourth Wednesday, except December, 7:30 P.M. Warren Clark, 889 Lurine Dr, Foster City, CA 94404. Tel: (415) 574-6074.

Santa Barbara

Bonsai Club of Santa Barbara. Meets at the Goleta Valley Community Center, 5679 Hollister Ave., Goleta, CA, second Tuesday, except August and December, at 7:30 P.M. Contact Joe Olson, PO Box 3703, Santa Barbara, CA 93103. Tel: (805) 964-0869, or Email: joeyuccaseed@verizon.net.

Santa Maria

Santa Maria Bonsai Club. Meets at Japanese Cultural Center, 134 N. Western, second Sunday, 9:00 A.M. to noon. Chris Ehrler, Tel: (805) 489-9046.

Santa Rosa

Redwood Empire Bonsai Society. Meets at the Veterans Memorial Hall, 1351 Maple, Santa Rosa, Ca. (across from the fairgrounds) the fourth Tuesday of each month at 7:30 P.M. Website: www.rebsbonsai.org. Email: President@rebsbonsai.org.

Temple City

Baiko-en Bonsai Kenkyukai. Meets at 5118 Barela Ave., second Sunday, 1:00 to 4:00 P.M. Marty Hagbery, 5009 N. Willow Ave., Covina, CA 91724. Tel: (818) 331-8382.

Vacaville

Vaca Valley Bonsai Club. Meets at Community Presbyterian Church, 425 Hemlock St., second Tuesday, 7:00 P.M. John Jackson, 4681 Midway Rd., Vacaville, CA 95688. Tel: (707) 446-1720. Mailing address: 592 Cottonwood, Vacaville, CA 95688.

Van Nuys

Sansui Kai of So. California. Meets the first Wednesday, 7:30 P.M., at the Japanese Garden, shares address with Donald C. Tillman Water Reclamation Plant, 6100 Woodley Avenue, Van Nuys. Workshop 6:30 P.M. Dick Beltran, 10100 Keokuk Ave., Chatsworth, CA. 91311. Tel: (818) 349-0508.

Westlake Village

Conejo Valley Bonsai Society. Meets the third Thursday of every month, 7:30 P.M., at the Westlake Village City Hall/Community Room, 31200 Oakcrest Drive, Westlake Village, CA. Contact: Ken Fuentes, pres., Tel: (805)495-7480.

Colorado

Colorado Springs

Pikes Peak Bonsai Society. Meets at the Senior Center (Ceramics Room), 1514 N. Hancock, 10:00 A.M., second Saturday of each month. Website: http://www.phoenixbonsai.com/PikesPeakBonsai.html. Email: rjb@phoenixbonsai.com.

Denver

Rocky Mountain Bonsai Society. Meets at the Denver Botanic Gardens on the first Tuesday of each month at 7:30 P.M. except in December. Website: www.rockymtnbonsai.org.

Fort Collins

The Bonsai Society of Northern Colorado. Has meetings on the fourth Tuesday of each month at 7:00 P.M., and workshops on the second Saturday of each month, 1:00 to 3:00 P.M. Shows are at Fort Collins Nursery, 2121 E. Mulberry in Fort Collins. Contact: Barbara Rich, Tel: (970) 663-3046.

GRAND JUNCTION

The Western Colorado Bonsai Society of Grand Junction. Information, Email: trehaus@excite.com.

CONNECTICUT

HARTFORD

Bonsai Society of Greater Hartford. Meets at the Pond House at Elizabeth Park, Asylum and Prospect Avenues, in West Hartford on the third Monday of every month at 7:00 P.M. Contact: Diana Majchrzak. Website: www.greaterhartfordbonsai.com.

NEW HAVEN

Bonsai Society of Greater New Haven. Meets at Edgerton Garden Center, 145 Edgehill Rd., second Tuesday at 7:30 P.M. Contact: Ms. Nancy Mack, 36 Mulberry Hill St., Hamden, CT 06517, Tel: (203) 288-6744, or Lois Simeone, 30 Coachman Lane, Woodbridge, CT, Tel: (203) 393-0433. Website: www.angelfire.com/art/bonsaict.

NEW LONDON

China Trade Bonsai Society. Meets the first Wednesday of each month, March through November, from 6:00 P.M. to 8:00 P.M. at Conn College, New London Hall, 270 Mohegan Ave., Rt. 32, New London, Connecticut. Website: www.chinatradebonsaisociety.org.

STAMFORD

Yama Ki Bonsai Society. Meetings are held monthly, usually at the Bartlett Arboretum, 151 Brookdale Rd., Stamford, CT 06903, the second Saturday at 1:00 P.M. Check our *website* for actual location. Contact: Norm Geisinger, Tel: (203) 746-3200.

DELAWARE

WILMINGTON

Brandywine Bonsai Society. Meets every third Saturday of the month (except December) at the Brandywine Town Center, Wilmington, West Chester Pike (Rte 202) and Naamans Road (Rte 92), at 10:00 A.M. Contact: Steve Ittel, Tel: 302-778-4546. Web site: http://www.gobbs.org. Email: BrandywineBonsai@comcast.net.

DISTRICT OF COLUMBIA

Potomac Bonsai Association. Meets every other month at the National Arboretum, 3501 NY Ave., NE, Washington, D.C. 20002. Tel: (301) 871-5768. Contact: Chuck Croft, 5256 Queens Wood Drive, Burke, VA 22015. Tel: (703) 978-6841. Website: http://www.potomacbonsai.com/.

Washington Bonsai Club. Meets at Administration Bldg., U.S. National Arboretum, second Saturday, except July and August, 2:00 P.M. Dorothy Miller, c/o National Arboretum, 3501 NY Ave. NE, Washington D.C. 20002. Contact, Ross Campbell, Email: campbellr@gao.gov.

FLORIDA

BOCA RATON

Lighthouse Bonsai Society. Meets at the Boca Raton Community Center, 150 N. W. Crawford Blvd., Boca Raton, FL, fourth Saturday, 9:30 A.M. Contact: Rita Rosenberg, Tel: (516) 251-1802. Email: riritobyrose@aol.com. Annual membership is $25.

BUNNELL

Kawa Bonsai Society. Meets at Flagler County Agricultural Extension Office, Sawgrass Road, Bunnell, FL, third Friday, 7:30 P.M. Contact: Carol Partelow, Tel: (386) 586-3437. Email: GPartelowl @cfl.rr.com. Website: http://www.kawabonsai.com/.

DAVIE

Broward Bonsai Society. Meets the third Saturday of each month at 11:00 A.M. at Flamingo Gardens, 3750 Flamingo Rd., Davie, FL. Contact: Art Cid, Tel: (954) 261-0135. Website: http://www.browardbonsai.com.

FORT LAUDERDALE

Gold Coast Bonsai Society. Meets at City of Sunrise Parks and Leisure Department, 6800 Sunset Strip, Sunrise, FL, the second Saturday, 9:30 A.M. Contact: Ed Trout, Tel: (954) 432-8208. Website: http://www.goldcoastbonsai.com.

FORT MEYERS

Bonsai Society of Southwest Florida. Meets the third Saturday of each month at the SPALC Building, 6281 Metro Plantation Road, between Daniels Parkway and Colonial Boulevard, at 9:00 A.M. Becky Bodnar, Tel: (239) 463-4102, Email: beckybodnar@msn.com. Website: http://www.thebonsaisswfl.com.

FORT PIERCE

Treasure Coast Bonsai Society. Meets at St. Lucie Agriculture Center, 8400 Picos Rd., second Tuesday, 7:30 P.M. Jim Smith, Vero Beach, FL. Tel: (772) 562-5291.

FT. WALTON BEACH

Ft. Walton Beach Bonsai Society. PO Box 224, Shalimar FL 32579-0224, meets at Okaloosa County Extension Bldg., 125 Hollywood Blvd. NW, Ft. Walton Beach, FL 32548, first Tuesday and Third Thursday, 7:00 P.M.

GAINESVILLE

Gainesville Bonsai Society. PO Box 15383, Gainesville, FL 32604-5383. Meets at Kanapaha Botanical Gardens, 4700 SW 58th Dr., Gainesville, third Saturday, 9:30 A.M.

HOMOSASSA

Buttonwood Bonsai Club of Crystal River. 10 Boxelder Ct., Homosassa, FL 34446. Meets at First Presbyterian Church, U.S. 19, Crystal River, FL, second Saturday, 9:30 A.M.

LAKELAND

The Bonsai Society of Lakeland. Meets at 7:00 P.M., the third Thursday of every month at the First United Methodist Church at 72 Lake Morton Drive in Lakeland. Website: lakelandbonsai.com.

MIAMI

Bonsai Society of Miami. Meets at Fairchild Tropical Garden, 10901 Old Cutler Rd., second Tuesday, 7:30 P.M. Call Glenn Hilton, Tel: (305) 796-2525 for more information. Mailing address: Bonsai Society of Miami, 17850 SW 289 St., Miami, Fl 33031. Web site: http://www.bonsaisocietyofmiami.org. Email: bonsaimiami@bellsouth.net.

NAPLES

Bonsai Society of Naples. Meets twice monthly at various locations. Ernie Fernandez, P.O. Box 704, Bonita Springs, FL 33959. Tel: (813) 947-3552 (home) or (813) 992-0800 (0fc).

ORLANDO

Central Florida Bonsai Club. Meets at Orange County Agricultural Center at the corner of Conway and Judge Rd. in Orlando. Meetings are the second and fourth Friday each month, 7:30 P.M. Contact Adam Lavigne, Tel: (407) 399-1224. Email: president@centralfloridabonsaiclub.com.

PALM BAY

Bonsai Society of Brevard. 1263 Serenade St. NW, Palm Bay, FL 32907. Meets at Melbourne Public Library, Fee Ave, Melbourne, FL, third Saturday, 2:00 P.M. Website: http://www.bonsaisocietyofbrevard.org/.

PENSACOLA

Pensacola Gulf Coast Bonsai Society. Meets at Gulf Breeze Library, 1060 Shoreline Dr., Gulf Breeze, FL 32561, first Thursday, except July, 7:30 P.M. Jean Jongewaard, 5262 Pale Moon Dr., Pensacola, FL 32515. Tel: (904) 492-1305.

PORT CHARLOTTE

Charlotte Ichiban Bonsai Kai. Meets at Port Charlotte Cultural Center, Community Room, 2280 Aaron St., Port Charlotte, Florida 33952 on the fourth Tuesday, 7:00 P.M. Jerry Oseland, Tel: (813) 625-6468 or Robert Clifton, Tel: (813) 743-0829, or write to Charlotte Ichiban Bonsai Kai, PO Box 8023, Port Charlotte, FL 33952-8023.

ST. PETERSBURG

Suncoast Bonsai Society. Meets at Unitarian Universalist Church, Arlington Avenue North, in St. Petersburg, FL, the fourth Monday of each month from 7:00 to 9:00 P.M. Contact: Mick, Tel: (727) 522-1879. Website: http://www.suncoastbonsai.com/.

SARASOTA

Sho Fu Bonsai Society. Meets the first Thursday of each month, at 7:30 P.M. at Waterside Retirement Estates, 4540 Bee Ridge Road, Sarasota, FL 34233. Email: info@shofubonsai.com.

TALLAHASSEE

Tallahassee Bonsai Society. Meets second Saturday at the LeMoyne Art Foundation, Gadsden and Call Sts. Regular meeting starts at 2:00. President: James Houston.

Wee Arbor Study Group. Meets at 7582 Bowling Green Dr., second Sunday, 2:00 to 5:00 P.M. C. Duane Clayburn, 7582 Bowling Green Dr. Rt. 19, Box 1073, Tallahassee, FL 3230l. Tel: (904) 893-4442.

TAMPA

Hukyu Bonsai Society of Tampa. Meets at USF Botanical Gardens, 4202 E. Fowler Ave, SCA 238, third Saturday, 10:00 A.M. William B. Henderson, 10704 Lake Carroll Way, Tampa, FL 33618-4236. Tel: (813) 932-3714.

WEST PALM BEACH

Bonsai Society of the Palm Beaches. Meets at 7:30 P.M. the first Tuesday of each month at the Mount's Botanical Building, 551 N. Military Trail, West Palm Beach, FL. Contact: Dick Miller, Tel: (561) 432-1230.

GEORGIA

ATLANTA

Atlanta Bonsai Society. The College Park Presbyterian Church is located on the corner of Main Street and John Calvin Avenue in College Park. For more information, contact: Dennis McHugh, Tel: (770) 436-5747, Email: dennismchugh@charter.net. Website: http://www.atlantabonsaisociety.com.

HAWAII

HONOLULU

Club 100 Bonsai. Meets at Club 100, 520 Kamoku St., fourth Thursday, 7:00 P.M. Warren Yamamoto, 1526C Pukele Ave., Honolulu, HI 96816. Tel: (808) 523-4603 (bus.). Affiliate of Club 100, the 100th Infantry's Veterans organization. Membership restricted.

Pacific Bonsai Club. Meets at 2907 Alphonse Place, third Tuesday, 7:00 P.M. Lyle Takeuchi, Tel: (808) 737-0408.

Rainbow Bonsai Club. Meets at 2673 East Manoa Rd., second Sunday, 9:00 A.M. Wayne Arita, 2673 East Manoa Rd., Honolulu, HI 96822. Tel: (808) 988-7775.

Wahiawa-Waialua Bonsai Club. Meets monthly at 94-074 Akualele Place. Richard Andrzejewski, Tel: (808) 625-1885.

PEARL CITY

Pearl City Bonsai Club. Meets at 852 Second St., third Tuesday, 7:00 P.M.

Idaho

Boise

Boise Bonsai Society. For more information, please contact: Barbara Gough, 893 E. Twin Willow Court, Boise, ID 83706. Tel: (208) 336-5769. Email: blg@cableone.net. Website: www.boisebonsai.com.

Illinois

Glencoe

Midwest Bonsai Society. Meets at Chicago Botanic Garden, 1000 Lake Cook Rd., Glencoe, IL, the first Monday of each month at 7:30 P.M. Contact: Midday Bonsai Society, P.O. Box 1373, Highland Park, Il 60036. Email: midwest.bonsai@yahoo.com.

Glen Ellyn

Prairie State Bonsai Society. Meets at College of DuPage, fourth Monday, 7:30 P.M. President: Mark Karczewski. Contact: Prairie State Bosai Society, P.O. Box 2634, Glen Ellyn, IL 60138-2634. Tel: (630) 257-7586. Website: www.prairiestatebonsai.com.

Oak Park

Near West Bonsai Society. NWBS meets on the third Monday (February-November) at Maze Branch Library, 845 S. Gunderson Ave, Oak Park, IL 60304. 7:00 P.M. to 8:30 P.M. Contact: Roger D. Thompson, Email: Roger@mindspring.com, Tel: (708) 383-5267. Website: Groups.msn.com/NearWestBonsaiSociety/.

Peoria

Bonsai Club Heart of Illinois. Meets at Bio Center, Glen Oak Park, third Thursday, 7:30 P.M. J. Horvath Jr., 109 W. Almond Dr., Washington, IL 61571. Tel: (309) 745-5256.

Rock Island

Quad City Bonsai Club. Meets at Deere-Wyman Carriage House, Moline, last Thursday, except December, 7:30 P.M. Website: www.qcbonsai.org. Email: mail@qcbonsai.org.

Rockford

Rock River Bonsai Society. Meet at the Rock Valley Greenhouse and Garden Center, 785 N Bell School Road, Rockford, IL, the third Thursday of each month at 7:00 P.M. Contact: Robert Seele, Tel: (815) 631-3956.

Sandwich

De La Ke Bonsai Society. Meets at Fox Valley Older Adult Center, 1406 W Suydam Rd., Sandwich, IL, the second Saturday, 10:00 A.M., year-round. Please contact: Kevin H. Johnson, 215 19th Ave Naplate, IL 61350. Email: de_la_ke_bonsai_society@yahoo.com.

Springfield

Springfield Bonsai Society. Meets at Washington Park Botanical Garden, 1740 W. Fayette, second Monday of each month at 7:00 P.M. Contact: Gary Trammell, Tel: (219) 741-4849. Email: trammell.gary@uis.edu. Website: http://www.bonsaisbs.com/.

Indiana

Elkhart

Wellfield Bonsai Study. Meets the second Sunday of each month at 2:00 P.M. Meetings are held at the Wellfield Botanic Gardens, 1000 N. Main St. in Elkhart, IN. Contact: Liz Borger, Email: Elkbonsai532@Gmail.com.

Evansville

Bogans Bonsai Study Group. Meets at Dave Bogans home on the first Saturday of the month, 10:00 A.M. Contact: Dave Bogan, 101 Terry Lane, Lynnville, IN 47619. Tel: (812) 922-5451. Email: bogans bonsai@verizon.net.

Ft. Wayne

Ft. Wayne Bonsai Club. Meets the fourth Saturday of each month at 10:30 A.M. Contact Kathy Lee, Tel: (260) 637-6242. Email: igarden2@aol.com. Website: http://fortwaynebonsai.org.

Indianapolis

Indianapolis Bonsai Club. Meets first Wednesday of each month at 7:00 P.M. at the Garfield Park Conservatory, 2450 Shelby St., Indianapolis, IN. President Mark Fields, Email: maf71459@yahoo.com. Vice-President Carl Wooldridge, Email: carl wool@hotmail.com. Website http://www.indybon sai.org/.

Iowa

Cedar Rapids

Eastern Iowa Bonsai Association. Meets at Noelridge Park Greenhouse, third Thursday, except December/January, 7:00 P.M. Craig Bean, Tel: (319-390-0274). Website: www.geocities.com/bonsai bean2000/index.html.

Des Moines

Iowa Bonsai Association. Meets at Des Moines Botanical Center, 909 E River Dr., third Tuesday, except December, 7:00 P.M. David Lowman, Email: lowman@netins.net. Tel: (515) 769-2446 or (800) 528-2827.

Kansas

Mission

The Bonsai Society of Greater Kansas City. Society members meet each month (except July) at the Garden Center in Loose Park, 5200 Pennsylvania, Kansas City, MO. Meeting dates are irregular, check website. Contact: Brad Short.

Wichita

Wichita Bonsai Club. Members meet the second Monday of each month at 7:00 P.M. at The Botanica, 701 Amidon, Wichita, KS. Contact: William Burrow, Tel: (316) 267-8247.

Kentucky

Henderson

Greater Evansville Bonsai Society. Meets at the Henderson County Public Library, first Wednesday, 6:30 P.M. Dave Bogan, Tel: (812) 922-5451.

Louisville

Greater Louisville Bonsai Society. Meets monthly at the Bon Air Regional Library, 2816 Del Rio Place, Louisville, KY. Check website for date/time of meetings: www.louisvillebonsai.org.

Louisiana

Baton Rouge

Louisiana Bonsai Society. Meets at Baton Rouge Garden Center, 7950 Independence Blvd, third Tuesday at 7:00 P.M. Contact: Howard Merrill, Tel: (225) 275-2917.

Lafayette

Bonsai Society of Acadiana. Meets at the University of Louisiana at the Lafayette Horticulture Center, Johnston St., first Wednesday, 7:00 P.M. Contact: Bonsai Society of Acadiana, P.O. Box 51906, Lafayette, LA 70505-1906. Johnny Hardcastle, Tel: (337) 365-4829. Email: jmh6344@louisiana.edu.

Lake Charles

Lake Charles Bonsai Society. Meets at McNeese State Univ., Frasch Hall, Lecture Hall 101, Beauregard Drive at Ryan Street, third Tuesday, 7:00 P.M. Contact: Dennis Corley, president, P.O. Box 1652, Lake Charles, LA 70602. Tel: (409) 866-5803. Email: awbonsai@bellsouth.net. Website: www.LCBSbonsai.org.

New Orleans

Greater New Orleans Bonsai Society. Meets at St. Andrews Church hall, 8017 Zimple St., second Tuesday, 7:30 P.M. Johnny Martinez, Tel: (504) 467-2857. Website: www.gnobs.org.

Shreveport

Shreveport Bonsai Society. Meets monthly at the Barnwell Art and Garden Center, 801 Clyde Fant Memorial Parkway, on the second Saturday, 1:00 P.M. Annual spring show and workshop. For more info contact: Robert Specian, Tel: (318) 227-0744. Email: rspecian@comcast.net. Website: http://shreveportbonsai.org/.

Maine

Bangor

Bangor Area Bonsai Society. Meets third Sunday, 3:00 to 6:00 P.M. Barbara Friedman, 1229 Broadway, Box 417, Bangor, ME 04401. Tel: (207) 947-5588.

Maryland

Baltimore

Baltimore Bonsai Club. Meets at Cylburn Arboretum in the historic mansion, third Sunday, 1:00 to 4:00 P.M. Mike Ramina, Email: mmr2823@aol.com. Arschel Morell, Tel: (410) 744-6478.

Bethesda

Brookside Bonsai Society. Meets at Chevy Chase Recreation Center, third Thursday, 7:30 P.M. Jim Hughes, Tel: (301) 779-2891.

Bowie

Bowie Bonsai Club. Meets at Bowie Community Center, last Monday, 7:00 P.M. Terry Adkins, Tel: (301) 350-3586.

Mei-Hawa Penjing Society. Meets at Bowie Community Center, second Sunday, 1:00 P.M. Akey C. F. Hung, 12412 Shadow Lane, Bowie, MD 20715. Tel: (301) 390-6687.

Clinton

Kiyomizu Bonsai Club. Meets the fourth Sunday at 2:00 P.M. at the Clearwater Nature Center. Email: wilsone@howrey.com.

Shady Side

Shady Side Bonsai. Location: Shady Side, Maryland. Meetings: second Thursday of the month. Tachigi@aol.com. Website: http://shadysidemd.tripod.com/.

Massachusetts

Cape Cod

Cape Cod Bonsai Club. Meets every second Monday, 7:00 P.M., at the Yarmouth Senior Center on Forest Rd. Contact: Andy Amault, Email: A.Amault@comcast.net.

Hamilton

Northeast Bonsai Association. Meets at Hamilton Community House, 284 Bay Rd (Rt. 1A) So. Hamilton, MA. Contact: Charles Paraskevas (Act Cleaning), 37 Central St., Beverly, MA 01915. Tel: (978) 921-0286. Email: CEPHAS35@aol.com.

Martha's Vineyard

Martha's Vineyard Bonsai Club. Meets at the Polly Hill Arboretum, 809 State Road, West Tisbury, MA, on the second Tuesday of the month at 7:00 P.M. No meetings in December and January. Contact: Dan Harnen, P.O. Box 4919, Vineyard Haven, MA 02568. Tel: (508) 693-9788. Email: Tashmoodan@AOL.Com.

Springfield

The Bonsai Society of Greater Springfield. Meets at Springfield Technical Community College (STCC) at 7:15 P.M. every third Tuesday of the month (excluding July and August) in room 316 in the Putnam Hall building (Bldg. 17), located at 1 Armory Square. Contact: Sandy Saffer.

Stoughton

Bonsai Study Group of Massachusetts Horticultural Society. Meetings on the first Sunday of each month. Email: BonsaiStudyGroup@comcast.net for subject matter and meeting location. New England Bonsai Gardens, 914 South Main Street /Rte. 126, Bellingham, MA 02019, or Royal Bonsai Gardens, 1297 Park St., Stoughton, MA. Anne Karshis, Email: a.karshis@comcast.net.

Michigan

Ann Arbor

Ann Arbor Bonsai Society. Meets at Matthaei Botanical Garden, 1800 N. Dixboro Rd., fourth Wednesday of each month at 7:30 P.M. Contact: Ryan Liu, Tel: (313) 421-1917. Email: aabsnewsletter@yahoo.com. Website: http://annarborbonsaisociety.org/.

Bay City

The San Toshi Bonsai Club. Meets the third Thursday of each month at Bay Landscaping, 1630 N. Southeast Boutell, Essexville, MI. Anne Kemper, Tel: (517) 835-7730. Email: agkemper@hotmail.com.

Grand Rapids

West Michigan Bonsai Club. Meets each Saturday at the Frederik Meijer Gardens, 1000 East Beltline Avenue NE, at 9:00 A.M. Contact: Mollie Hollar, Tel: (616) 754-2351. Email: hollar@chartermi.net. Please check our website.

Kalamazoo

Bonsai Society of Kalamazoo. Meets the second Sunday of each month at 1:00 P.M. at the Girl Scout Headquarters, located at the corner of Maple and Crosstown in Kalamazoo. Contact: Eric Newton, Tel: (269) 731-3850. Email: newtsbonsai@tds.net. Founded in 1980.

Traverse City

Sakura Bonsai Society of Northern Michigan. Contact: Eric Hallman, Tel: (231) 932-7509. Email: e-dhallman@juno.com. Annual dues $20.

Tri-Cities

The San Toshi Bonsai Club. Meets the third Thursday of each month at Bay Landscaping, 1630 N. Southeast Boutell, Essexville, MI. Anne Kemper, Tel: (517) 835-7730. Email: agkemper@hotmail.com.

Troy

Four Seasons Bonsai Club. Meets the last Sunday of the month at 2:00 P.M. at Telly's Greenhouse and Nursery, 3301 John R. Road, Troy, MI. Todd Renshaw, Tel: 248-585-9916. Email: webmaster@mababonsai.org. Please check our website.

Minnesota

Minneapolis

Minnesota Bonsai Society. Meets the first Tuesday of the month (except January) at Jehovah Evangelical Lutheran Church, 1566 Thomas Ave., St. Paul, MN (Corner of Snelling and Thomas, four blocks north of University Avenue). Claude A. Worrell, P.O. Box 32901, Minneapolis, MN 55432. Visitors welcome.

Mississippi

Long Beach

Mississippi Gulf Coast Bonsai Society. Meets monthly at the Mississippi Gulf Coast Community College, in the building to the left of the Administration Bldg., in Long Beach, corner of Espy and "B" Street, Longbeach, MS, at 6:30 P.M., second Wednesday of each month. Tel: (985) 643-1573. Email: HylanderOB1@aol.com. Website: http://www.msgulfcoastbonsai.org.

Missouri

Kansas City

Bonsai Society of Greater Kansas City (MO). Meets at Loose Park Garden Center, 5200 Pennsylvania, Kansas City, MO, Saturdays and Sundays as scheduled, except August and December, 9:00 A.M. Gilbert Novak, 9842 Overhill Rd., Kansas City, MO 64134. Tel: (816) 762-2992.

Springfield

Ozarks Bonsai Guild. For information please contact: Jeff Germann, Tel: (417) 883-6782. Email: ozarksbonsai@gmail.com. Website: http://ozarks-bonsai.ning.com.

St. Louis

Bonsai Society of Greater St. Louis. Meetings are the first Tuesday or Wednesday of the month, 7:00 P.M., in the Beaumont Room at the Missouri Botanical Garden. Contact: Glenn Pauley, president, Tel: (314) 843-1312. Email: gkpauley@att.net.

Montana

Billings

Billings Bonsai Society. Meets at Gainan's Garden Center, Billings. For more information on meeting dates contact Wally Mclane, PO Box 288, Billings, Montana 59103. Tel: (406) 259-8676.

Kalispell

Big Sky Bonsai Society. At this time no regular meetings. For information contact Jerry Meislik, Tel: (406) 862-0387. Email: jerry@bonsaihunk.us.

Nebraska

No clubs exist in this area.

Nevada

Las Vegas

Las Vegas Bonsai Society. Meets at the Nevada Garden Club Center, Lorenzo Park, 3333 W. Washington Ave., in Las Vegas, the second Wednesday, 7:00 P.M. Contact: Bob Kovach, Tel: (702) 257-4768. Email: tubs78@cox.net.

Reno

Yukiyama Bonsai Kai. Meetings are held the first Saturday of the month, 10:00 A.M. to noon, at the Northeast Community Center, 1301 Valley Road, in Reno, NV. Contact: Pat Flynn, Tel: (775) 825-1858. Email: info@bonsairenp.org. Website: www.bonsaireno.org.

New Hampshire

No clubs exist in this area.

New Jersey

Closter

The Bergen Bonsai Society. Meets at Closter Nature Center, Ruckman Rd., Closter, NJ, third Sunday, 10:00 A.M. Contact: George LeBolt. Email: bonsaibygeorge@verizon.net. Website: http://www.bergenbonsai.netfirms.com/.

Middletown

Deep Cut Bonsai Society. Meets at the King of Kings Lutheran Church, 250 Harmony Rd., Middletown, NJ, on the third Thursday of each month at 7:30 P.M. Contact: Kenneth Olander, Tel: (732) 202-0677. Email: bowhunter444@verizon.net. Website: www.deepcutbonsaiclub.org.

Morristown

Great Swamp Bonsai Society. Meets second Tuesday of the month at 7:30 P.M. at the Frelinghuysen Arboretum, Hanover Ave., Morristown, NJ. John Michalski, Email: hounia@aol.com. Website: www.arboretumfriends.org/gsbonsai/.

Mt. Laurel

Bonsai Society of South Jersey. Meets second Wednesday each month at 7:00 P.M. at the Clover Garden Center, 1017 South Church St., Mt. Laurel, NJ. Tom De Simone, Tel: (856) 988-9094. Email: thomasrose@verizon.net.

New Mexico

Albuquerque

Albuquerque Bonsai Club. Meets at the Heights Cumberland Presbyterian Church, 8600 Academy Rd. NE, first Saturday at 9:00 A.M. Contact Susan Burns, president, Email: s.r.burns@comcast.net. Website: www.abqbonsai.org.

New York

Buffalo

Bonsai in Buffalo. Information, Email: 62myway@gmail.com. Website: http://sites.google.com/site/bonsaiinbuffalo/.

Buffalo Bonsai Society. Meets at 7:00 P.M. on the third Wednesday of each month (except July and December) at Menne's Nursery, 3100 Niagara Falls Blvd., Amherst, NY 14228. Email: info@buffalobonsaisociety.com. Website: www.buffalobonsaisociety.com.

Farmingdale

Farmingdale Chapter of Bonsai Society of Greater New York. Meets at Greenhouse, S.U.N.Y., Farmingdale, second Friday, 8:00 P.M.

Long Island

Long Island Bonsai Society. Meets at Planting Fields, Upper Brookville, NY, second Monday each month, except January/February meetings on second Sunday at 11:00 A.M. Website: longislandbonsai.org.

North Syracuse

Bonsai Club of Central New York. Meets at Pitcher Hill Community Church, 605 Bailey Road, North Syracuse, near Buckley Road, the second Wednesday of each month, 7:30 P.M. Iris Cohen, 6 Bevell Lane, North Syracuse, NY 13212, Tel: (315) 461-9226. Email: iriscohen@aol.com. Website: http://cnybonsai.googlepages.com/.

Queens

Queens Chapter of Bonsai Society of Greater New York. Meets at Queens Botanical Gardens, 4320 Main St., Flushing, Queens, fourth Wednesday, 8:00 P.M. Philip Tacktill, 1243 Melville Rd, Farmingdale, NY 11735. Tel: (516) 293-9246.

Rochester

Bonsai Society of Upstate New York. Meets at Brighton Town Park Lodge, 777 Westfall Rd. Contact: William K. Valavanis, 1070 Martin Rd., West Henrietta, NY 14586-9623. Tel: (716) 334-2595. Email: wnv@internationalbonsai.com. Large exhibit the end of May. Website: http://www.bonsai-upstateny.org.

Staten Island

Staten Island Bonsai Society. Meets at Blue Heron Nature Center, 222 Poillon Ave., Staten Island, each second Tuesday at 7:30 P.M. Contacts: Vito Morongiello, Tel: 718-984-9739, or Kevin Kilkenny.

Utica

Mohawk Valley Bonsai Club. Meets at the Unitarian Universalist Church, 10 Higby Road, just off Genesee Street, Utica, the second Saturday at noon. For more information contact Tom Martin, Tel: (315) 292-1140. Email: tmartin@twcny.rr.com. Club established in 2005.

West Charlton

Mohawk-Hudson Bonsai Society. Meets the last Sunday of each month at noon. Contact: Pauline Muth, 7 Western Ave, West Charlton, NY. Tel: (518) 882-1039. Email: pauline@pfmbonsai.com. Website: www.pfmbonsai.com.

North Carolina

Asheville

Blue Ridge Bonsai Society. We assemble around 1:30 with the program starting at 2:00 P.M. Yearly membership is $25. Meets at the Botanical Gardens in Asheville, 151 W. T. Weaver Blvd., Asheville, NC. Contact: Bob Thatcher, Tel: (828) 667-9563. Email: tman15@earthlink.net.

CHARLOTTE

The Bonsai Society of the Carolinas. Meets the second weekend of each month at the Bonsai Learning Center at 4416 Beatties Ford Road in Charlotte, NC. Contact: Bob Wymer, 8328 Kaplewood Ct., Charlotte, NC 28226. Tel: (704) 541-5776 or Tel: (24 hour bonsai hotline) (704) 552-6551. Website: http://www.bonsaicarolina.com.

RALEIGH, DURHAM, CHAPEL HILL

Triangle Bonsai Society. Meets at the Commons Building, Wake County Office Park, 4011 Carya Dr., Raleigh, NC. Meeting dates vary by month, please check the website for current information. Contact: Harold Johnson, 6806 Knotty Pine Dr., Chapel Hill, NC 27517.

WINSTON-SALEM

North Carolina Bonsai Association. Contact: Terry W. Brandsma, 4208 Brentonshire Ln., High Point, NC 27265.

NORTH DAKOTA

WEST FARGO

Bonsai of the North Society. Contact: Gregory A. Baumgartner, Email: threebs.nd@netzero.net.

OHIO

AKRON-CANTON

Akron-Canton Bonsai Society. Meets the first Thursday of every month at 7:00 P.M. at the Cuyahoga Valley Art Center, 2131 Front Street, Cuyahoga Falls, OH. On the Mall in downtown Cuyahoga Falls, just south of Portage Trail, near Rt. 8. For more information, Email: akroncantonbonsai@gmail.com. Website: http://picasaweb.google.com/akroncantonbonsai.

CINCINNATI

Bonsai Society of Greater Cincinnati. Meets at Civic Garden Center, 2715 Reading Rd., third Thursday, except December and January, 7:30 P.M. Website: http://cincinnatibonsai.com. Contact: Tom McCormack, 10931 Allenhurst Blvd. E., Cincinnati, OH 45241. Tel: (513) 563-0473.

CLEVELAND

Cleveland Bonsai Club. Meets at the Cleveland-Rockefeller Park Greenhouse, 750 E. 88th St. of Martin Luther King Blvd., Cleveland, OH , the fourth Saturday of the month, 9:30 A.M. to noon. Contact: Dale Harder, Tel: (440) 888-2163 after 5:30 P.M. (EST). Email: dale@hhr-lasers.com.

COLUMBUS

Columbus Bonsai Society. Meets at Franklin Park Conservatory, 1777 East Broad St., third Sunday of each month at 2:00 P.M. Contact: Mark Passerrello, 438 Mainsail Drive, Westerville, OH 43081. Tel: (614) 890-1995.

DAYTON

Bonsai Dayton. Meets at the OSU Extension Office in Montgomery County Fairgrounds, 1001 S. Main Street, third Wednesday except July and August at 6:30 P.M. Contact: Dave Billing, Tel: (937) 433-8432.

NEWARK

Pun Ching Bonsai Club. Meets at the Dawes Arboretum, 7770 Jacksontown Rd., SE, Newark, OH 43056, third Tuesday at 7:00 P.M. Contact: Jeff Carr, Tel: (740) 323-2355. Email: jcarr@stasel woodbonsai.com.

SANDUSKY

Sandusky Bonsai Club. Meets at 306 Wayne St., first Tuesday, except January, 7:30 P.M. Send mail to Parkview Barber Shop, 306 Wayne St., Sandusky, OH 44870, or call Paulette Grahl, Tel: (419) 626-2703.

WILLOUGHBY

Ohio Great Lakes Bonsai Society. Meets second Saturday of each month. Contact Albert Vlasar, 5278A Liberty Lane, Willoughby, OH 44094. Tel: (440)585 4867.

OKLAHOMA

NORMAN

Association of Oklahoma Bonsai Hobbyists. Meets on the first Sunday of the month from 1:00 to 4:00 P.M., usually at the Firehouse Art Center in Norman, Oklahoma. Contact: Randy Jones, Email: rj@randysbonsai.com. Tel: 405.364.8960.

OKLAHOMA CITY

Central Oklahoma Bonsai Society. Meets at 3400 NW 36th St., second Tuesday, 7:00 P.M. June show and bazaar. Contact: Dale Haworth, 10874 S. Sante Fe Ave., Edmond, Oklahoma. Tel: (405) 844-2513. Email: dalehaworth@cox.net.

TULSA

Northeast Oklahoma Bonsai Association. Meets at Tulsa Garden Center, 2435 S. Peoria, second Monday, 7:00 P.M. Glen Miller Jr., 1708 S. College Ave., Tulsa OK 74104.

Tulsa Bonsai Society. Meets at Tulsa Garden Center, 2435 S. Peoria, first Monday, 7:00 P.M. Dennis Chandlee.

OREGON

COOS BAY/NORTH BEND

Bay Area Bonsai Society. Meets at Coos Bay Public Library, 525 Anderson, second Monday, except July and August, 7:00 P.M. George and Eva Ahuna, 1434 N Tenth Court, Coos Bay, OR 97420, Tel: (503) 269-9696, or Kenneth Windred,

3013 Pigeon Point Rd., Coos Bay, OR 97420, Tel: (503) 888-3634.

CORVALLIS

Corvallis Bonsai Society. Meets at Chintimini Senior Center, 2601 NW Tyler Ave., fourth Tuesday, 7:00 P.M. Ruth Musil, Tel: (503) 757-8261.

EUGENE

Eugene Bonsai Society, Inc.. Meets at Eugene Garden Club, 1645 High St. in Eugene, first Thursday, except January, July, and August, at 6:30 P.M. Contact: Dean Burkhart, Tel: (541) 744-1919. Email: burkhaks@aol.com. Website: www.eugene bonsai.org.

MEDFORD

Cascade Bonsai Society. Meets the third Thursday of each month at 7:00 P.M. at Eastwood Baptist Church Annex, 675 N. Keene Way, Medford, OR. Contact: Jan Bailey, Tel: (541) 857-2627. Email: bondoxies@charter.net.

PORT ORFORD

Far-West Bonsai Society. Meets at Alfonso Travel Park, first Monday, 7:00 P.M. DeBoyd and Eileen Smith, 95650 Sixes River Rd., Sixes, OR 97476. Tel: (503) 332-7633.

PORTLAND

The Bonsai Society of Portland. Meets on the fourth Tuesday of the month at St. Phillips Neri Parish located at 2408 SE 16th Avenue, Portland. No meetings July, August and December. Contact: Arlene Sigourney, PO Box 10615, Portland, OR 97296-0615. Tel: (503) 667-0148. Email: portland-bonsai@hotmail.com. Website: www.portlandbon sai.org.

SALEM

Willamette Valley Bonsai Society. Meets at the Marion County Fire District #1, 300 Cordon Road NE, Salem, on the second Tuesday, 7:00 P.M. Contact: Ron Phair, Tel: (503) 932-2165. Email: phairest@hotmail.com. Website: http://willAMet tevalleybonsai.org.

PENNSYLVANIA

ERIE

Great Lakes Bonsai Society. Contact Mike Golab for meeting dates and locations: Tel: (814) 456-6186. Email: mikego6194@msn.com.

HARRISBURG

Susquehanna Bonsai Club. Meets third Monday, 7:00 P.M. Contact James and Mary Kay Doyle, 1451 Pleasant Hill Rd., Harrisburg, PA 17112 for meeting locations. Tel: (717) 545-4555.

HUNTINGDON VALLEY

Pennypack Bonsai Society. Meets the second Thursday of every month at Pennypack Ecological Restoration Trust, 2955 Edgehill Road, Huntingdon Valley, PA. Website: http://greenfield.fortunecity.com/panda/121/.

LANCASTER

Lancaster Bonsai Society. Meets at historic Conestoga House and Gardens at 1608 Marietta Pike (Rt. 23), just west of Lancaster. The club meets in the library every second Wednesday of the month, except for December, at 7:00 P.M. Email: ulrich51 @excite.com.

LEHIGH VALLEY

Bonsai Society of Lehigh Valley. Meets at Bethlehem Area Vocational Technical School, Horticultural Room, 3300 Chester Ave., Bethlehem, last Tuesday, 7:00 P.M., except July, August, and December. Jim Gillespie: (610) 837-6688. Mailing address: PO Box 1684, Bethlehem, PA 18016-1684.

PHILADELPHIA

Pennsylvania Bonsai Society. Meets at Greater Plymouth Community Center, 2910 Jolly Rd., Plymouth Meeting, PA, third Friday, 7:00 P.M. Linda Brant: (610) 948-6380. Email: lbrant@comcast.net. Website: http://pabonsai.org.

PITTSBURGH

Pittsburgh Bonsai Society. Meets at Pittsburgh Civic Garden Center, 5th and Shady Ave., third Wednesday, 7:00 P.M. Don Gould, 239 James St., Wilkins Twp, PA 15145. Tel: (412) 823-2090.

READING

Reading Bonsai Society. Club Meetings are held the first Monday of each month at 7:00 P.M. in the Reading Public Museum Auditorium. Enter through the back security entrance. For more information contact Alan Groff, Tel: (610) 927-2272. Email: alang@inter-graphic.com. Website: www.RedRival.com/rbc.

WEST MITON

Augusta Bonsai Club. Meets on the second Monday of each month at 6:30 P.M. at the United Christ Church, White Deer Churches, West Milton, PA. Contact: John Bierley, Tel: (570) 546-7811. Email: quietspiritarts@hotmail.com.

WILMINGTON, DELAWARE (also serves Southeast Pennsylvania)

Brandywine Bonsai Society. Meets every third Saturday of the month (except December) at the Brandywine Town Center, Wilmington-West Chester Pike (Rte 202) and Naamans Road (Rte 92), at 10:00 A.M. Contact: Steve Ittel, Tel: 302-778-4546. Email: BrandywineBonsai@comcast.net. Website: http://www.gobbs.org.

PUERTO RICO

TRUJILLO ALTO

Federacion Puerto Rico de Bonsai. Presidente Pedro J. Moarales, P.O. Box 1620, Trujillo Alto, Puerto Rico 00977-1620. Tel: 787 765 6680, Res.

787 755 3362, Fax: 787 767 1888, Res. 787 761 3394. Email: futago@prtc.net.

BAYAMON

Club de Bonsai de Puerto Rico–Capitulo de San Juan. Meets the third Tuesday of each month at 7:30 P.M. at Centro Cumunal Crown Hills, Winston Churchill Ave., El Senorial, San Juan. Jose Rivera, Email: josorl@prw.net. Website: www.geocities.com/cbpr2000.

RHODE ISLAND

W. KINGSTON

Rhode Island Bonsai Society. PO Box 40935, Providence, RI 02940. Website: www.rhodeislandbonsaisociety.org. Email: president@rhodeislandbonsaisociety.org.

SOUTH CAROLINA

COLUMBIA

Bonsai Club of South Carolina. Meets at 10 A.M. on the third Saturday of each month at the Garden Club Council of Greater Columbia Building at Maxcy Gregg Park (near Five Points), Columbia, SC. Website: http://members.aol.com/SCbonsai/Bonsaipages/SCBS.html. Email: SCBonsai@aol.com.

SEABROOK ISLAND (outside Charleston)

Coastal Carolina Bonsai Club. Meets at Property Owners Community Room, Seabrook Island, second Monday every other month beginning January, 7:30 P.M. Jeanne P. Thompson, 2384 High Hammock Rd., Johns Island, SC 29455, Tel. (803)768-2192. We have a security gate. One must be invited or ask for entrance from the contact person.

SUMMERVILLE

Summerville Bonsai Study Group. Meets at 2:00 P.M. on the third Sunday of each month at the Cuthbert Community Center in Azalea Park on West 5th South Street. Contact: Ron Martin.

SOUTH DAKOTA

No clubs exist in this area.

TENNESSEE

KINGSPORT

Mid-Appalachian Bonsai kai. Meets the third Monday of each month, for location and directions please contact Anita Bausman, Tel: (423) 239-7602.

KNOXVILLE

Knoxville Bonsai Society. Meets at various members' homes typically on the second Saturday of each month from 9:30 A.M. to noon. Contact: Tom Bjorholm: Tel: (865) 922-0825. Email: bjorholmt@juno.com. Website: www.bjorvalabonsai.com/kbs.

MEMPHIS

Memphis Bonsai Society. Meets at the Memphis Botanical Gardens Goldsmith Civic Center (750 Cherry Road, Memphis, TN) on the fourth Tuesday of each month (unless a special activity dedicates otherwise). The meetings start at 7:00 P.M. Email: mphsbonsai@aol.com. Website: www.memphisbonsai.com.

NASHVILLE

Nashville Bonsai Society. Meets at Cheekwood Botanic Gardens, 1200 Forrest Park Drive, Nashville, TN, on the first Tuesday of each month at 7:00 P.M., except during the months of December and January. Contact: Barbara Bogan, Tel: (615) 337-4728. Email: bogansbonsai@verizon.net.

TEXAS

ABILENE

Big Country Bonsai Club. Meets at Abilene Garden Club, 300 Westwood, second Tuesday, 7:00 P.M. Evelyn Mayfield, 1425 Tanglewood Rd., Abilene, TX 79605. Tel: (915) 692-1665.

AUSTIN

Austin Bonsai Society. The club meets on the second Wednesday of each month at 7:00 P.M. social and 7:30 meeting at the Zilker Garden Center in Austin. Contact: Elaine, Tel: (512) 266-2655. Email: ewbonasi@austin.rr.com.

BEAUMONT

Southeast Texas Bonsai Club. Meets at Garden Center, Terrell Park, first Tuesday, 7:00 P.M. Contact: Mark Lee: Tel: (409) 722-9287.

CORPUS CHRISTI

Corpus Christi Bonsai Club. Meets every fourth Thursday of the month, January through October, 7:00 P.M., at the Garden Senior Center, 5325 Greely Street. Contract: Yvonne Padilla, Tel: (512) 992-0009. Email: myforest@sbcglobal.net. Website: http://corpuschristibonsaiclub.org.

DALLAS

Bonsai Society of Dallas. Meets first Saturday of each month at 9:00 A.M. at North Haven Gardens, 7700 North Haven Road. George Straw, Email: bonsaistraw@aol.com. Tel: (214) 357-3048. Website: http://www.bonsaisocietyofdallas.com.

FORT WORTH

Fort Worth Bonsai Society. Meets at Fort Worth Botanic Garden Conservatory, 3220 Botanical Garden Dr., second Thursday, 7:00 P.M. Suzanne Scott, 3130 Woodland Hts., Colleyville, TX 76034. Tel: (817) 283-5985.

HOUSTON

Houston Bonsai Society, Inc. Meets monthly on the first Wednesday at the Houston Garden Center in Hermann Park, 1500 Herman Dr., 7:00 P.M. Contact: Donald Green, HBS, P.O. Box 540727, Houston, TX 77254-0727. Email: zgreen3@comcast.net. Tel: (713) 771-1442. Website: www.houstonbonsai.com.

San Antonio

San Antonio Bonsai Society, Inc. Meets at 7:00 P.M. on the second Thursday of each month, at the Lion's Field Adult and Senior Citizens Center located at 2809 Broadway (corner of Broadway and Mulberry). Contact: Donna Dobberfuhl, 2009 SABS president, Email: two2views@yahoo.com. Postal Mailings: P. O. Box 39161, San Antonio, TX 78216.

Weslaco

Rio Grande Valley Bonsai Society. Meets second Sunday of the month (with some exceptions to accommodate outside speakers) at 2:00 P.M. in the Hoblitzelle Building of the Texas A & M Research Center in Weslaco, TX. Contact Rick Choate, Tel: (210) 580-4303, evenings and weekends.

Utah

Salt Lake City

Bonsai Club of Utah. Meets at Sugar House Park Garden Center, 1676 E. 21st South, fourth Wednesday, 7:30 P.M. Jean Schroeder, PO Box 58975, Salt Lake City, UT 84158. Website: http//users.burgoyne.com/~dainge.

St. George

Southern Utah Bonsai Society. Meetings are every third Thursday at Star Nursery, 385 W Telegraph St, Washington, UT at 7:00 P.M. Casey Niederhauser, Tel: (435) 668-0844. Email: casey@subonsai.com. Website: http//www.subonsai.com.

Vermont

Central to Northern Vermont

Green Mountain Bonsai Society. Meets in members' homes or at Williston Federated Church, third Sunday, 3:00 P.M. Trudy Anderson, RD 1, Box 129, Jericho, VT 05465. Tel: (802) 899-3487.

Northeastern Vermont

Northeast Vermont Bonsai Club. Meets at New England Art Glass Studio every fourth Thursday of the month. Contact: Tim Byrne, RR#1, Box 4, Derby Vermont, 05829. No meetings November–February.

Virginia

Arlington

Northern Virginia Bonsai Society. We meet every second Saturday of the month, 9:00 A.M. at the Walter Reed Community Center, 2909 16th St. S. Arlington, VA. John Fitzsimons, Email: jfitzsimons@verizon.net.

Hampton

Peninsula Bonsai Society. Meets the second Tuesdays, 7:00 P.M., at the Peninsula Council of Garden Clubs building in Hampton. Contact: Bob Owens, Tel: (757) 877-3515. Email: Bowensai@aol.com.

Lynchburg

Central Virginia Bonsai Society. Usually meets at Grove Street Recreation Center, 301 Grove St., the fourth Thursday during growing season at 7:00 P.M. Contact: Julian R. Adams, 1721 Langhorne Road, Lynchburg, VA 24503. Tel: (434) 384-7951. Email: jra@adAMsbonsai.com.

Norfolk

Virginia Bonsai Society. We meet in the Holly Room of Baker Hall at Norfolk Botanical Gardens, 6700 Azalea Garden Rd., first Thursday of each month, 7:00 P.M. Contact: Walter Lisicki (president), Tel: (757) 486-3422. Email: info@virginiabonsai.org. Website: www.virginiabonsai.org.

Richmond

Richmond Bonsai Society. Meets at Imperial Plaza Auditorium, 1717 Bellevue Ave., fourth Monday at 7:00 P.M. Randi Sharp, Tel: (804) 840-5565. Email: richmondbonsaisociety@yahoo.com. Website: http://richmondbonsaisociety.org/.

Roanoke

Hinoki Bonsai Club. Meets at Roanoke Council of Garden Clubs Bldg., 3640 Colonial Ave., third Wednesday of each month, except August, at 7:30 P.M. Contact: Ken Clubb, Tel: (540) 362-2725. Email: kclubb43@cox.net.

Virgin Islands

No clubs exist in this area.

Washington

Olympia

Olympia Bonsai Club. Meets at 7:00 P.M. on the second Thursday of each month at the American Legion Post #3, 3201 Boston Harbor Rd. NE, Olympia, WA. Our mailing address is Box 2682, Olympia, WA., 98507-2682. Gene Tsuji, Tel: (360) 491-0593.

Seattle

Puget Sound Bonsai Association. Meets at Center for Urban Horticulture at Univ. of Wash., 3501 NE 41st St., fourth Monday, February, March, April, May.

Sequim

Dungeness Bonsai Society. Meets at Pioneer Park, 387 E Washington Street, in Sequim. First Tuesday in February, March, April, May, September, October, November, 10:00 A.M. to noon. Contact President Robert Stack, Dungeness Bonsai Society, PO Box 1441, Sequim, WA 98382.

Spokane

Inland Empire Bonsai Society. Meets at Manito Park meeting room (4W, 21st Ave) on the third Sunday of every month at noon. Hal Allert: Tel: (509) 869-4583. Email: info@inlandbonsai.com. Website: http://www.inlandbonsai.com/.

YAKIMA

Yakima Valley Bonsai Society. Meetings are held at 7:30 P.M. the last Tuesday of each month from February through October at the Yakima Area Arboretum, 1401 Arboretum Dr., Yakima WA. Email: Ernie Smith Racee@wolfenet.com.

WEST VIRGINIA

MORGANTOWN

Mountaineer Bonsai Society. Meetings are held on the third Thursday of every month at 7:00 P.M. in the Evansdale Greenhouse Division of Plant and Soil Sciences, West Virginia University. Morgantown, West Virginia 26506. Tel: (304) 293-4480. Current president: Tom Simonyi. Email: mistermoyogi@yahoo.com.

WISCONSIN

APPLETON

Fox Valley Bonsai Society. Meets at the Gardens of the Fox Cities in Appleton, WI, the second Tuesday, at 7:00 P.M. Leroy Frahm, Tel: (414) 832-6722. Email: leroyfrahm@hotmail.com.

GREEN BAY

Bay Area Bonsai Society. Meets at The Senior Center in downtown Green Bay, WI, second Wednesday, except January, July, November, and December, 7:00 P.M. Sandra Keller, Tel: (920) 865-7546, or Bay Area Bonsai Society, PO Box 12244, Green Bay, WI 54307-2241.

LACROSSE

The Coulee Region Bonsai Club. Meets at Asbury Methodist Church, 19 and Redfield St., third Monday, except December, 7:00 P.M. Tony Buchda, 400 Monitor St., LaCrosse, WI 54601. Tel: (608) 782-4231.

MADISON

Badger Bonsai Society. Meetings are at 7:00 on the second Thursday of every month at Olbrich Gardens (3330 Atwood Avenue, Madison, WI), except for January and July, when the club has a special dinner meeting. Ronald Fortmann, Tel: (262) 490-8733. Email: aabonsai@charter.net. Website: www.badgerbonsai.net.

MILWAUKEE

Milwaukee Bonsai Society. Meets on the first Tuesday at 7:00 P.M. at Grace Church, 3030 W Oklahoma, Milwaukee, WI. Pam Woythal: Tel: 414-299-9229 or write PO Box 198, Brookfield, WI 53008-0198. Website: www.milwaukeebonsai.org. Email: mbsweb@hotmail.com.

WYOMING

GILLETTE

Gillette Bonsai Study Group. Meets at various dates and times. Contact Gerald Gardner, 912 Cherry Lane, Gillette, WY. Tel: (307) 685-2041. Email: ggardner@vcn.com.

LARAMIE

Laramie Bonsai Study Group. Contact Gerald Gardner, 912 Cherry Lane, Gillette, WY. Tel: (307) 685-2041. Email: ggardner@vcn.com.

Bonsai Nurseries—

ALABAMA

(no locations found)

ALASKA

(no locations found)

ARKANSAS

Bella Vista, Bonsai Gardens of North West Arkansas

Van Buren, American Bonsai

ARIZONA

Tucson, The Bonsai Center

CALIFORNIA

Fresno, Nee-Hai Bonsai

Gardena, Chikugo-En Nursery

Hayward, Grove Way Bonsai

Kelseyville, Evergreen Garden Works

Lakeland, *Kuma Bonsai*

Los Angeles, Yamaguchi Bonsai

Modesto, Blue Oak Nursery

Newcastle, Matsuda Bonsai and Landscape Nursery

Northridge, Kimura Bonsai and Landscape Nursery

Placerville, Lotus Bonsai

Sebastopol, Miniature Plant Kingdom

Sylmar, Fuji Bonsai Nurseries

COLORADO

Engelwood, Bonsai Nursery Inc.

Wheat Ridge, Colorado Bonsai

CONNECTICUT

Stamford, Shanti Bithi Bonsai Nursery

DELAWARE

(no locations found)

FLORIDA

Bokeelia, Wigert's Mango Grove and Nursery

Deland, Mike Roger's Bonsai Studio

Holly Hill, Schley's Bonsai

Lakeland, Korean Bonsai Nursery

Miami, Miami Tropical Bonsai

Sanford, Japan Nursery Inc.

GEORGIA

Cleremont, Plant City Bonsai

Conyers, Bonsai by the Monastery

Port Wentworth, Bonsai Beginnings Green World

Hawaii

Kurtistown, Fuku Bonsai
Waimanalo, Hawaii Bonsai Cultural Center (Dragon Garden Nurseries)

Idaho

Lewiston, American Bonsai Nursery

Illinois

Edwarsville, Cass Bonsai Gardens
Willowbrook, Hidden Gardens Nursery

Indiana

(no locations found)

Iowa

Kelley, DaSu Bonsai Studios

Kansas

(no locations found)

Kentucky

Sheperdsville, Bonsai West

Louisiana

Covington, Bonsai Northshore

Maine

Woolwich, Maine Bonsai Gardens

Maryland

Baltimore, Black Pines Nursery
Brandywine, Celestial Bonsai
Rohrersville, Meehan's Miniatures
Shady Side, Shady Side Bonsai

Massachusetts

Bellingham, New England Bonsai Garden
Harwich, Cape Cod Bonsai Studio
Littleton, Bonsai West
Stoughton, Royal Bonsai Garden

Michigan

(no locations found)

Minnesota

Forest Lake, BMK Bonsai
Prior Lake, Five Stone Garden

Mississippi

Olive Branch, Bussel's Bonsai Nursery

Missouri

(no locations found)

Montana

(no locations found)

Nebraska

(no locations found)

Nevada

(no locations found)

New Hampshire

(no locations found)

New Jersey

Egg Harbor Twp, Okami Gardens
Flemington, AllShapes Bonsai

New Mexico

(no locations found)

New York

Avon, Hollow Creek Bonsai
Brooklyn, Bonsai of Brooklyn
Northport, Green Garden Nursery
Queensbury, Northland Gardens
Rochester, International Bonsai
Smithtown, Bonsai Boy of New York

North Carolina

Charlotte, Bonsai Learning Center
Cherryville, The Growing Grounds
Fuquay Varina, Matsu Momiji Bonsai Nursery
Wilmington, Painted Lady Bonsai

North Dakota

(no locations found)

Ohio

North Canton, Ken's World of Bonsai
North Dayton, North Dayton Garden Center

Oklahoma

Blanchard, Sonlight Nursery

Oregon

Corvallis, Wee Tree Farm
Portland, Koyama Bonsai

Pennsylvania

Danielsville, Sho Fu En Bonsai
East Berlin, Sleepy Hollow Bonsai
Harrisburg, Nature's Way Nursery
Honeybrook, Old Mill Bonsai Studio
New Hope, Rosade Bonsai Studio

Rhode Island

Tiverton, Eagleville Bonsai, LLC

South Carolina

Charleston, Working with Nature Bonsai
Greenville, Green Thumb Bonsai
Summerville, Tokonoma Bonsai

South Dakota

(no locations found)

Tennessee

(no locations found)

Texas

Garland, Dallas Bonsai
Wimberley, Jade Gardens

Utah

Salt Lake City, Ben's House of Bonsai

Vermont

(no locations found)

Virginia

Christiansburg, Higo Garden Bonsai
Dumfries, Little Trees Bonsai Nursery
Lynchburg, Adam's Bonsai
Vienna, Wolf Trap Nursery

Washington

Bremerton, Elandan Gardens
Kent, Asia Pacific Gardening Inc.
Seattle, Bonsai Northwest

West Virginia

(no locations found)

Wisconsin

(no locations found)

Wyoming

(no locations found)

• Canada •

Bonsai Societies—

Alberta

EDMONTON

Bonsai Society of Edmonton. Meets the third Wednesday each month, Japanese Cultural, 6750 88 St. at 7:30 P.M. Contact: Les Dowdell, 3536 104A St., Edmonton, AB T6J 2N2. Tel: (403) 437 0530. Email: les.dowdell@agric.gov.ab.ca.

LETHBRIDGE

Bonsai Society of Southern Alberta. Meetings second Tuesday each month except July and August at Lethbridge Public Library at 7:00 P.M. Contact: Carmen Pfiffner, 1912 — 9A St., Coaldale, AB T1M 1B2. Tel: (403) 328 3855. Website: www.lethbridgelibrary.ab.ca

British Columbia

British Columbia Bonsai Clubs Federation. Roger Low 3230 East 15th Ave., Vancouver, BC V5M 2L4. Tel: (604) 435 5737.

CRANBROOK

Cranbrook Bonsai Club. Meets at Mount Baker High school, Room 107, on the third Wednesday of each month, except April. Contact: Kevin Masson: Email: bonsaitreeman@yahoo.ca. Tel: (250) 489-5785.

DUNCAN

Cowichan Bonsai Club. Meets second Monday of each month at 7:00 P.M. at Providence Farm (main building). Don, Tel: (250) 748-9798. Email: islandbonsai@telus.net.

KELOWNA

Kelowna Bonsai Club. Meets first Monday each month, February–June and September–November, Okanagan University College, 1000 KLO Road, at 7:00 P.M. Tom, Tel: (250) 868-3368. Ed, Tel: (250) 860-7099.

PENTICTON

Penticton Bonsai. Contact: Dan Muesh, Kelowna Bonsai Club, 1034 Martin Ave., Kelowna, BC Y1Y 6V5. Tel: 250 492 5323.

RICHMOND

Wakayama Kenji Kai Bonsai Club. Meets second and fourth Tuesday each month, Steveston Japanese Canadian Cultural Centre at 7:30 P.M. Jim Tanaka, 7571 Montana Rd., Richmond, BC V7C 2K7. Tel: (604) 274 1684.

SURREY

British Columbia Bonsai Society. Meets first Thursday each month from February through December, 7:00 P.M. to 9:00 P.M., at Sunnyside Hall, 1845 154th Street, Surrey, BC. Jim McAusland, Tel: (604) 533 6685.

Omiya Bonsai Club. 1686 150th St., Aldergrove, BC V0X 1A0. Phil Johnston, Tel: (604) 683 8600, Fax: (604) 683 8614.

VANCOUVER

Chinese Penjing Society of Canada. Meets the third Sunday of each month, Chinese Cultural Center, at 2:00 P.M. Ian Wang, Tel: (604) 272-5971.

Japanese Gardeners Association Bonsai Club. Meets fourth Friday each month, 7:30 P.M. at West Coast Garden Coop, 4289 Slocan Ave. Contact: Roy Haroda, 996 Cloverley Ave., Vancouver, BC V7L 1N3. Tel: (604) 980 5840.

Hon. David Lam Gardening Society. Meets first Tuesday of each month at the Van Dusen Garden, 37th and Oak. Contact: Tony Wu, Tel: (604) 473 9837, or Sam Law, Tel: (604) 437 3828. Sam Law, 3F Metrotown Centre, 4820 Kingsway, Burnaby, BC V6H 4J2.

Dr. Sun Yat Sen Classical Chinese Garden Penjing Club. 578 Carrall St., Vancouver, BC V6B 5K2 Pin Lee or Kathy Gibler, Tel: (604) 730 2611.

Taguchi Bonsai Club. Meets on the third Monday of each month, except July, August and January, Van Dusen Botanical Garden, 37th St. and Oak, at 7:30 P.M. Sandor Knoll, 2706 Highbury St., Vancouver, BC V6R 3T5. Tel: (604) 224 1343.

Taiwanese Canadian Cultural Society Bonsai Club. Meets second Saturday each month, Room

#202, 8853 Sekirk St., at 7:30 P.M. Ruey Lin, Tel: (604) 267 0901 or (604) 267-0902.

Vancouver Bonsai Association. Meets irregularly on Saturday mornings at the Van Dusen Botanical Gardens, 37th St. and Oak. Pauline Nielson, 1949 37th Ave. W., Vancouver, BC V6M 1N5. Tel: (604) 261 6060.

Vancouver Sumi Bonsai Club. Meets second Wednesday of each month, except January and August, Van Dusen Botanical Gardens, 37th Ave. and Oak St., at 7:30 P.M. Tats Fukuda, Tel: (604) 275-8749.

West Coast Bonsai Society. Meets first Friday of each month, 7:30 P.M., at the Van Dusen Botanical Gardens, 37th St. and Oak. Roger Low, 3230 E. 15th Ave., Vancouver, BC V5M 2L4. Tel: (604) 435 5737.

VERNON

Vernon Bonsai Club. Meets fourth Monday each month at the Vernon Arts Centre, 2704A Hwy #6, Vernon, BC . Spring and fall shows. Ray Evans, Tel: (250) 542-7254. Email: rrevans@shaw.ca.

VICTORIA

Vancouver Island Bonsai Club. Meets the third Monday of each month at the Garth Homer Society Bldg., 813 Darwin Ave., Victoria, BC, 7:30 P.M. Annual show at Hillside Shopping Centre in early May. Randy Kowalchuk, Pres. PO Box 8674, Victoria, BC V8W 3S2. Tel: (250) 370-7562. Email: randyko@shaw.ca. Website: www.victoriabonsai.bc.ca.

MANITOBA

WINNIPEG

Winnipeg Bonsai Society. Meets on the second Monday each month September to May, Assiniboine Park Conservatory at 7:00 P.M. Paul Collard, Tel: (204) 488-3234. Email: pcollard@shaw.ca. Website: http://www.bonsaiwinnipeg.ca.

NEW BRUNSWICK

No clubs exist in this area.

NEWFOUNDLAND AND LABRADOR

No clubs exist in this area.

NOVA SCOTIA

No clubs exist in this area.

NORTHWESTERN TERRITORY

No clubs exist in this area.

ONTARIO

BRANTFORD

Brant Bonsai Society. Meets fourth Monday each month except July, August and December at Tranquility Place (basement), 436 Powerline Road, Brantford at 7:30 P.M. Bruce Little, 29 Tanglewood Terrace, Brantford, Ontario Canada N3R 3R8. Tel: (519) 756-0585. Email: brantbonsai@hotmail.com.

ETOBICOKE

Misseto Bonsai. Meets on the third Thursday of each month at the Islington United Church, 25 Burnamthorpe Rd., in Etobicoke at 7:00 P.M. Thomas Balsillie, Tel: (416) 807 6124. Email: missetobonsai@yahoo.com.

GUELPH

Guelph Bonsai Club. Meets first Wednesday each month except January, July, and August, Bovey Bldg. at 7:00 P.M. Contact: David Wolyn, Bovey Bldg., University of Guelph, Guelph, ON N1G 2W1. Tel: (519) 824 4120, ext. 3092. Email: dwolyn @evbhort.ca.

HAGERSVILLE

Haldimand Bonsai Society. Meets irregularly at above address. Shows with the Guelph Bonsai Club. Contact: Alice Barker, RR #6, Hagersville, ON N0A 1H0. Tel: (905) 768-3864. Email: adeschen@enbhort.uoguelph.ca.

NIAGARA ON THE LAKE

Niagara Bonsai Society. Meets on the third Sunday of each month at the Niagara College Campus Garden Centre, corner of Glendale Ave and Taylor Road, at 1:30 P.M. Contact: Brenda Dennis, Tel: (905) 892-3646. Email: bdennis1@gmail.com.

NORTH BAY

North Bay Bonsai Society. Meets first Monday of each month, Community Centre, Swale St., Callander, ON, at 7:00 P.M. Annual show third week of August. Albert Cobb, RR#4, 1212 Memorial Park Dr., Powassan, ON P0H 1Z0. Tel: (705) 724 5665. Email: tedreed@onlink.net.

OSHAWA

Matsuyama Bonsai Society. Meets the second Tuesday each month, September thru June, Faith Place, 44 William St., Oshawa at 7:00 P.M. Contact: Grace Wicht, RR#1, Locust Hill, ON L0H 1J0. Tel: (905) 683 2568.

OTTAWA

Ottawa Bonsai Society. Our monthly meeting is held at Building 72 — Central Experimental Farm (Arboretum), the third Monday of the month (except December, July, August) at 7:30 P.M. Contact: Robert Smith, 40, Rue Imbeault, St-Alphonse de Rodriguez, PQ J0K 1W0. Tél: (450) 883-1196. Fax: (450) 883-1040. Email: info@bonsaigrosbec.com. Website: http://www.ottawabonsai.org.

TORONTO

The Toronto Bonsai Society. Meets the second Monday of each month except July and August, Dunnington Grubb Floral Hall, the Civic Garden Center, 777 Lawrence Ave. E., at 7:15 P.M. Contact: Dick Morton, 14 Lyncroft Dr., West Hill, ON M1R 1X7. Tel: (416)284 1215. Fax: (416) 775 3259.

WATERLOO KITCHENER

Waterloo Bonsai Club. Meets the third Wednesday of each month except December, July and August, Adult Recreation Centre, King and Allen St., Waterloo at 7:30 P.M. Eldon Leis, 184 Herbert St., Waterloo, ON N2J 1T5. Tel: (519) 743 3763.

PRINCE EDWARD ISLAND

No clubs exist in this area.

QUEBEC

MONTREAL

Société de Bonsai et Penjing de Lanaudière. Contact: Robert Smith, 40, rue Imbeault, St-Alphonse de Rodriguez, QB&J0K 1W0. Tel: (450) 883-1196. Fax: (450) 883-1040.

Société de Bonsai et Penjing de Montreal. Meets on the last Thursday of each month except June, July and August at the Montreal Botanical Garden. Contact: Administrative Secretary, 4101 Rue Sherbrooke, West, Montreal, QC H1X 2B2. Tel: (514) 872-1782.

QUEBEC

Le Groupe Bonsai Quebec. Meets the first Monday of each month at Laval University, 2480 Blvd. Hochelaga, in Quebec. J. P. Monette, Tel: (418) 887-3988. Email: jPM@bonsaiquebec.com. Website: www.bonsaiquebec.com.

SASKATCHEWAN

No clubs exist in this area.

YUKON

No clubs exist in this area.

Bonsai Nurseries—

The Angelgrove Tree Seed Company. Tree seeds, garden seeds catalog, Email: angelgrove@nf.sympatico.ca. (Anti-Spam: Please include the word "Seeds" in your subject line). Website: http://treesseeds.com. Website: www.AngelgroveSeeds.com. Fax: 709-596 2296. Tel: 1 888 596 4053. Business Hours: Monday to Friday 10:00 A.M. to 4.30 P.M. (EST). You can also try us on Saturdays.

Bonsai Store Canada. Website: http://www.bonsaistore.ca. Bonsai, air plants and lucky bamboo.

Great Canadian Bonsai. Store Shopping. Website: http://www.bonsaicanada.com

MishoBonsai.com. Website: http://www.mishobonsai.com. Trees and bonsai seeds.

Natural Bonsai. Website: http://www.naturalbonsai.com. Japanese bonsai tools, pots and supplies. Ships throughout Canada.

Peninsula Flowers Nursery. Website: http://www.bonsaibc.ca. Bonsai, pre-bonsai and bonsai containers located in B.C. Canada on southern Vancouver Island.

Sunny Bonsai & Orchid Greenhouse. Website: http://www.sunnybonsai.com

• *Mexico* •

Societies—

Asociacion de Bonsai Tropical de Mexico. Contact: Enrique Castano, CICY, Calle 43 no 130 colonia Chuburna de Hidalgo, Merida, Yucatan, Mexico. Tel: 9813914 ext. 242, Cell: 9991659980. Email: enriquec@cicy.mx. Website: http://www.bonsaitropical.com/.

Asociación Mexicana de Bonsai, Mexico City. Av. Acoxpa No. 545-101B Col. Prado Coapa, Mexico D.F.14350, Mexico. Tel: +52 (55) 5603 2798. Fax: +52 (55) 5603 2863. Email: emigdiot@excite.com.

Club Bonsai Guadalajara. Website: http://www.bonsaiguadalajara.4t.com/.

Bonsai Calli Guadalajara. Instituto Cultural Cabanas. Direccion: Calle Cabanas, en la Plaza Tapatia. Lugar: Guadalajara, Jalisco, Mexico. Horario: Domingos de 10:00 a 12:00 hrs.

Europe

• *Austria* •

Ing. Karl Heinz Unterweger. Linzerstrasse 14. Tel: +43 (0)7223 / 80792. Email: k_unterweger@aon.at. Website: http://www.bonsai-austria.at/.

Nurseries and Supplies—

Little Bonsaiworld — Bonsaizentrum Wien. A-2201 Gerasdorf Bei Wien — Siedlung Kapellerfeld Ost, Kantgasse 17-19. Tel: +43 650 694 21 55. Öffnungszeiten: MO von 14.00 to 18:00, DI von 9:30 to 13:00. MI geschlossen DO von 9:30 to13:00 und 14:00 to 18:00 FR von 14:00 to 18:00 SA-SO u. Feiertag sowie ausserhalb der Öffnungszeiten nach telefonischer Voranmeldung: Tel: +43 650 694 21 55.

• *Belgium* •

Frieda Joris, Baaskouter. Tel: 32-2-452.99.91. Fax: 32-2-452.99.91. Email: friebonsai@hotmail.com. Website: www. bonsai-abbc-belgium.be.

Bonsai Nurseries and Supplies—

Bauwens Bonsai. Kalenbergstrat 70 BE-1700, Dilbeek Belgium. Tel: +32(0)25 69 26 12. Email: bauwens.marc@skynet.be.

Bonsai Ateljee Callaert. Tel: 0032 (0)52 20 16 78. Sint-Onolfsdijk, 71 C, B 9200—Dendermonde. Email: info@bonsaiateljee.be.

Gingko Bonsai Center. Heirweg 190 (N445)—927, Laarne—Belgium. Tel: +32-9-355.14.85. Fax: +32-9-355.26.15.

Noya-En. Website: www.noya-en.eu.

Sugi Bonsai. Meir 51, 1840 Steenhuffel—Londerzeel, GSM: 0476 28 85 32. Email: sugibonsai@scarlet.be.

• *Czech Republic* •

Bonsai Zahrada Kunice. Kunice 132, 251 63 Strán ice. Tel: 607201454. *Otvírací doba:* So, Ne—10-18 hod Mapa, doprava *ZDE.* Website: Tel: domluva možná.

Karel Müller. Nam.Svobody 1518. Tel: +420-774.536.561. Email: karel68@volny.cz. Website: http://www.cz-bonsai.cz/.

• *Denmark* •

Bonsai Værkstedet. V/ Hans Jørgen Nielsen, Strynøvej 36, 6710 Esbjerg V—Denmark. Tel & Fax: (+45) 75156734. Mobil 40746734. Email: bonsai@Email.dk. Åbning tider. Mandag to Fredag 16:00 to19:00, Lørdag 10:00 to 14:00, Søndag efter aftale hele året.

Morten Albek. Freltoftevej 43, Freltofte. Tel: +4562 22 25 21, Cell phone: +45 24 79 50 64. Email: albek@shohin-europe.com. Website: http://www.bonsai-danmark.dk/.

• *France* •

Jean Marc Pouillon. 179 rue des Plattieres. Tel: +336 08 89 52 71. Email: president@ffb-bonsai.org. Website : www.ffb-bonsai.org/.

Bonsai Nurseries and Supplies—

Charlane Bonsai. 95, avenue de Villiers—75017 Paris. Tel: 01 42 27 17 04. Email: info@charlane-bonsai.com.

Paris Bonsai. Contacter Sylvain DeLannoy ou Isabelle Bernard au 01 45 32 22 69. De 11h to 19 h du Lundi au Samedi.

Pepeniere Maillot Bonsai. LeBoisFrazy, .01990 Relevant, France. Tel: +33 (0)4 74 55 23 48. Fax: +33 (0)4 74 55 21 18. Email: info@maillot-bonsai.com.

• *Germany* •

Bonsai and More. Website: http://www.bonsai-and-more.de/index.html.

Bonsai Garten Allgau. Anderstaigel-87549 Rettenberg. Email: info@bonsai-garten-allgaeo.

Bonsai Shop.com. Telefon: 039363-97721.

Bonsai-Zentrum Münsterland GmbH. Raiffeisenstrasse 22, 59387 Ascheberg. Tel: 02592-95. Fax: 02593-95 87 15. Mo to Fr: 9:00–18:00 Uhr, Sa: 9:00 to 16:00 Uhr, letzter Sonntag im Monat: 10:00 to 16:00 Uhr. Email: info@bonsai.de.

Jürgen Carocci. Birkenweg 31. Tel: +49 62 207 279. Fax: +49 62209 133 45. Email: Carocci.altenbach@gmx.de. Website: http://www.bonsai-club-deutschland.de/.

Yixing Lotus. Zhang Import & Export Glück-Auf-Str. 30 57271 Hilchenbach-Müsen Tel: 02733/61848. Email: shop@bonsai-lotus.de.

• *Ireland* •

Marcia Wright. Amberwood House, Rathgrangher, Hollymount, County Mayo, Ireland. Marcia, Tel: +353 (0) 86 1700086. Dennis: Tel: +353 (0) 86 639 0294. Email: marcia@AMberwoodbonsai.com.

• *Italy* •

Amatori Bonsai Trieste. Via Cataro, 6, 34100 Trieste, Italia, Tel: +39 040 303176.

Bonsai Olivo. di Proce Sonia, Via Oberdan 6,73057 Taviano (LECCE) Italy. Tel: 0833-914282. Email: bonsai@bonsaiolivo.it.

Centre S.A.S. Certrè Sas di Mario Remeggio & C.—31050 Via Edison 87 Villorba, Treviso, Italy. Tel: 0039.0422.910006.

Centro Bonsai Roma. Via Cantani Snc Roma, Tel, Fax: 06 45420831. Cell: 338 2059319. Email: bonsairoma@bonsairoma.it.

Marino Nikpal. Via Villa Glori 7. Tel: +39 0586 400916.

• *Malta* •

Bonsai Clubs. 3, Old Mint Street, Valletta VLT 11,Malta. Annual exhibition, usually on the first Saturday of June. President: Paul Debono.

The Garden Shop. San Gwann, Malta.

Zammit Nurseries. Santa Venera, Malta.

• *Monaco* •

Bernard Jaworowicz. 4 rue Harpignies, Tel: +33-04.93.57.01.07. Mobile : +33-608.87.17.68. Email: jaworowicz@wanadoo.fr. Website: www.bonsaiclubmonaco.free.fr. Website: http://www.ubi-bonsai.it/. Email: nikpal@ubibonsai.it.

• *Netherlands* •

Bonsai Design Holland. Huizen, Netherlands. William Vlaanderen, Tel: +31(0)6-546-83862. +31 (0)356-935553. Fax: +31 (0)35-691 4897. Skype:

William Vlaanderen Huizen NL CET. Email: info@samurai.nl. 09.00 to 18.00 KvK Nr. 28098525.

Bonsai Studio Kengai. Winterdijk 27, 5141 KE Waalwijk, Tel: 0416-652098. Mobiel: 0653-436920.

Espaflor Bonsai. 4281ND, Duizendmogen 10a, Andel, Nederland. Website: styledbynature.nl.

Janssen-Koopsman. Past. Vullinghsstraat 435985, PH Grashoek NL. (Vanaf 1-1-2010 gem. Peel en Maas). Tel: +31 (0)77-3072957. Email: info@bonsaistudio.nl.

Omiya Bonsai. M. L. Witteman, Ter Aar. Tel: +31(0)625436118. Fax: +31(0)172605771. Email: info@omiya.nl.

Oriental Bonsai Center B.V. Anjerweg 10, 2665 LN Bleiswijk, Tel: 0031(0)10-5211600. Fax: 0031(0) 10-5218166. Email: info@orientalonline.nl.

Tom Van Wanum. Rivierlaan 5. Tel: +31 (0) 181 625538, Mobile: +31 (0) 6 44 69 44 97. Email: tomvanwanum@xs4all.nl. Website: http://www.bonsainederland.nl/.

Tropical Bonsai Holland. Michael de Ruiter: Tel: +31 6 1101 4822. Email: info@tropicalbonsai.nl

• *Poland* •

Wlodzimierz Pietraszko. Ul. Kurpiow 14, Tel: +48(71)3681193. Fax: +48 (71) 3687027. Email: pietraszko@bonsai.pl.

• *Portugal* •

Rui Tavares. Rua das Andorinhas 2. Email: tavares@bio.uminho.pt. Website: Federação Portuguesa de Bonsai.

• *Slovakia* •

Vladimir Ondejcik. Pri Synagoge 3, Bonsai Centrum Nitra. Tel: 00421-37-6522582. Fax: 00421-37-7417074. Email: bonsai@e-bonsai.sk. Website: http://bonsai-sba.sk.

• *Slovenia* •

Tomaž Kovšca. Brilejeva 6. Tel: +386412 41224. Email: tomaz.kovsca@rtvslo.si.

• *Spain* •

Rolf Beyebach. El Jacal, El Pison, Camino de los Prunos, 25. Tel: 34-985-36.60.46. Email: beyebach@wanadoo.es. Website: www.aebonsai.org/. Website: http://www.bonsajklub.si/.

• *Sweden* •

Maria Arborelius-Rosberg. Plantagegatan 18. Tel: +46-4015.96.79. Email: maria.arborelius-rosberg@telia.com. Website : www.bonsaisallskapet.nu/.

• *Switzerland* •

Chris Mathys. Tannenweg 3.Tel: +4179 208 46 91. Email: chris-mathys@ggs.ch. Website: http://www.bonsai-vsb.ch/.

• *United Kingdom* •

Dr. Malcolm Hughes. The Woodlands, New Hall Drive, Walmley. Tel: +44-01213784837. Fax: +44-0121 311 1912. Email: mkhughes567@btopenworld.com. Website: http://www.fobbsbonsai.co.uk/.

Ambion Bonsai Club. Meets last Thursday of every month except June and December at the Hatters Space Community Centre, Upper Abbey Street, Nuneaton, Warwickshire CV11 5DN. Contact David Cheshire, 07974 219825.

Artistic Bonsai Circle. Small group based in South Wales but with online gallery.

Association of British Bonsai Artists (A.B.B.A.)

Bedfordshire Bonsai Society. Toddington

Berkshire Bonsai. Barkham

Bonsai Clubs International. Worldwide membership. Non-profit educational organization.

Bonsai Group. Meets at Capel Manor, Enfield, Middlesex.

Bonsai Kai. Greycoat Street — London SW1.

Bonsai Magazine. Czech Bonsai Association; bonsai, suiseki, etc.

British Shohin Association. Based in Willowbog Nursery, Northumberland.

Cardiff Bonsai Club. Based in South Wales.

Cheshire Bonsai Society. Little Budworth, near Tarporley, Cheshire

Colchester Bonsai Society. Colchester, Essex

Cornwall Bonsai Society.

Dragon Bonsai Society. Formerly known as Swansea & District Bonsai Society.

Erin Arts Centre Bonsai Society. Isle of Man

European Bonsai Association (EBA). Co-ordinating body for associations in Austria, Belgium, Czechia, Denmark, France, Germany, Italy, Luxembourg, Monaco, the Netherlands, Poland, San Marino, Slovakia, Slovenia, Spain, Sweden, Switzerland, and the UK.

Federation of British Bonsai Societies (F.O.B.B.S.). Co-ordinating body for member societies in the UK, details and links to contacts in local societies.

Glynderi Bonsai Club. South Wales

Grampian Bonsai Society. Aberdeen

Heart of England Bonsai Society. Leamington Spa, Warwickshire

Japanese Garden Society. International membership, UK regional meetings.

Maidstone Bonsai Society. Maidstone, Kent

Manchester Bonsai Society. Stockport

Mid Herts Bonsai Club. Meets in the Backhouse Room, Handside Lane, Welwyn Garden City, Herts.

National Bonsai Collection. Collection originally set up in Birmingham by Federation of British Bonsai Societies.

National Bonsai Society. Based in Southport, NW England.

Norfolk Bonsai Association. Reviews of bonsai tools and other equipment.

Northamptonshire Bonsai Society. They have an online site.

North Devon Bonsai Society. Barnstaple

Northern Classical Bonsai Group. Small group based in North of England.

North West Kent Bonsai Society. Swanley, Kent

Potteries Bonsai Group. Stoke on Trent, Staffs.

Salisbury Bonsai Society. Laverstock Village Hall, Wilts.

Satsuki Azalea Society. National membership.

Solent Bonsai Society. Fareham, Hants.

South Devon Bonsai Society. The society meets twice monthly at Youth Hall, St Paul's Church, Torquay Road, Preston, Paignton, Devon, on first Monday evening at 7:30 P.M. and third Saturday morning at 10:30 A.M.

South Yorkshire Bonsai Society. Sheffield

South Worcestershire Bonsai Society. Meets on the second Tuesday of every month at Claines British Legion, Cornmeadow Lane, Worcester.

Sussex Bonsai Group. Wivelsfield Green Village Hall, West Sussex

Swindon Bonsai Society. Wiltshire

Vale of Clwyd Bonsai Society. St. Asaph, Clwyd. Wales

Waltham Forest Bonsai Club. Walthamstow, London. Meetings third Tuesday of each month.

World Bonsai Friendship Federation.

Bonsai Nurseries and Suppliers—

Bonsai Garden. Bonsai trees and supplies. Tel: 01202 887797. Email: bonsaidirect@aol.com.

Bonsai Supplies. Tel: 01751 432773. Email: john @jfkms.fsnet.co.uk.

Cherry Blossom Bonsai. Bonsai Nursery. Tel: 01933 665383. Website: www.cherryblossombonsai.co.uk. Email: info@cherryblossombonsai.co.uk.

China Mist. Alan Harriman. Handmade bonsai dishes. Website: www.chinamist.co.uk.

Craig Coussins. Website: www.tokonomascrolls.com.

Exeter Bonsai Supplies. Bonsai trees, pots and supplies. Tel: 01392 437525. Email: brian@bonsai2000.freeserve.co.uk.

Gordon Duffet. Hand-built bonsai pots. Tel: 02076 358859.

Greenwood Gardens. Bonsai, trees, tools, books, videos, DVDs. Tel: 01159 205757. Website: www.bonsai.co.uk. Email: office@bonsai.co.uk.

John Pitt Bonsai Ceramics. Tel: Fax: 01283 733479. Mobile: 07940 580634. Website: www.johnpittbonsaiceramics.co.uk. Email: john@john pittbonsaiceramics.co.uk.

Kaizen Bonsai. Online shop. Tel: 01493 655038. Website: www.kaizenbonsai.com. Email: info@kai zenbonsai.com.

Larchfield Bonsai. Tel: 02476 258802. Website: www.larchfieldtrees.com. Email: maples@larch fieldtrees.com.

Lee Verhorevoort Bonsai. Tel: 01322 528458. Website: www.lvbonsai.co.uk. Email: info:lvbon sai.co.uk.

Observatory Bonsai Nursery. Tel: 02920 484892. Website: www.observatorybonsai.co.uk.

Pete Witcomb. Trees for bonsai. Tel: 02476 614137. Email: petewitcomb@fsmail.net.

Pots by Baillie. Tel: 01875 852887. Email: jackybaillie@aol.com.

Reid Bonsai. Tel: 01945 464822. Email: sandy.reid@norfolk.gov.uk.

Totally Bonsai. Tel: 01452 381240. Email: johnbonsai@dsl.pipex.com.

Walsall Studio Ceramics. Tel: 01922 645707. Website: www.walsall-studio-ceramics.com. Email: sales@walsall-studio-cerAMics.com.

Windybank Bonsai. Bonsai trees, tools, pots and accessories. Tel: 02086 698847. Website: www.windybankbonsai.co.uk. Email: info@windybank bonsai.co.uk.

South America, Central America, and the Caribbean

• *Argentina* •

Asociación Bonsái del Centro Argentino–San Francisco

Asociación Platense de Bonsai "Los Tilos"

Asociación Santafesina de Cultivadores de Bonsai

Centro Cultural Argentino de Bonsai

• *Brazil* •

Associação Bonsai do Rio Grande do Sul — Bonsai Sul

Escuela Europea Bonsai Brasil, Nova Lima Brazil

• Chile •

Asociación Chilena de Bonsai Chile, Santiago
Bonsai Nebari, Santiago
Club Bonsai Chile, Santiago
Club de Bonsai de Chile, Instituto Chileno Japones, Santiago
Escuela Bonsai Kenzo, Santiago

• Colombia •

Asociación Vallecaucana de Bonsai, Cali, Colombia
Kibo Bonsai
TAO Bonsái, Antioquia, Colombia

• Costa Rica •

Asociación Costarricense de Bonsai, San José, Costa Rica, Acobonsai

• Dominican Republic •

Asociación Dominicana de Bonsai, Santo Domingo, Dominican Republica
Club Dominicano de Bonsai — Domsai

• Ecuador •

Club Bonsai de Guayaquil, Guayaquil, Ecuador
Club de Bonsai Cuenca, Ecuador

• Guadalupe •

Karukéra Bonsai Club

• Guyana Francesa •

Tipie Bwa

• Martinique •

Tropik Bonsai Club, Martinique, F.W.I.

• Panama •

Asociación Bonsai de las Cumbres
Asociación Bonsai de Panama, Panamá City, Panamá

• Peru •

Club Peruano de Bonsai, Lima, Peru

• Puerto Rico •

Federación Bonsai de Puerto Rico, San Juan, Puerto Rico

• St. Lucia •

Bonsai Society of St. Lucia, Castries, W.I.

• Venezuela •

Club Zuliano del Bonsai y la Conservación
Sociedad Conservacionista y de Bonsai, Valencia, Venezuela
Sociedad Venezolana de Bonsai, Caracas Venezuela

Asia

• Japan •

Nippon Bonsai Association. Contact: Mrs. Hisako F. Saito in the International Division or Ms. Dambara, their English speaking contact person. 8–1, Ikenohata 2-chome, Taito-ku, TOKYO 110 Japan. Tel: +81 3821 3059. Fax: +81 33828 9150. Website: http://www.bonsai-kyokai.or.jp/.

Nippon Suieski Association. http://www.suiseki-assn.gr.jp/

Omiya Bonsai Villages. There is a Bonsai Village (Bonsai-cho) near Omiya Koen station, there is also a smaller Bonsai village in Someya a suburb of Omiya City. Website: http://www.bonsaishoponline.com/bia/country/japan/omiya.shtml.

Fuyo-en. 96 Bonsai-cho, Tel: 048-666-2400.

Shouto-en. 90 Bonsai-cho, Tel: 048-652-1033. Bonsai tools, pots, and scissors.

Seikou-en. 268 Bonsai-cho, Tel: 048-663-3991.

Mansei-en. 285 Bonsai-cho, Tel: 048-663-3991.

Kyuka-en. 131 Bonsai-cho, Tel: 048-663-0423. Original tools sold here.

Tojyu-en. 247 Bonsai-cho, Tel: 048-663-3899

Ryuho-en. 236 Bonsai-cho, Tel: 048-663-2267.

Fukushima-en. 1515 Toro-cho, Tel: 048-663-2400.

The House of the Four Seasons. Tel: 048-664-1636.

Cherry Tree Street Kanraku-en. 261 Bonsai-cho. Tel: 81 48 663 3308.

Kanaderu Bonsai. 113 Bonsai-cho. Tel: y81 48 651 4162.

Ikko-en. 479 Bonsai-cho. Tel: 81 48 663 7943.

Taiko-en. 89 Bonsai-cho. Tel: 81 48 665 3443.

Shoto-en. 90 Bonsai-cho, Tel: 81 48 652 1033.

Bonsai Shiki-no-ie. 267-1 Bonsai-cho, Tel: 81-48-664-1636.

Minuma Green Center & Citizens' Garden. 2-94 Minuma Tel: 81-48-664-5915.

The Omiya Bonsai Art Museum, Saitama. 2-24-3 Toro-cho, Kita Ward, Saitama City, Saitama, 331-0804. Tel: 048-780-2091. Website: http://www.bonsai-art-museum.jp/index.php.

Kinashi Bonsai Village-Shikoku Island

Koju-en Nursery — Kyoto. Mini-Bonsai, pots. Located at 19 Karahashi Isono-cho, Minami-ku, Kyoto. Tel: 601-8462.

Major Bonsai Exhibition in Kyoto each year. Contact to your nearest JAL office for more details.

Koju-en Nursery. Has a webpage that contains a Bonsai exhibition schedule for Japan and information in English about the "All Japan Shohi-Bonsai Association."

World Bonsai Contest — Japan. International Bonsai Photo Contest. Mr. Saburo Kato, chairman of Nippon Bonsai Association.

The Taikan (Bonsai Museum). Obuse — near Nagano. Open 9:00 A.M. to 4:00 P.M., closed on Mondays and Tuesdays, the year-end and New Year holidays. Located at: 10-20 Dainichido, Obuse-machi. Tel: 026-247-3000. Website: http://www.bonsaishoponline.com/bia/country/japan/taikan.shtml.

Plum and Bonsai exhibitions of Keiunkan — Nagahama, Shiga. Located at 2-5 Minato-cho Nagahama, Shiga, Japan. Time 9AM to 4PM. Tel: 0749-62-4111.

All Japan Shohin-Bonsai Association. Located at 19 Karahashi Isono-cho, Minami-ku, Kyoto. Website: http://mini-bonsai.com/http://www.shohin-bonsai.org/.

Yamamoto — Garden Plant Producing Center. Located a walk from Yamamoto Station on the Hankyu Railway Takarazuka line. Takarazuka City Hyogo Prefecture.

Tokoname Bonsai Pottery. Located at 3-8 Sakae-machi, Tokoname, Aichi Prefecture. Tel: 0569-35-4309. Website: http://www.tokoname.or.jp/bonsai/.

Shunka-en Bonsai Garden — Tokyo. Open from 10:00 AM to 5:00 PM Tuesday through Sunday. For more information: Tel: (81) 3-3670-8622. Fax: (81) 3-3670-5884. Website: http://www.kunio-kobayashi.com/.

• *China* •

North China Region —

Beijing Botanical Garden. Located at the base of the Fragrant Hills, open from 6:30 A.M. to 8 P.M. every day. Take bus 360 (from the Beijing Zoo), bus 333 (from the Summer Palace), or direct your taxi to "Wofosi" or "Zhiwuyuan." Tel: 62591283. Website: http://www.bonsaishoponline.com/bia/country/china_north/beijing-botanical-garden.shtml.

Summer Palace (Yiheyuan). Located in Haidian District, some 12 kilometers northwest of the downtown. Website: http://www.travelchinaguide.com/cityguides/beijing/summer.htm.

BeiJing Bonsai — Beijing. Address: BeiJing Kyushu Hui Tong flower market, Bonsai Exhibition Area. Tel: 13439030118. Mr. Shi. Website: bonsai@beijingbonsai.com. Email: BeiJingbonsai@126.com.

Central China Region —

Shanghai Botanic Garden — Penjing Garden. http://www.bonsaishoponline.com/bia/country/china_central/shanghai-botanic-garden-p.shtml.

Garden and Display Greenhouses. 1100 Long Wu Road, Shanghai 200231. China. Tel: 86 21-64365523. Fax: 86 21-64703460. Email: shbg@gate.uninet.co.cn.

Suzhou — City of Gardens. Address: Gongyuan Road 12, Suzhou, Jiangsu, China, 215006. Tel: 0086-512-5219953. Fax: 0086-512-5223937. Email: szgarden@public1.sz.js.cn. Website: http://www.bonsaishoponline.com/bia/country/china_central/suzhou-city-of-gardens.shtml.

Wuhan City —

Yellow Crane Tower Pagoda, Wuhan City, Hubei Province

Cultural Stone Museum, Wuhan, Hubei Province

Hangzhou Bonsai Information. Across the street from the Tomb of Yue Fei. There is also Bonsai Garden near Huagang Park and Bonsai in the Hangzhou Flower Nursery.

Hangzhou Yongchin Trade Co., Ltd. Bonsai pot supplier located in China Garden City, Hangzhou, Zhejiang.

Yunfeng Gardens — Huzhou, Zhejiang — Zhejiang Yunfeng Gardens Co., Ltd. Nursery address: No. 1 Wanshan Road, Huzhou, Zhejiang, China (313000). Office: Room 4048 Guanfeng Building, South Street, Huzhou, Zhejiang, China (313000). Tel: 0086-572-2033665 or 0086-572 2058027. Fax: 0086-572-2033877. General Manager: Li Zhiliang. Contact Mrs. Jenny Wong: yunfenggardens@yahoo.cn.

Yixing, Jiangsu Bonsai.

Yixing Hongqi Pottery & Horticulture Co., Ltd. Shanqian Road Dingshu Yixing Jiangsu China PC:214221. Phone: 0086-510-7417328 or 0086-21-58926207. Fax:0086-510-7417328 or 0086-21-58926207. Mobile: 013301708755. President: Wu Zi Cheng: Email: hongqipottery@163.com. Vice President: Dai Zhen Hui: Email: Yixinghongqi@163.com.

South China Region—

BeiJing Bonsai—Beijing. Address: BeiJing Kyushu Hui Tong flower market Bonsai Exhibition Area. Tel: 13439030118. Mr. Shi—Email: bonsai @beijingbonsai.com. Email: BeiJingbonsai@126. com. Website: http://www.bonsaishoponline.com/ bia/country/china_north/beijing-botanical-garden. shtml.

Hong Kong and Kowloon—

The Man Lung Bonsai Garden. Located in the Hong Kong Baptist University, Kowloon Tong, Kowloon, Hong Kong. Tel: (852) 2339 7960. Websites: http://www.manlungpenjing.org/ and http://www.hkbu.edu.hk/spotlight/penjing2.htm.

Dr Wu's garden. Contact : Ms. Chan (secretary): Tel: 2524-2221. Website: http://www.bonsaishop online.com/bia/country/china_hk/dr-wus-garden. shtml.

Hong Kong Bonsai Association. Tel: 2785 9178.

Hong Kong Bonsai International Society. Tel: 2474 6702.

Kowloon Walled City Park—Kowloon. Open: 6.30 A.M.–11 P.M. daily; free admission. Website: http://www.lcsd.gov.hk/parks/kwcp/en/.

Ching Chung Koon Temple—New Territories. The temple complex is adjacent to Ching Chung LRT Station. Website: http://www.discoverhong kong.com/eng/touring/hkiidistricts/ta_dist_tuenl. jhtml.

More Information about Bonsai in China—

Suzhou Agrotechnical Secondary School. Wang Zhong Liang, president; 11 Xiyuan Road, Suzhou.

Pan Zhong Lian—Great Master of Miniature Trees and Rockery of China. Miniature Trees and Rockery Art Research Society of Zhejiang, Room 15-204, Fourth Building, Shuguang Xincun, Hangzhou. Ceng Ci Ping—East Gate, Dongjiao Park, Zhongshan Avenue.

Guangshou. Mr. Wang Xiao Ying—president. Yixing Lotus Pottery and Horticulture Co., Ltd, Shanghai Office No 4, Lane 2060 Xie Tu Road, Shanghai. Wu Jian Qiang—deputy director, Yixing Lotus Pottery and Horticulture Co Ltd, Dingsham, Yixing, Jiangsu 214221. Luo Guo-Xiong—director.

Shanghai Botanic Gardens. 1100 Long Wu Road, Shanghai. Jin Wan Li—director.

Nursery of Minhang. No 3045 Hu Min Road, Beiqiao, Shanghai.

Shanghai Flowers and Plants Co-op. Zhang Xing Taug—vice director, No 1621 North Bridge, Hu Ming Road, Shanghai.

• *The Philippines* •

Sagay City Bonsai Club, Inc. Sagay City, Negros Occidental, Philippines. Contact Persons: 1. Dr. Diego De Ocampo, Cueva St., Sagay City, Negros Occidental, Tel: 034 488 0186 2. Mr. John Delleva Jr., Purok Pasil, Zone 1, Cadiz City, Negros Occidental, Tel: No. 63 034 493 1624. Mobile: 63 921 489 3721. Email: landscape_johndel@yahoo.com. ph or bonsai_johndel@yahoo.com.ph.

Northern Cebu Bonsai Society. Society (NCBS) meets every first Sunday of the month. The venue is at the member's garden assigned by the group. Contact details and more information is available on their website.

Cebu Bonsai Society. The current president is Joselito M. Alansalon.

Mt. APO Bonsai Society. We are headquartered in Davao and meet on the last Sunday of every month. For the meeting venue or more information, please contact Rudy Cuba, PO Box 80422, Davao City 8000, Island of Mindanao. Tel/Fax: (6382) 235-1159. Email: rudycuba@yahoo.com.

Eastern Pangasinan Bonsai Club. Headed by Mr. Melchor Noynay and Mr. Jomer Pascua. The group meets every Saturday. For more details Email: jomeratsea@yahoo.com.

Mindanao Bonsai Society. Four chapters: *Metro Kidapawan Chapter* (2nd district of North Cotabato); *Midsayap-PALMA Chapter* (1st District of North Cotabato province; *Socsarge Chapter* (Southern Philippines); *Metro Davao Chapter* (Eastern Mindanao). MBS Officers: President—Herden Pedrajas, Vice Pres.—Antonio Bacus, Secretary—Eliezer Varon, Treasurer—Marcel Calungsud, MBS Advisor—Atty. Poncevic Ceballos.

Angeles Bonsai Club. Bonsai club in Angeles City, Pampanga.

Angono Bonsai Club. Bonsai club in Angono, Rizal.

Pangasinan Bonsai Society. Headed by Michael Morden.

Baguio-Benguet Bonsai Group. Headed by Dr. Noel de Leon.

Northern Luzon. Based in La Union and headed by Cliff Coloma.

La Union Bonsai Society. Bonsai Club in San Fernando City.

• *Taiwan* •

Chung Hua Bonsai, Suiseki & Old Pottery Association. 3rd Floor, No.128, Chun Hsiao E. Road, Sec.4, 106, Taipei, ROC. Tel: 886-2-2771-4323. Fax: 886-2-2771-0234. Website: http://www.cbsa. com.tw/.

Bonsai Association R.O.C. Taiwan. 13th Floor N° 179 DUN HWA, S. Road, Sec 1, Taipei, Taiwan. Fax: 886-2-2771-0234.

National Bonsai Association of Taiwan. No 110, 7F, Tien Mu East Rd, Taipei, Taiwan. Tel: 886-2-2874-3802 or 886-2-2871-8108. Email: a9728946 @ms8.hinet.net.

Taipei Bonsai & Artistic Stone Association. Tel: 886 2 2823 3043. Fax: 886 2 2821 2720.

Chang Ta-ch'ien's Memorial Residence. In the grounds of The National Palace Museum. Located at 221 Chi-shaun Rd, Sec 2, Wai-shuang-hsi, Taipei. Open Monday–Friday except National Holidays. Please call or write in advance to arrange a visit. Tel: 2881-2021 ext 384. Website: http://www.npm.gov.tw/english/live/nvs/le.htm.

Jianguo Weekend Flower Market. The five National Bonsai Associations are as follows: Chung Hua Bonsai, Suiseki & Old Pottery Association; Taiwan Bonsai, Creator Association; Far Fong Bonsai Association; Chang Hua Ficus Bonsai Association; Ya Fong (Mini-size) Bonsai Association.

• *Korea* •

The Korea Bonsai Association. Lists Bonsai growers, Pot and tool suppliers all across Korea. Address: 84-23, Poongsan-dong, Hanam City, Kyonggi, Korea. Tel: 82-347-794-5082, FAX: 82-347-794-5101. Website: http://www.koreabonsai.com/.

Achim Goyo Arboretum (Morning Calm). Near Seoul; for information and inquiries: Tel: 031-584-6703 (Kor). Website: http://www.morningcalm.co.kr (Kor/Eng). Hours: (May–October) 09:00–20:00 /(November-April) 09:00 to 18:00. During special exhibition periods or holidays the opening hours may be extended. See also: http://www.bonsaishoponline.com/bia/country/korea/achim-goyo-arboretum-morn.shtml.

Korean Bonsai Museum — Seocho-gu, Seoul—Korean Bonsai Research Institute. Address: 205-6, Woo Myun-Dong, Seocho-Gu, Seoul. Tel: 02 577-0001-3 Mobile: 017-244-9191 Website: http://www.bonsaitv.com/.

Sun You Bonsai Nursery. Near Seoul; address: E-1 Goyang Hwa Hwe Danji. 1262 Won Dang-Dong, Deok Yang-Gu, Goyang-Si. Tel: +82 31 966 2228. Fax: +82 31 966 2298.

• *India* •

The Indian Bonsai Association–Delhi. Contact: Dr. Hari Om Ahuja, B-17, D.D.A Flats, Saket, New Delhi 110017, INDIA. Tel: 98100 01697. Email: hariom.ahuja@gmail.com.

Friends Bonsai Society. In the State of Andhra Pradesh; Dr. Pushpa Jaywant.

Ahmedabad Bonsai Club (ABC), Gujarat, India. The website has information.

Bonsai Club of Ahmedabad, Parag Mehta. Located at: 22, Laxminagar Society, Opp. D.K. Patel Hall, Naranpura, Ahmedabab — 380 013. Tel: 9227207984. Email: bonsai@bonsaiclubofahmedabad.com.

Bonsai Society in Jamshedpur. Address is Sidhartha Marketing Co., Rekhi Mansion, Diagonal road, Bistupur, Jamshedpur 831001. Tel: 2435998, 221448, 09334825981. Fax: 2438462. We are also running a Bonsai society in Jamshedpur. Contact Naresh Agarwal at the above address or Email: smcjsr77@gmail.com.

Bonsai Club of Baroda. Baroda City & in the Gujrat state of India. Contact: Pravin Baviskar. Email: p_baviskar@hotmail.com.

Bonsai Club (India)–Chandigarh. Contact Anil Kaushik, 5749 Sector 38 West, Chandigarh 160014 (India). Tel: +91 172 93165 95050. Email: anilkaushik@hotmail.com.

Bonsai Society of Madhya Pradesh–Bhopal. Contact: Bonsai Society of Madhya Pradesh, E-5/76 Arera Colony, Bhopal (M.P.) 462016 or Vivek Shukla. Email: shuklavivek@mailcity.com.

Vriksha Bonsai Club–Banglore. Contact: Tel: 91-80-2250474 or Anita Agrawal. Email: natnagar@yahoo.com.

Bonsai Club of India–Nanital, U.P. Contact: C/O Bonsai Hut, Forest Colony, D-2 F.T.I., Rampur Rd, Haldwani, Nanital, U.P. Tel: 05946-21855,20853 (ext-251). Email: jsuhag@yahoo.com.

Kerala Bonsai Association. Gen. Secretary K. P. Sairaj. Email: kp_sai@yahoo.com.

Ansaris Bonsai Society. Email: loveeu_ansari@yahoo.com.

Amateur Bonsai Growers–Bilaspur (CG). Dr. S. K. Gidwani.

Avadh Bonsai Association–Charbagh, Lucknow. C/o Santosh Arora, Vidya Vihar, 8-A.P. Sen Road, Charbagh, Lucknow 226001,INDIA. Contact: Santosh Arora Tel: 91-522-2635 702. Email: kkarora15@sify.com.

Bonsai Study Group–Mumbai. Preyas, 20 Dadyseth Road, Babulnath, Mumbai, 400007, INDIA. Tel: 91-22-3679762. Fax: 91-22-3878639. Email: nikunjyo@bom2.vsnl.net.in.

India Friendship Bonsai Society–Mumbai. 102, Nilgiri, Lokhandwala Complex, Andheri (West) Mumbai, Maharastra 400053,India. Contact: Sujay Shah Tel: +91-22-6345813. Fax: +91-22-6314106. Email: rupas@vsnl.com.

Bonsai Lovers of Bihar–Patna. Dr. K. M. Singh, project director, Agril. Technology Management Agency, Collectorate Campus, Vikas Bhawan, Patna-1, Bihar. Email: krish_sinh@sify.com or Email: krish-sinh@hotmail.com.

Mrs. SuryaNarmada Inbavijayan–Chennai. D 103/A, Sowbagya Colony, K. K. Nagar, Chennai — 600 078, Tamilnadu, India. Tel: +91-98402 13912. Email Mrs. SuryaNarmada. Email: suryanarmada@yahoo.com.

Kishkinda Moolika Bonsai Garden–Mysore. Sri Avadhoota Datta Peetha in Mysore, India. Website: http://www.bonsaishoponline.com/bia/country/india/kishkinda-moolika-bonsai.shtml.

Naresh Agarwa–Jamshedpur. Address is Sidhartha Marketing Co., Rekhi mansion, Diagonal road, Bistupur, Jamshedpur 831001. Tel: 2435998, 221448, 09334825981. Fax: 2438462. We are also running a Bonsai society in Jamshedpur. Contact Naresh Agarwal at the above address or: Email: smcjsr77@gmail.com. Website: http://www.nare shagarwala.com/.

Ssurup Bonsai Village–Panvel. Website: http:// www.bonsaishoponline.com/bia/country/india/ssu rup-bonsai-village.shtml.

Bonsai Wonder. Display at NTR Memorial Park, Hyderabad.

Bonsai_Rao.com–Hyderabad & Secunderabad. Website: http://www.geocities.ws/bonsai_rao/index -2.html.

Kapilaa's Creations — Pimpri–Pune–Maharastra. Tel: (020) 27464082. Website: http://www.kapi laascreations.com/gallery.html. Email: kapilaas@ yahoo.co.in.

BonsaiIndia.net–Shamsher and Kanwaljit Deol. Website: http://bonsaiindia.net/.

The Mughal Gardens–Rashtrapati Bhavan. Mughal Gardens is attached to the main building of the Rashtrapati Bhavan. The Mughal Gardens are open to the public February–March every year. The entry and exit into the gardens will be regulated from Gate no. 35 of the President's Estate, which is located near the North Avenue, at the western end of the Church Road.

The Agri Horticultural Society of India–Kolkata. Located at 1 Alipore Road, Kolkata. Website: http://www.agrihorticultureindia.com/bonsai.html.

Bonsai World, A. M. Mohammed. good quality bonsai pots and tools

Green Grower Garden Centre–Mumbai. Our bonsai exhibition is open Monday through Saturday from 9:30 A.M. to 6:00 P.M. Mahatma Gandhi Sewa Mandir, Opp. Bandra Talao, S.V. Road, Bandra (West), Mumbai–400 050. INDIA. Tel: 91-22-2641 5985 or 2642 7094. Fax: 91-22-2643 6029. Email: ggrower@pcil.co.in.

• *Thailand* •

Thailand's Bonsai Capital–Ratchaburi Province. Khao Raeng District–Ratchaburi province is 120 km southwest of Bangkok.

Suan Chatuchak Market–Bangkok. Located on Phahonyothin Road diagonally opposite the Northern Bus Terminal. The Weekend Market is open on Saturdays and Sundays from 7:00 A.M. to 6:00 P.M.

Chatuchak (Jatujak) Plants Market–Bangkok. Near Chatuchak Market

Thewet Market–Bangkok. Found off Samsen Road, on Khlong Phadung Krung Kasem, Bangkok.

Pak Khlong Talat Market–Bangkok. Located on Maha Rat Road near the Memorial Bridge.

Million Years Stones Park & Crocodile Farm–Pattaya. Located 9 kilometers from Pattaya township. The hours of operation are 8:30–18:00 daily. Website: http://www.welkominnthailand.com/ epg_crocol farm.htm. See also: http://www.bon saishoponline.com/bia/country/thailand/chiang-mai.shtml.

• *Vietnam* •

The Vietnam Natural and Traditional Beauty Association (SIVACAVINA). Website: http://www. geocities.com/bonsai-in-asia/vietnam4.html.

Bonsai garden at Binh Hoa Phuoc Island–Vinh Long. Website: http://www.bonsaishoponline. com/bia/country/vietnam/Vietnam-Bonsai-garden. shtml.

Mr. Giao's house and Bonsai garden–Vinh Long. Rent a boat and travel on the Mekong 30 minutes from Vinh Long to Mr. Giao's house and Bonsai garden. (Binh Thuan II Hamlet, Hoa Ninh Village, Vinh Long Province; no phone).

Bonsai Tours Viet Nam. Tel: 84. 82247.8282 or 84. 913.915.974. Email: info@bonsaitoursvn.com. Website: http://www.bonsaitoursvn.com/.

Bonsai in Ho Chi Minh City–Saigon—Thanh Tam Nursery. The address is: 8/2 Thuan Kieu Hamlet (Tan Thoi Nhat Village–Hoc Mon); Tel: 920779.

Bonsai and Silk Embroidery Pictures–Ho Chi Minh City (Saigon). Call first. The address is: A13/32 Hung Vuong, An Lac, Binh Chanh, Ho Chi Minh City. Tel: 87544345 or Mobile: 090805545.

Bonsai Garden–Sa Dec. Head south from Ho Chi Minh City.

• *Pakistan* •

Pakistan Bonsai Society. PBS meets six times. 7-10 Hina Palace, Civil Lines, Hoshang Road, Karachi — 75530. Pakistan. Tel: 5689823-25, 5685070. Fax: 5685070. Mr. Muhammad Ovais. Email: sbsnet@cyber.net.pk.

• *Singapore* •

Singapore Penjing & Stone Appreciation Society. President: Mdm. Chua Kwei Foon. Vice President: Lim Keow Wah. Members meet in Singapore every Sunday from 2:00 to 6:00 P.M. at 200 Turf Club Road, Turf City (near Car Park C), Singapore 287994. Tel: 65 97363710. Website: http://www. bonsaishoponline.com/bia/country/singapore/index. shtml.

• *Malaysia* •

Malaysia Bonsai and Suiseki Society–Kuala Lumpur. The Society holds bonsai workshops every Sunday from 10:00 A.M. to noon at its current club premises at Pyrus Garden, 32, Jalan Nyaman 12, Bukit Indah, off Jalan Kelang Lama, 58200 Kuala Lumpur. Malaysia Bonsai & Suiseki Society, No 95, Jalan Rukun Lima, 58200 Kuala Lumpur, Malaysia. Tel: 603-79809706. Fax: 603-79840548. Email: rsee@nasioncom.net. Website: http://members.tripod.com/~ahassan_2/index/index.html. See also: http://www.bonsaifun.com/.

Classic Bonsai and Suiseki Collection Enterprise–Kuala Lumpur. 2, Jalan Bukit Maluri 8 (Jalan 8/37), Taman Bukit Maluri, Kepong, Kuala Lumpur. Mr. S. L. Ong, Tel: 03-62769192 or 012-3325793.

Pusat Bonsai Hobby–Petaling Jaya. No: 1, Sek 10/1, Jalan Gasing, Petaling Jaya, 46000. Selangor. Mr. Yap Choo: Tel: 603-79568639 or 019-442544.

Zheng Buk Bonsai Nursery Centre–Kuala Lumpor. 50, Kepong Ulu, Kepong, 52100 Kuala Lumpor. Tel: 019-2136089.

Caines Nursery & Bonsai Centre–Pegtalin Jaya. 62, Jalan SSI/32, 47300 Pegtalin Jaya, Selangor. Tel: 603-78751362 or 78769871. Fax: 603-78751650.

Kejuteraan Kesenian Hua May (M) SDN BHD–Kuala Lumpur. No: 138-E, Batu 3, Jalan Kelang Lama, 58000 Kuala Lumpur. Tel: 603-7821211. Fax: 603-7800422.

Lee Nursery & Bonsai Centre–Kuala Lumpar. Batu 7, Jalan Puchong, Mukim Petaling, 57100 Kuala Lumpar. Tel: 012-2152055 or 012-3788761.

Sri Taman Nursery & Florist–Kuantan. Lot 1/3547, Jalan Tengku Mohamad, 25050 Kuantan, Pahang D.M. Tel: 09-5684616 or 010-9890911.

Taman Sui Mei Bonsai Centre–Melaka. No: 1, Jalan Zahir 8, 75250 Melaka. Tel: 06-3359698, 011-662297 or 019-6550199.

Ah Peng Bonsai Centre–Melaka. 317-1, Lorong Tiga, Pokok Mangga, Batu 3, 75200, Melaka, Malaysia.

Taman Bunga Loh–Melaka. 5896-C, Bt 4, Klebang Besar, 75200 Melaka. Tel: 06-3152385.

Min Hoe Yuen Bonsai Nurseries–Melaka. 28-C, Tanjong Minyak, 75250 Melaka. Mr. Pang Hoi Chan, Tel: 06-3355620 or 012-6810628.

Pang Siew Yew Father & Son Bonsai Garden–Melaka. I C, Bertam Ulu, 76450 Melaka. Tel: 06-3123973 or 06-3121348.

Seremban–Seremban. Mr. Raymond Chew, Wisma CE, No: 340–342, Taman Bukit Emas, Jalan Tampin, 70450 Seremban. 019-6610198.

Pin Bonsai Nursery Centre–Perak. Lot 65582, Jalan Raja Musa Mahadi, Sri Ampang, 31650 lpoh, Perak. Tel: 05-3129452 or 019-5131116.

Winson Gardening Supplies–Johor. No: A2, Jalan Mengkibol, 86000 Kluang, Johor. Tel: 07-7731437 or 019-7755005. Mr. Chiang Kim Soon, No: 28, Jalan Seladang 2, Taman Mohd Yassin, 86200 Simpang Rengam, Johor. Mr. Choo Hock Hee: Tel: 07-7556306.

Kebun Bunga Meng Bonsai Dan Landscape–Johor. Batu 4 1/2 Jalan Kluang, Batu Pahat, Johor. Tel: 07-4347055 or 010-7264177.

Great Dragon Bonsai Centre–Mantin. 1180, Batu 12½, 71700 Mantin, Negeri Sembilan Darul Khusus.

Parklane Bonsai–Sibuga. 1732, Jalan 3, Taman Sibuga.

Yi Fong Stone Gallery–Kajang. 137, Taman Sg, Chua, 43000 Kajang, Selangor Darul Ehsan. Tel: 03-87370585.

• *Indonesia* •

The Indonesian Bonsai Association (PPBI). Website: http://www.bonsaishoponline.com/bia/country/indonesia/the-indonesian-bonsai-ass.shtml.

Cebu Bonsai Society and Cebu Suiseki Society–Bali-Sanur. Nurseries are located in Sanur close to main tourist areas. Website: http://www.bonsai-in-asia.com/bali/index.shtml.

Jakarta–Utara–Pluit Bonsai Centre. Located at Jl. Taman Pluit Putra Putri, Jakarta Utara.

Aneka Bonsai Unggulan–Jakarta. Jl. Taman Pluit Putra Putri Blok-III, Jakarta Utara. Tel: +62-21-6693956. Mobile: +62-818-810018. Fax: +62-21-6620640. Email: bonsaiindonesia@netscape.net.id.

Bonsai Indonesia–Jakarta. Sulistyo, Budi, Sentra Bonsai Pluit Blok 3 Kav 1, Jl Pluit Putri Raya, Jakarta 14450. Tel: (62) 811861046. Fax: (62) (21) 5814783. Email: budisulistyo@yahoo.com.

Aries Bonsai–Jakarta. Jl. Budi Raya Terusan, Komplek Pajak (Kemanggisan), Jakarta Barat, Tel:+62-812-9198822.

Bonsai Pluit Prima–Jakarta. Jl. Taman Pluit Putra Putri, Blok-A II & B II Kav. 22-24,Jakarta Utara. Tel: +62-21-5802204. Mobile: +62-816-1162006. Email: rinsteve@centrin.net.id.

Flora mega–Jakarta. Jl. Taman Pluit Putra Putri, Blok-A II & B II Kav.41-42, Jakarta Utara. Tel: +62-21-64700505. Mobile: +62-816-1368555.

Harmonic Tropical Bonsai–Jakarta. Jl. Taman Pluit Putra Putri, Blok-A II Kav. 46-48, Jakarta Utara. Tel:/Fax: +62-21-5404094. Mobile: +62-811-878020.

Ideal Flora–Jakarta. Jl. Taman Pluit Putra Putri, Blok-A II Kav.34-35, Jakarta Utara. Tel: +62-21-6601354. Fax: +62-21-493886. Mobile: +62-818-161009.

Indraloka Bonsai–Jakarta. Jl. lndraloka III No. 30, Kav. Polri Blok-G XI, RT 005/06,Kel. Wijaya Kusuma Jakarta 11460. Tel: +62-21-5604379.

Jakarta Bonsai Centre–Jakarta. Jl. Taman Pluit Putra Putri, Jakarta Utara. Tel: +62-816-861881.

Nobel Gallery Bonsai–Jakarta. Jl. Budi Raya Terusan Kebon Jeruk (Kemanggisan), Jakarta Barat, Tel: +62-21-9212210 or 8755088, Mobile: +62-816-1914846.

Marka Bonsai Appliances Centre–Jakarta. Jl. Taman Pluit Putra Putri, Blok-A II & B II Kav. 29-31, Jakarta Utara. Tel: +62-21-3863076 or 34833358 or 34833359. Fax: +62-21-3459486 or 6599033. Email: markAMtr@cbn.net.id.

Subur Bonsai–Jakarta. Jl. Taman Pluit Putra Putri, Blok-A II Kav. 20-21, Jakarta Utara. Mobile: +62-818-197485.

Wahyu–Jakarta. Jl. Surya Nirmala Blok 0 No.14, Sunrise Garden, Kedoya, Jakarta 11520—Indonesia. Tel: +62-21-580220 or 580440 or 5806103, Fax: +62-21-5800528 or 5806102.

Tangerang—West Java—

Sams Bonsai–Tangerang. Bonardo Sianturi, Menjual Bahan Bonsai, bonsai 1/2 jadi dan Bonsai Koleksi. Graha Raya Bintaro, Cl. Fedora blok J3/11, Serpong-Tangerang. Tel: 088-8837-8838 or 021-98597343. Email: bosian2002@yahoo.com.

Kiki Bonsai–Tangerang. Jl. Perintis Kemerdekaan I No. 2, Tangerang–Jawa Barat. Tel: +62-21-5915391.

Hari Bonsai–Tangerang. Jl. Perintis Kemerdekaan I No. 1, Tangerang–Jawa Barat. Tel: +62-21-5530139.

Puncak—West Java—

Nuansa Bonsai Pasekon–Jawa Barat. Jl. Gadog I Farmasi No. 43, Cipanas, Cianjur 43253–Jawa Barat. Tel: +62–263–516860. Mobile: +62–816–1810858.

Gariand Landscaping & Nurseries–Jawa Barat. Kampung Pasir Madin RT 08 No. 4, Cisarua–Jawa Barat. Tel: +62–251–253492.

Bandung—

Bonsai Star Gallery–Jawa Barat. Jl. Cibaligo No. 38, Cimahi, Bandung–Jawa Barat. Tel: (62)-(022)-6030030. Email: bunjasmal711@bdg.centrin.net.id.

Tedy Boy Bonsai–Bangung. Ruko Jl. Sanggar Kancana 27 No.2, Komp Sanggar Hurip, Soekamo Hatta–Bangung 40286. Tel/Fax: 62–22–7304238 or 62–8122025958. Email: bigboybonsai@bdg.centrin.net.id.

Istana Bonsai–Jawa Barat. Jl. Cibaligo No. 38 Km. 1, Cimahi, Bandung–Jawa Barat. Tel: +62-22-6030027. Fax: +62-22-6033180.

Beauty Bonsai Nursery–Jawa Barat. Jl. Cilamaya No. 3, Bandung 40115–Jawa Barat. Tel: +62-22-4205364. Fax: +62-22-4218145

Central Java—

Antik Jaga Furniture–Jawa Tengah. Prayitno, Agus (or) Sydorov, Yevgeniy, Raya Batealit, Bawu RT 07/02, Batealit, Jepara 59461, Central Java. Tel: +62 291 595920 or 596138. Fax:+62 291 595920.

Griya Puspita Bonsai–Jawa Tengah. Jl. Raya Bandungan, Dsn. Kemloko, Kel. Bergas Kidul Kec. Bergas, Bandungan–Jawa Tengah. Tel: +62-298-522088.

East Java—

Aldy Bonsai Gallery. Jl. Raya Mojorejo No. 99 Batu, Malang–Jawa Timur Tel: +62-341-598734.

Ud "Artha." Jl. Bukit Berbunga Sidomulyo No. 1 (Jl. Brantas Sidomulyo No. 1) Bumiaji, Batu, Malang—Jawa Timur. Tel: +62-341-591681.

Jambi—Sumatra—

Bajubang Nursery. Bajubang, Jambi. Tel: +62-743-21364. Mobile:. +62-811-744566.

Australia and New Zealand

Auckland Bonsai Society (NZ). Address: The Secretary, AABC Ltd, PO Box 513, Ascot Vale VIC 3032. Email secretary@aabcltd.org.

Avon Bonsai Society (NZ). Address: The Secretary, AABC Ltd, PO Box 513, Ascot Vale VIC 3032. Email: secretary@aabcltd.org.

Bairnsdale Bonsai Group–Ascot Vale. Public Contact Address: The Secretary, AABC Ltd, PO Box 513, Ascot Vale VIC 3032. Email: juliet.miskin@gmail.com. Club regular meetings alternate months.

Ballarat Bonsai Society Inc.–Ballarat. Public Contact Address: The Secretary, PO Box 614 W, Ballarat West VIC 3350. Email: rhaines@vic.australis.com.au. Regular club meetings on the first Thursday of the month (except January), at 7:30 P.M., at the Robert Clarke Centre, Ballarat Botanical Gardens, Ballarat.

Bayside Bonsai Club–Ascot Vale. Address: The Secretary, AABC Ltd, PO Box 513, Ascot Vale VIC 3032. Email: ernmacl@bigpond.com.au. Regular club meetings on the second Saturday of each month, 1:00 P.M. to 4:00 P.M.

Bendigo Bonsai Club Inc.–Bendigo. Address: The Secretary, PO Box 889, Bendigo VIC 3550. Email: bendigobonsaiclub@bigpond.com. Regular club meetings on the fourth Saturday of the month, at the Community of Christ Hall, 60 Havlin Street West, Bendigo (except December and January).

Bimer Bonsai Club Inc.–Geebung. Address: The

Secretary, PO Box 64, Geebung QLD 4034. Email: info@bimerbonsai.org.au. Regular club meetings first Saturday of the month, from 1:30 P.M. to 4:30 P.M., at the Church Hall, Jaguar Street, West Chermside (except January).

Bonsai Interest Group–Ascot Vale. Address: The Secretary, AABC Ltd, PO Box 513, Ascot Vale VIC 3032. Email: mike.robyn@bigpond.com.

Bonsai Northwest Inc.–Yarraville. Address: The Secretary, PO Box 222, Yarraville VIC 3013. Email: information@bonsainorthwest.com.au. Regular club meetings occur the first Monday of the month, at 8.00 P.M., at the Yarraville Club, 135 Stephen Street, Yarraville, except January.

Bonsai Society of Australia Inc.–Ascot Vale. Address: The Secretary, AABC Ltd, PO Box 513, Ascot Vale VIC 3032. Email: dare37@bigpond.com. Regular club meetings first Tuesday of the month, at 8:00 P.M., at the West Pennant Hills Community Centre, 42A Hill Road, West Pennant Hills (except December).

Bonsai Society of Queensland Inc.–Banyo. Address: The Secretary, GPO Box 212, Banyo QLD 4014. Email: mail@bonsaisocietyqld.asn.au. Regular club meetings occur on the third Saturday of the month, at 1:30 P.M., at the Mt. Gravatt Show Grounds (except December).

Bonsai Society of Sydney Inc.–Ascot Vale. Public Contact Address: The Secretary, AABC Ltd, PO Box 513, Ascot Vale VIC 3032. Email: secretary@aabcltd.org. Regular club meetings occur at the Imperial Gardens and Bonsai Art, 18 Myoora Road, Terrey Hills.

Bonsai Society of the Central Coast Inc.–Wamberal. Address: The Secretary, PO Box 3676, Wamberal NSW 2260. Email: deniseallen@westnet.com.au. Regular club meetings second Tuesday of the month, from 7:30 P.M. to 10:00 P.M., at the Gosford City Arts Centre, Webb Street, East Gosford (except January).

Bonsai Society of Victoria Inc.–Diamond Creek. Address: The Secretary, PO Box 118, Diamond Creek VIC 3089. Email: secbonsaivic@optusnet.com.au. Regular club meetings occur on the fourth Monday of the month at 8:00 P.M. at Kew Masonic Centre, 31–33 Strathalbyn Street, East Kew (except December).

Bonsai Society of Western Australia Inc.–Myaree. Address: The Secretary, 10 Choules Place, WA 6154. Email: commitee@bonsaisocietywa.com. Regular club meetings occur on the last Monday of each month, at 7:30 PM, at the Collins Street Centre, Corner Collins and Shaftesbury Streets, South Perth (except December).

Bonsai Study Group–Lindfield. Address: The Secretary, PO Box 201, Lindfield NSW 2070. Email: jtapner@bigpond.net.au.

Cairns Bonsai Society Inc.–Cairns. Address: The Secretary, AABC Ltd, PO Box 513, Ascot Vale VIC 3032. Email: secretary@aabcltd.org. Regular club meetings occur on the first Saturday of the month, from 12:30 P.M. to 4:30 P.M., at the C.W.A. Hall, Grove Street, Cairns (except January).

Campbelltown Bonsai Group Inc.–Ascot Vale. Address: The Secretary, AABC Ltd, PO Box 513, Ascot Vale VIC 3032. Email: secretary@aabcltd.org. Regular club meetings occur every Monday night for four terms a year at the Ruse Community Centre, Oberon Street, Ruse. Starting at 7:30 P.M. until approximately 9:30 to 10:00 P.M.

Canberra Bonsai Society Inc.–Woden. Address: The Secretary, PO Box 800, Woden ACT 2606. Email: secretary@cbs.org.au. Regular club meetings first Saturday of each month, from 9.30 A.M. to 1:30 P.M., at the Hughes Community Centre, Wisdom Street, Hughes. Website: www.cbs.org.au.

Christchurch Bonsai Society (NZ)–Ascot Vale. Address: The Secretary, AABC Ltd, PO Box 513, Ascot Vale VIC 3032. Email: secretary@aabcltd.org.

Coffs Harbour Inc.–Coffs Harbour. Address: The Secretary. AABC Ltd, PO Box 513, Ascot Vale VIC 3032. Email: secretary@aabcltd.org. Regular club meetings first Saturday of the month, at 1:30 P.M., at the Fellowship Hall, Uniting Church, Gordon Street, Coffs Harbour.

Friends of the Orange Botanic Gardens Bonsai Group–Ascot Vale. Address: The Secretary, AABC Ltd, PO Box 513, Ascot Vale VIC 3032 Email: secretary@aabcltd.org.

Geelong Bonsai Club Inc.–Ascot Vale. Address: The Secretary, AABC Ltd, PO Box 513, Ascot Vale VIC 3032. Email: secretary@aabcltd.org. Regular club meetings occur on the first Monday of each month at Memorial Hall, Reserve Road, Grovedale (except January). Other Information: The Geelong Bonsai Club Inc. Website: http://www.geelongbonsaiclub.tk/.

Gold Coast Tweed Bonsai Club Inc.–Mudgeeraba. Address: The Secretary, PO Box 257, Mudgeeraba QLD 4213. Email: the.tarrants@bigpond.com. Regular club meetings occur on the second Saturday of the month, at 1:30 P.M., at the Elanora Community Hall, Galleon Way, Currumbin Waters.

Goldfields Bonsai Club–Ascot Vale. Address: The Secretary, AABC Ltd, PO Box 513, Ascot Vale VIC 3032. Email: secretary@aabcltd.org.

Goulburn Bonsai Society Inc.–Goulburn. Address: The Secretary, PO Box 580, Goulburn NSW 2580. Email: kachmica@goulburn.net.au. Regular club meetings occur on the last Sunday of each month (except December and January) at the Guide Hall, Faithful Street, Goulburn.

Hamilton Bonsai Club (NZ)–Hamilton. Address: The Secretary, AABC Ltd, PO Box 513,

Ascot Vale VIC 3032. Email: moyogi@xtra.co.nz. Regular club meetings are on the second Wednesday of the month, at 7:30 P.M., October to April. They are on the second Sunday of the month at 2:00 P.M., May to September. Location: Glenview Community Centre, Hamilton, New Zealand.

Illawarra Bonsai Society Inc.–Gymea. Address: The Secretary, PO Box 294, Jannali NSW 2226. Email: secretary@aabcltd.org. Regular club meetings occur on the third Monday of each month at 7:30 P.M., February to December, at the Gymea Community Centre, 39 Gymea Bay Road, Gymea.

Launceston Bonsai Workshop–Ascot Vale. Address: The Secretary, AABC Ltd, PO Box 513, Ascot Vale VIC 3032. Email: secretary@aabcltd.org. Regular club meetings occur on the first and third Wednesday evenings, from 7:00 P.M. to 9:00 P.M., from March to November at Riverside. Contact Lynne Farrell, Tel: 0417 581 080.

Mackay Bonsai Society–Mackay. Address: The Secretary, AABC Ltd, PO Box 513, Ascot Vale VIC 3032. Email: secretary@aabcltd.org. Regular club meetings occur on the last Sunday of each month, at 1:30 P.M., at the Botanical Gardens Room, Lagoon Street, Mackay. At times the Mackay Botanical Gardens are unavailable in which case please call Tel: (07) 4954 8447 for alternate arrangements.

Mornington Peninsula Bonsai Society Inc.–Rosebud. Address: The Secretary, PO Box 79, Rosebud VIC 3939. Email: byers@satlink.com.au. Regular club meetings first and third Wednesday of the month, at 7:30 P.M., at the Moorooduc Hall, corner Bentons and Derrill Rds., Moorooduc, Victoria (except December).

Mount Gambier Bonsai Society Inc.–Ascot Vale. Address: The Secretary, AABC Ltd, PO Box 513, Ascot Vale VIC 3032. Email: secretary@aabcltd.org. Regular club meetings occur on the third Tuesday of the month.

Nepean Bonsai Society Inc.–Penrith. Address: The Secretary, PO Box 1176, Penrith NSW 2751. Email: info@nepeanbonsaisociety.org. Regular club meetings fourth Sunday of each month, at 2:00 P.M., at North Penrith Community Centre, 66B Illawong Avenue, Kingswood Park (except December).

Newcastle Bonsai Society Inc.–Kotara. Address: The Secretary, PO Box 521, Kotara NSW 2289. Email: d.wood@internode.on.net. Tel: 0418 226 068. Regular club meetings second Saturday of the month and an all day workshop commencing at 10:00 A.M., at the Mt Hutton Girl Guides Hall, Lamington Drive (off Burton Road), Mt Hutton.

Otago Bonsai Society (NZ)–Ascot Vale. Address: The Secretary, AABC Ltd, PO Box 513, Ascot Vale VIC 3032. Email: secretary@aabcltd.org.

Peel Valley Bonsai Club–Tamworth. Address: The Secretary, Tamworth Regional Craft Centre, 109 Peel St, Tamworth NSW 2340. Email: secretary@aabcltd.org. Regular club meetings occur on first Saturday of the month at the Tamworth Regional Craft Centre, 109 Peel Street, Tamworth.

Redlands Bonsai Society Inc.–Victoria Point. Address: The Secretary, PO Box 5291, Victoria Point QLD 4164. Email: secretary@aabcltd.org. Regular club meetings first Saturday of the month, from 1:00 P.M. to 5:00 P.M., at the Scout Hall, Cnr Gordon and Bainbridge Streets, Ormiston.

Sakura Bonsai Studio Inc.–Brookvale. Address: The Secretary, AABC Ltd, PO Box 513, Ascot Vale VIC 3032. Email: secretary@aabcltd.org. Regular club meetings second Sunday of each month, at the Manly-Warringah Rugby League Club, unlicensed premises at Federal Parade, Brookvale (first floor of car park).

Sale Bonsai Club Inc.–Ascot Vale. Address: The Secretary, AABC Ltd, PO Box 513, Ascot Vale VIC 3032. Email: secretary@aabcltd.org. Regular club meetings occur on the first Saturday of the month (except January). Please contact the secretary for the location.

Shoalhaven Bonsai Club–Werri Beach. Address: The Secretary, AABC Ltd, PO Box 513, Ascot Vale VIC 3032. Email: secretary@aabcltd.org. Regular club meetings third Sunday of the month, at 2:00 P.M., at Werri Beach, Progress Hall on Pacific Avenue, Werri Beach (except December).

South Australian Bonsai Society Inc.–Goodwood. Address: The Secretary, PO Box 159, Goodwood SA 5034. Email: secretary@aabcltd.org. Regular club meetings first Tuesday of the month, at 8:00 P.M., and the third Tuesday of the month, at 7.30 P.M., at the Goodwood Community Centre, Rosa Street, Goodwood.

Southern Bonsai Club Inc.–Ascot Vale. Address: The Secretary, AABC Ltd, PO Box 513, Ascot Vale VIC 3032. Email: secretary@aabcltd.org.

Southlakes Bonsai Club Inc.–Ascot Vale. Address: The Secretary, AABC Ltd, PO Box 513, Ascot Vale VIC 3032. Email: secretary@aabcltd.org.

Suiseki Australia Inc.–North Rocks. Address: The Secretary, AABC Ltd, PO Box 513, Ascot Vale VIC 3032. Email: secretary@aabcltd.org. Regular club meetings third Wednesday of every month, to coincide with school holidays, at the Don Moore Community Centre, North Rocks Road, North Rocks, NSW.

Summerland Bonsai Society Inc.–Lismore. Address: The Secretary, AABC Ltd, PO Box 513, Ascot Vale VIC 3032. Email: kol83669@bigpond.net.au. Regular club meetings second Saturday of the month, at 1:30 P.M., at the Uniting Church Hall, Keen Street, Lismore.

Sunshine Coast Bonsai Society Inc.–Woombye. Address: The Secretary, AABC Ltd, PO Box 513, Ascot Vale VIC 3032. Email: secretary@aabcltd.org. Regular club meetings fourth Saturday of each month, 1:30 P.M. (doors open at 1:00 P.M.), at the School of Arts Hall, in Woombye, except December and January.

Sydney City Bonsai Club Inc.–Beaconsfield. Address: The Secretary, AABC Ltd, PO Box 513, Ascot Vale VIC 3032. Email: secretary@aabcltd.org. Regular club meetings second Tuesday of the month, at 7:00 P.M., at Green Square Community Church, 182 Victoria Street (corner of Collins Street), Beaconsfield (except January).

Tasmanian Bonsai Society–Wynyard. Address: The Secretary, C/-233 Old Bass Highway, Wynyard TAS 7325. Email: secretary@aabcltd.org. Regular club meetings occur on the last Wednesday of each month.

The School of Bonsai Inc. Address: PO Box 4510, North Rocks NSW 2151. Email: schoolofbonsai@yahoo.com.au. Classes meet at The Don Moore Community Centre, North Rocks Road (corner of Farnell St), North Rocks NSW.

Toowoomba Bonsai Group Inc.–Toowoomba. Address: The Secretary, PO Box 7359 Toowoomba MC, Toowoomba. Email: secretary@aabcltd.org. Regular club meetings occur on the first Saturday of the month at the Toowoomba Education Centre, Baker Street, Toowoomba.

Townsville Bonsai Society Inc.–Mundingburra. Address: The Secretary, AABC Ltd, PO Box 513, Ascot Vale VIC 3032. Email: secretary@aabcltd.org. Regular club meetings first Sunday of the month, from 2:00 P.M. to 4:00 P.M., at St Joseph's School, 65 Ross River Road, Mundingburra, except January.

Twin Lakes Bonsai Society–Ascot Vale. Address: The Secretary, AABC Ltd, PO Box 513, Ascot Vale VIC 3032. Email: secretary@aabcltd.org. Regular club meetings occur on the second Sunday of the month at 10:00 A.M.

Urimbirra South Coast Bonsai Society Inc.–Dapto. Address: The Secretary, AABC Ltd, PO Box 513, Ascot Vale VIC 3032. Email: secretary@aabcltd.org. Regular club meetings second Tuesday of the month, at 7.00 P.M., in the "Laurel Room" Ribbonwood Centre, Prince's Highway, Dapto.

Wagga Wagga Bonsai Society Inc.–Wagga Wagga. Address: The Secretary, PO Box 5771, Wagga Wagga NSW 2650. Email: secretary@aabcltd.org. Regular club meetings occur on the first Tuesday each month, at 7:30 P.M., ARCC Hall, 131 Tarcutta Street, Wagga Wagga NSW.

Wauchope Bonsai Workshop Group Inc.–Wauchope. Address: The Secretary, PO Box 131, Wauchope NSW 2446. Email: wauchope.bonsai@optusnet.com.au. Regular club meetings occur on the first Saturday of the month, from 11:00 A.M. to 3:00 P.M., at the Wauchope Showground Hall, High Street, Wauchope.

Waverley Garden Club–Bonsai Group Inc.–Mount Waverley. Address: The Secretary, PO Box 926, Mount Waverley VIC 3 149. Email: bruceandkaye@iprimus.com.au. Regular club meetings occur on the third Tuesday of the month, January to December, at 8:00 P.M., at the St John's Church Hall, Virginia Street, Mt. Waverley.

Weston Creek Bonsai Group Inc.–Weston. Address: The Secretary, PO Box 3852, Weston Creek ACT 2611. Email: *secretary@aabcltd.org.* Regular club meetings second Saturday of each month, at 1:30 P.M. at the Weston Creek Community Centre, Parkinson Street, Weston.

Yarra Valley Bonsai Society Inc.–Mount Evelyn. Address: The Secretary, PO Box 345, Mount Evelyn VIC 3796. Email: info@yarravalleybonsai.org.au. Regular club meetings occur on the second Tuesday of the month, at 7:00 P.M., at Japara House, Montrose, Victoria (Melway 52 D7).

Africa

• *South Africa* •

Name, location, meeting information and email—

Blaauwberg Bonsai Kai. Blaauwberg; last Saturday; mrjade@mweb.co.za

Bloemfontein Bonsai Kai. Bloemfontein; 2nd Saturday; vian@fxsos.co.za

Boland Bonsai Kai. Stellenbosch; last Saturday; cjjbrand@snowisp.com

Border Bonsai Kai. Gonubie; 2nd Saturday; cjjbrand@snowisp.com

Cape Bonsai Kai. Cape Town–Claremont; 3rd Thursday; tony@nanoson.co.za

Durban Bonsai Society. Durban; 2nd Sunday; BorresenE@velavke.co.za

Eastern Bonsai Society. Highlands North, Johannesburg; 2nd Saturday; bonsai@pixie.co.za

Eastern Province Bonsai Kai. Port Elizabeth; 2nd Saturday

East Rand Bonsai Kai. Boksburg; 1st Saturday; erbk@telkomsa.net

Fish Eagle Bonsai Kai. Richards Bay; 2nd Saturday; betsydj@mweb.co.za

Kalahari Bonsai Kai. Upington; 1st Saturday; Kalaharibonsai@gmail.com

Kat River Kai. George; 2nd last Saturday; toblen@mweb.co.za

Kengai Bonsai Kai. Assegay; last Sunday mistymoonbonsai@gmail.com

Kierieklapper Bonsai Kai. Boksburg; 2nd Saturday 14:00; boshoffm@ekurhuleni.gov.za

Midway Bonsai society. Midrand; 3rd Saturday; centuref@icon.co.za

Oyama Bonsai Kai. Cape Town–Plumstead; 2nd Wednesday; nelhj@global.co.za

Pietermaritzburg Bonsai Society. Pietermaritzburg; 2nd Saturday; nuss@telkomsa.net

Platberg Bonsai Kai. Harrismith; 2nd Saturday; pieta.pretorius@wspgroup.co.za

Pretoria Bonsai Kai. Pretoria; 1st Saturday; org@ntp.co.za

Rustenburg Bonsai Kai. Rustenburg; 3rd Saturday; antonc@angloplat.com

Shibui Bonsai Kai. Emmerentia; 3rd Saturday; bonsaikebana@mweb.co.za

Southern Bonsai Society. Alberton; 2nd Saturday; kareldup@netralink.com

Tzaneen Bonsai Kai. Tzaneen; 3rd Saturday; midas@inx.co.za

Waterberg Bonsaiklub. Mookgophong (Naboomspruit); 3rd Saturday; hansieb@lantic.net

Zululand Bonsai Society. Richards Bay; 2nd Saturday; cllrliz@mweb.co.za

Antarctica

I was unable to locate any bonsai societies in Antarctica.

Appendix C: Light and Soil Requirements of Some Trees

Trees	Light	pH
Acacias	Full Sun	Acid
Apple	Full Sun	Acid
Arborvitae	Full Sun	Acid
Ash	Full Sun	Acid
Azalea	Partial Sun	Acid
Bamboo	Full Sun	Acid
Beech	Full sun	Acid
Birch	Full sun	Acid
Blueberry	Full Sun	Acid
Boxwood	Full Sun/ Partial Shade	Alkaline
Bougainvillea	Full Sun	Acid
Camellia	Semi-shade	Acid
Cherry	Full sun	Acid
Chestnut	Full Sun	Acid
Citrus	Full Sun	Acid
Coffee	Partial Shade	Acid
Cotoneaster	Full sun	Acid
Crabapple	Full sun	Acid
Cranberry	Full sun/ Partial shade	Acid
Crepe myrtle	Full sun	Acid
Cypress	Full sun	Acid
Dogwood	Partial Sun	Acid
Elm	Full Sun	Acid to Alkaline
Ficus	Full sun	Acid
Florida poinciana	Full sun	Acid
Fukien tea	Full sun	Acid
Gardenia	Full sun	Acid
Gingko	Full sun	Acid
Hawthorn	Full sun/ partial shade	Acid or Acid or alkaline
Hemlock	Full sun/ shade	Acid
Hibiscus	Full sun	Acid
Holly	Full sun/ partial sun	Acid
Huckleberry	Full sun	Acid
Jasmine	Full sun	Acid
Jade	Semi-shade	Acid
Joshua tree	Full sun	Alkaline
Juniper	Full sun	Acid
Kumquat	Full sun	Acid
Larch	Full sun	Acid
Magnolia	Full sun	Acid
Mahogany	Full sun	Acid
Maple	Full sun	Acid
Mimosa	Full Sun/ partial shade	Acid
Mulberry	Full sun	Neutral
Oak	Full sun/ partial shade	Acid
Osage orange	Full sun	Acid

Trees	Light	pH	Trees	Light	pH
Persimmon	Full sun	Acid	Tamarind	Full sun	Acid
Pine	Full sun	Acid	Texas ebony	Full sun	Acid to alkaline
Pomegranate	Full sun	Acid to alkaline	Walnut	Full sun	Acid
Poplar	Full sun	Acid	Willow	Full sun	Acid to alkaline
Quince	Full sun	Neutral			
Serissa	Slight shade	Acid	Wisteria	Full sun	Acid
Spruce	Full sun	Acid	Yew	Full sun	Acid
Tamarack	Full sun	Acid	Zelkova	Full sun	Acid

Bibliography

Anderson, Miles. *The Complete Illustrated Guide to Growing Cacti & Succulents.* London: Lorenz, 2008.

Batchelder, Brian. *New Horizons in Bonsai.* Miami: B. Batchelder, 1990.

Capon, Brian. *Botany for Gardeners.* Portland, OR: Timber Press, 2005.

Courtier, Jane, and Graham Clarke. *Indoor Plants: The Essential Guide to Choosing and Caring for Houseplants.* Pleasantville, NY: Reader's Digest, 1997.

Jahn, Victoria. *Simon & Schuster's Guide to Bonsai.* New York: Simon and Schuster, 1990.

Koide, Nobukichi, Saburo Kato, and Takeyama Fuzaso. *The Master's Book of Bonsai.* New York: Kodansha International, 1989.

Lesniewicz, Paul. *Bonsai: The Complete Guide to Art and Technique.* Poole, Dorset, UK: Blandford Press, 1984.

Lewis, Colin. *Bonsai Survival Manual.* Pownal, VT: Storey Communications, 1996.

Mattison, Steve. *The Complete Potter: The Complete Reference to Tools, Materials, and Techniques for All Potters and Ceramicists.* Hauppauge, NY: Barron's Educational Series, 2003.

McDowell, Jack, ed.. *Bonsai: Culture and Care of Miniature Trees.* Menlo Park, CA: Lane Books, 1966.

Murfitt, Stephen. *The Glaze Book:* Iola, WI: Krause Publications, 2002.

Murphy, Wendy B. *Japanese Gardens.* Alexandria, VA: Time-Life Books, 1979.

Norman, Ken. *Essential Bonsai: The Complete Handbook for Creating and Growing Your Own Bonsai.* New York: Barnes and Noble Books, 2003.

Pessey, Christian. *Introducing Bonsai.* New York: Smith, 1989.

"Pinching and Pruning." *Bonsai Today* 10 (November-December, 1990): 19–45.

Price Jon, and Leroy Price. *The Art of Crystalline Glazing: Basic Techniques.* Iola, WI: Krause Publications, 2003.

Resnick, Susan M. Bachenheimer. *Bonsai.* London: Tiger Books International, 1995.

Samson, Isabelle, and Remy Samson. *The Creative Art of Bonsai.* London: Hamlyn, 2000.

Sibley, David Allen. *The Sibley Guide to Trees.* New York: Alfred A. Knopf, 2009.

Smittle, Delilah, ed. *Care-Free Plants.* Pleasantville, NY: Reader's Digest, 2002. Tomlinson, Harry. *Bonsai.* Pleasantville, NY: Reader's Digest, 1995.

Walker, Jacqueline. *The Subtropical Garden.* Portland, OR: Timber Press, 1996.

Warren, William. *Tropical Plants for Home and Garden.* New York: Thames and Hudson, 2006.

Yashiroda, Kan. *Bonsai: Special Techniques.* Brooklyn, NY: Brooklyn Botantical Garden, 1988.

Index

Numbers in ***bold italics*** indicate pages with photographs.